Exploring Young Children's Agency in Everyday Transitions

Transitions in Childhood and Youth

Series Editors: Marilyn Fleer, Mariane Hedegaard and Megan Adams

The series brings together books that present and explore empirical research and theoretical discussion on the themes of childhood and youth transitions. Special attention is directed to conceptualizing transitions holistically so that societal, institutional and personal perspectives are featured within and across books. Key to the series is presenting the processes of transitions between practices or activities and their relationship to the person, in contexts such as intergenerational family practices, the processes of care, a person's development, the learning of individuals, groups and systems, personal health, labour and birthing and ageing. All books take a broad cultural-historical approach of transitions across a range of contexts and countries and when brought together in one place make an important contribution to better understanding transitions globally. Books in the Transitions in Childhood and Youth series offer an excellent resource for postgraduate students, researchers, policy writers and academics.

Advisory Board:

Anne Edwards (University of Oxford, UK)
Fernando Gonzalez-Rey (University Center of Brasília, Brazil)
Jennifer Vadeboncoeur (University of British Columbia, Canada)
Anna Stetsenko (City University of New York, USA)

Also available in the series:

Children's Transitions in Everyday Life and Institutions, edited by Mariane Hedegaard and Marilyn Fleer
Developmental Dynamics and Transitions in High School, Sofie Pedersen
Qualitative Studies of Exploration in Childhood Education: Cultures of Play and Learning in Transition, edited by Marilyn Fleer, Mariane Hedegaard, Elin Eriksen Ødegaard and Hanne Værum Sørensen
Supporting Difficult Transitions: Children, Young People and Their Carers, edited by Mariane Hedegaard and Anne Edwards
A Cultural-Historical Approach towards Pedagogical Transitions: Transitions in Post-Apartheid South Africa, Joanne Hardman

Exploring Young Children's Agency in Everyday Transitions

Pernille Juhl

BLOOMSBURY ACADEMIC
LONDON • NEW YORK • OXFORD • NEW DELHI • SYDNEY

BLOOMSBURY ACADEMIC
Bloomsbury Publishing Plc
50 Bedford Square, London, WC1B 3DP, UK
1385 Broadway, New York, NY 10018, USA
29 Earlsfort Terrace, Dublin 2, Ireland

BLOOMSBURY, BLOOMSBURY ACADEMIC and the Diana logo
are trademarks of Bloomsbury Publishing Plc

First published in Great Britain 2023
Paperback edition published 2024

Copyright © Pernille Juhl, 2023

Pernille Juhl has asserted her right under the Copyright,
Designs and Patents Act, 1988, to be identified as Author of this work.

For legal purposes the Acknowledgements on pp. vii–viii constitute
an extension of this copyright page.

Series Design by Joshua Fanning
Cover image: © Elliot Elliot/ Getty Images

All rights reserved. No part of this publication may be reproduced or transmitted in any form or by any means, electronic or mechanical, including photocopying, recording, or any information storage or retrieval system, without prior permission in writing from the publishers.

Bloomsbury Publishing Plc does not have any control over, or responsibility for, any third-party websites referred to or in this book. All internet addresses given in this book were correct at the time of going to press. The author and publisher regret any inconvenience caused if addresses have changed or sites have ceased to exist, but can accept no responsibility for any such changes.

A catalogue record for this book is available from the British Library.

A catalog record for this book is available from the Library of Congress.

ISBN: HB: 978-1-3501-8829-7
PB: 978-1-3501-8833-4
ePDF: 978-1-3501-8830-3
eBook: 978-1-3501-8831-0

Series: Transitions in Childhood and Youth

Typeset by Integra Software Services Pvt. Ltd.

To find out more about our authors and books visit www.bloomsbury.com
and sign up for our newsletters.

Contents

Series Editors' Foreword	vi
Acknowledgements	vii

Part 1

1	Staging the Problem	3
2	Children's Agency – a Topic in a Diverse Research Field	15
3	Theorizing Young Children's Agency in Everyday Living	33

Part 2

4	Children's Everyday Life in ECEC Contexts	65
5	Transitioning Between Everyday Life Contexts	101

Part 3

6	Young Children's Family Life	121
7	Parents' Self-understanding and Agency	161

Part 4

8	Summing-up and Future Perspectives	187

Notes	207
References	208
Index	227

Series Editors' Foreword

In this book series we have chosen to focus on transitions through the lens of cultural-historical theory. Specifically, transition is conceptualized to encompass the changes in daily activity settings, the changes in everyday moves between different institutional practices and the changes on entering new practice through life course trajectories, such as going to school, leaving school, entering the work force or entering into parenthood. Through transition into new practices, children and young people meet new challenges and demands that may give them possibility for development.

Important for a cultural-historical conception of transition is the person's agency or intentions, which can be used as analytical tools for gaining the person's perspective during microgenetic transitions between activity settings within an institution, such as indoor play, lunch and outdoor activities in kindergarten, in daily moves between home and kindergarten, school or work, and during macro-transitions that involve new practices. As the person or people take forward their intention within the daily transitions or the new institutions that they attend, a dynamic interplay between the person and the institution can be observed. Cultural-historical studies of transitions across a range of contexts and countries are brought together in this book series, where they can make an important contribution to better understanding transitions globally.

Acknowledgements

First and foremost, I would like to thank the parents and children, in the book, who allowed me to become a part of their everyday lives and private spheres at all times and in situations when only the few would like to have visitors – not to mention observers. I have learned so much from you all, and this book and the knowledge I hope it offers would not have been possible to gain without your trust in me and allowing me to present your perspectives. I am deeply grateful for your trust, courage and the knowledge you shared.

I wish to extend my special thanks to Professor Mariane Hedegaard and Professor Marilyn Fleer for encouraging me to write this book and for inspiring me along the way. For sure this book would not have been written if it was not for you.

Moreover, I would like to thank the publisher and staff at Bloomsbury Academic for the kind and generous help I was offered during the process. I would like to thank Carlsberg Foundation which granted me a monograph fellowship. This gave me the necessary time to finish the book. And relatedly, a special thanks to Associate Professor Trine Østergaard Wulf-Andersen, who took on extra work when I more or less vanished in order to write.

Thank you to all my wonderful colleagues at the Department of People & Technology, Roskilde University. First and foremost, I wish to thank my colleagues in the research group Subject, Technology and Social Practice (STP). Thank you for the invaluable support and continuous encouragement from colleagues and friends: Jo Krøjer, Dorte Kousholt, Allan Westerling, Trine Østergaard Wulf-Andersen, Sofie Pedersen, Niklas Chimirri. Thank you to Peter Busch-Jensen, Ernst Schraube, Charlotte Højholt, Dorte Kousholt, Mariane Hedegaard, Agnes Andenæs and Ole Dreier for the inspiration all of your work has been to me and for your support.

Thank you to my children, Anna, Aksel and Erika, and my parents and all my wonderful friends for bearing with me in yet another writing project that took a great deal of my time. Thank you for supporting me and trusting in me at any times. Thank you, Peter for our great teamwork. I am forever grateful for your support, and I could not wish for a better co-parent in crime. You mean the world to me, you always will.

A special thank you to my besties, Marianne and Louise, for always being around and helping me preserve my sanity most of the time – I would not have been able to survive the last couple of years if it was not for your endless love and support.

Allan, thank you for always, already loving me and for believing in me, even when I do not believe in myself.

Part One

1

Staging the Problem

This book is about young children's agency. This research interest descends from a methodological ambition to study young children (age one to five) as agentic beings situated in their everyday life across various contexts (e.g. family and day care). I conducted participant observations of young children in their everyday life contexts as a situated approach to the study of children's development and well-being (Juhl, 2014, 2015). While collecting empirical evidence I was struck by the fact that even very young children make a continuous effort to orientate themselves and act in relation to the differences they experience across everyday life contexts and in relation to the various people, conditions and demands they encounter. I became aware of how these orientation processes were a pivotal part of their development of agency. I found that the prevailing conceptualizations of agency, however, are not sufficiently precise for the study of the youngest group of children. Consequently, in this book, I suggest the analytical concept of embodied orientation as fruitful for an exploration of the interrelation between the youngest children and their world. In this way, encountering a methodological problem in exploring young children has led me to focus on the processes of orientation as essential to understanding agency in relation to how young children make the world respond to what they contribute. I will elaborate the analytical concept embodied orientation in more detail in Chapter 3.

The endeavour to develop situated knowledge about children in their everyday lives has been pursued in psychological research since the early 1900s (Stern, 1914), but interest in everyday life was abandoned in the name of cognitive and behavioural research, which embraced experimental designs throughout most of the 1900s (Chimirri, Kitmøller & Hviid, 2015). However, in recent decades, situated, contextualized explorations of the child as an active subject situated in the world have been pursued across various critical research traditions (e.g. socio-cultural developmental psychology, cultural psychology, poststructuralism and phenomenology). However, existing research on children's agency primarily involves children above the age of three (Lam & Pollard, 2006; Thorne, 2008). In the last decade, though, a growing body of literature has evolved surrounding the field of young children below the age of three as situated in their everyday lives – some scholars even arguing that the term babyhood should be used (e.g. Orrmalm, 2020a, b). Inspired by other scholars, my approach to agency is in terms of how young children influence the activities they are part of in their various everyday life contexts (Hedegaard & Fleer, 2019; Højholt & Kousholt, 2018; Røn Larsen & Stanek, 2015). I identified daily transitions as a productive empirical area for the exploration of such agentic processes – and particularly by focusing on the processes of embodied orientation as the following example from my empirical observations of a young boy in his nursery illustrates:

> Daniel (20 months) picks up one of his boots and carries it into the kitchen. He sits down and struggles a bit before finally getting it on. He gets up and walks further into the room with the boot on one foot. Ann (childminder) stops him, takes off the boot and kindly, but determinedly, says: 'We don't wear boots inside'. She carries the boot back into the hallway and then returns to the kitchen. Daniel goes back to the hallway and picks up the boot again. Ann takes it from him once more and puts it back. Daniel picks it up a third time; Ann laughs and asks Daniel if he wants to go for a walk. He gets up and runs around while squealing and sounds incredibly happy.

This example illustrates how Daniel persistently makes an effort to pursue his engagements in this situation. What is not evident in the example, however, is that Daniel utilizes his everyday life experiences from being outside playing in the rain earlier this morning on his way to nursery together with his mother (and me, doing participant observations). In this way, Daniel uses the process of a daily transition between different contexts and activities to pursue his engagements later that day when at the nursery. Daniel uses materials (boots) and his body (fetching the boots and putting one on) to orientate in the situations he is part of and also to communicate his intentions (going outside in the rain). He is communicating with his childminder, and he makes a continuous effort to hold on to his engagements to get the childminder (and later his peers) involved in going outside. I will elaborate on this example further in Chapter 4.

Based on the above and a large number of additional observations of five young children's everyday lives I argue that ethnographically observing the same group of children for a long time and across different situations, activities and contexts allowed me to explore the children's agency in terms of intentional actions and contributions to their development as situated in everyday living.

I also consider the daily transitions key events for exploring young children's agency since the conceptualization of transitions highlights the complexity children face and how they act in relation to this complexity when they move between activities and social relationships within and across different situations and contexts (Hedegaard & Fleer, 2019). I focus on the transitions children make as part of living their everyday lives within and across early childhood education and care (ECEC) contexts and family life contexts. Vogler, Crivello and Woodhead (2008, p. 2) term these daily transitions horizontal. I focus on the children's micromovements (Murray & Cortéz-Morales, 2019) to grasp the multiplicity and variability of the daily transitions that children make, not only in between various contexts but also within each of these contexts – for instance, when children move between various spaces, activities and situations.

In recent decades, young children's agency has been the object of increasing political attention (Alderson, Hawthorne & Killen, 2005; Vandenbroeck & De Bie, 2006). Article 12 of the Convention on the Rights of the Child[1] is evidence of this since the article entitles all children who are able to express themselves verbally and non-verbally to be informed, to be heard and to participate in decision-making processes concerning their well-being and other important matters in their lives (Lansdown, 2005). This type of political goal calls for paying attention to how to include young children's experiences and perspectives on their everyday living. However, the majority of research on the youngest children does not explore the topic of agency. Instead, the research mainly focuses on this age group of children as vulnerable, dependent beings, as I will illustrate in Chapter 2. Thus, numerous studies that include young children centre on exploring adversity or deviations in children's lives (Traum & Moran, 2016). This mainly comprises research that focuses on the attachment between caregivers and young children below the age of three (Steele & Steele, 2017; Wilson, 2001). A related strand of research addresses adversities and the risk of lopsided development as a consequence of young children's vulnerability and dependency on the caregiver's fulfilment of their needs in certain ways to avoid psychopathology (Grienenberg, Denham & Reynolds, 2015). Regarding daily transitions, strands of research address the risks related to these transitions between everyday life across the family and ECEC contexts (Kilgo, Richard & Noonan, 1989; Rimm-Kaufmann & Pianta, 2000). For instance, the research examines how being enrolled in ECEC jeopardizes the attachment in the parent-child relationship (Belsky & Pluess, 2013; Klein, Kraft & Shohet, 2010). In this way, the dominant strands of research on young children do not address young children's well-being and agency as related to possibilities for influencing their everyday life across contexts. However, in terms of building resilience in children, agency is discussed in terms of individual predispositions, capacities and robust human beings (Bernard, 1999; Masten & Barnes, 2018; Peterson & Yates, 2013), for example as a factor that can be cultivated, moulded and optimized through early childhood interventions (Callaghan, Fellin & Alexander, 2019) and in early learning programmes. Similarly, the issue of agency is being examined as a matter of obtaining personal freedom and independence (Steckermeier, 2019).

I argue that exploring and theorizing agency specifically in relation to young children is essential to gaining a more precise understanding of how they experience and actively relate to conditions in their everyday lives. This will work as an important first step in transcending a tendency to approach the youngest children in terms of them as either vulnerable and passive or resilient and robust individuals. Consequently, my approach to exploring the topic of agency draws on the work of scholars who conceptualized agency as inherently social. For this purpose, I take my point of departure in cultural-historical theory (Chaiklin, Hedegaard & Juul Jensen, 1999; Hedegaard, 2014; Hviid, 2008; Rogoff, 2003) and psychology from the standpoint of the subject (Dreier, 2008; Holzkamp, 2013a, b, c; Højholt & Kousholt, 2018; Tolman, 2009). These theoretical frameworks are useful because their conceptualization of the human-world relationship is a dialectical one that emphasizes how children are active subjects in their own lives. The latter framework uses the concept conduct of everyday life (Holzkamp, 2013b), which makes it possible to highlight the exploratory and creative processes involved in young children's everyday living across different contexts. The methodological consequences of these theoretical assumptions across both of these theoretical frameworks are that the phenomenon to be studied is the unit of child-in-context shared by a variety of theoretical traditions, as already mentioned. Consequently, I focus not only on children in transitions but also on the historical and societal everyday life contexts in which their transitioning is situated. In the book, I foreground how children actively orientate in such everyday life transitions. This approach contributes to my aim of understanding children as active subjects co-creating together with co-participants (e.g. parents, professionals and peers) the conditions under which they live, rather than as passively determined by these life conditions.

Moreover, I wish to emphasize the importance of supporting young children in experiencing that they have influence. Personal development, I argue, is not just a question of developing through social practices, but also one of contributing to the development and transformation of social practices (as also argued by others, e.g. Chimirri, 2013; Højholt & Kousholt, 2018; Kousholt, 2016;

Røn Larsen & Stanek, 2015; Stetsenko, 2020). Hence, my point of departure is that the development of personal agency is connected to increasing young children's influence on the circumstance under which they live. The social meanings of the children's contributions are mediated through how others (peers and caregivers) relate to and respond to these contributions, and how others use their contributions in the further development of common activities, and thereby developing social practices. Throughout this book I will unpack and discuss how I address such processes of young children's agency, and how these can be explored and theorized. I will illustrate how the prevailing concept of agency is not precise enough for sufficiently exploring agency from the children's perspectives situated in their everyday lives; that is, how young children make the world respond on their contributions. Applying the Vygotskian idea of microgenetic events (1988), it is possible to address both the multiple daily transitioning processes that children are part of and also how transitioning is part of their developmental conditions. I will elaborate this in Chapter 3.

Origin of the Empirical Data

The analyses in the book are based on empirical data retrieved from a year-long ethnographic study of five Danish children one to five years of age in Denmark from 2011 to 2012 (see Juhl, 2014, 2015, 2016). The study included multiple participant observations in each of the children's everyday life contexts, enabling detailed analysis of their perspectives. The children and their parents were recruited through local early intervention programmes (Juhl, 2016). Because of authorities' concerns about the parents' ability to provide proper care for their children, and to ensure their children's well-being, the children were categorized by the authorities as being at risk of lopsided development and distress. Local authorities assigned the children and their parents to early preventive interventions (e.g. home visits and support from a health visitor, social workers and respite family care[2]) in which various professionals, such as social workers, health visitors and caregivers in ECEC centres, worked to provide these children and their families with adequate help.

The concerns about the children's well-being that prompted the early preventive interventions were often not related to the children's particular everyday life situation but to circumstances in the parents' lives that were categorized as risk factors on a more general and abstract level, such as growing up in poverty or in a divorced family, or with a young, single mother (Juhl, 2016). In other words, the early childhood interventions did not necessarily take the concrete everyday lives of the children and parents as their starting point for understanding their difficulties when designing the interventions, even though everyday life literally comprises the contexts in which the interventions are supposed to work (Dreier, 2011). One reason for not taking concrete problems and conflicts in everyday life as a starting point for the early childhood interventions is that embedded in the very nature of early preventive interventions is that they are to provide appropriate support 'before problems become entrenched' (Robinson & Dunsmuir, 2010, p. 11), which is why they are most commonly initiated early, as regards both the child's age and the level of complexity, based on assumptions about what potentially can become problematic and entail risk for children's development and well-being. My study was designed as a response to these limitations. Consequently, I aimed to explore the situated meanings of the specific life situations of children and parents, and hence, what kinds of constraints and possibilities they encountered in their everyday living. My aim was not to try to assess the potential impact from isolated risk factors. Rather, I wanted to understand how conditions entailed various meanings to different children, depending on the entangled and complex circumstances and how young children actively live their lives and deal with their life conditions. I employed a variety of methods, for example, ethnographically inspired participant observations with children (e.g. Kousholt, 2011, 2016; Spradley, 1980), qualitative life mode interviews (Haavind, 2019) with the parents and qualitative interviews (Brinkmann & Kvale, 2015) with professionals about what kind of concerns about the children served as the basis for the interventions. Observing the children in their daily contexts allowed me to gain in-depth insight into their daily routines, engagements and favourite activities in a variety of situations across time and space. I also became familiar with the children and their various caregivers. Most of the time, I participated actively in the ongoing activities in assorted places; for instance, I would sit next to the children on the floor and play with them, go along to shop, eat together with the families, move from ECEC to family contexts with the child and parents, and vice versa. On other occasions, I mainly observed without participating in activities with the children. During the life mode interviews with the parents, my questions focused on their everyday life routines and what they perceived as a good life for their children, how they prioritized and organized everyday family life and how they experienced being enrolled in early interventions.

While doing the study the children's daily transitioning and their orientation processes in relation hereto attracted my attention as significant in relation to understanding young children's well-being. In this book I use the empirical data produced in that study to specifically focus on exploring agency in relation to young children's transitions in daily living. I consider the empirical accounts of the children's transitions as an opportunity to contribute with novel understandings of the youngest group of children – even when in difficult life situations – as active subjects dealing with their specific life situations and circumstances. This focus reveals how the children, although very young, make daily efforts to orientate in and contribute to developing and transforming the different situations they take part in across activities and contexts. Hence, agency is important in relation to young children in order to be able to understand the personal meanings of difficult life conditions in everyday life anchored in social practices. My ambition is to produce knowledge that enables early childhood interventions to target conditions in everyday life instead of individualizing the problems children and parents experience.

I observed five children and started with Anthony when he was twelve months, Daniel twelve months, Oscar fifteen months, Emily three years old and Toby four. My analytical focus in the book will be on how these children orientate as an important part of participating in influential ways as a key to exploring and conceptualizing processes of agency. I specifically pursue issues such as what kinds of activities the children engage in, what they try to accomplish and what kinds of opportunities and issues they face in common everyday life situations and how the children move between various situations and relationships with peers and adults.

Contributions

The ambition of the book is twofold: (1) to contribute to existing research and theoretical endeavours in terms of conceptualizing agency to account for young children in more precise ways, and (2) to contribute with analytical concepts that can support professionals in approaching and including young children as agentic beings – for instance, in early childhood interventions.

The situated analysis in the book contributes to addressing the problem that, whenever young children's development and well-being become the subject of concern, the children are pictured as vulnerable creatures with certain needs to be fulfilled in certain ways. Clearly young children need to be taken care of, but I wish to transcend the understanding of a vulnerable, passive creature by illustrating how young children – even when their life conditions are difficult – act in intentional, agentic ways. An additional and even more pivotal ambition is to argue that the various subjective meanings of life conditions and problems must be explored from the children's perspectives as situated in their specific configurations of everyday life. In this way, the same situation entails a variety of personal meanings to different children. For this reason, I argue that it is crucial to develop analytical tools that can help explore and include the perspectives of very young children. As a result, a key point in the book is that young children – despite their life situations and problems – need to be taken seriously as intentional subjects engaged in the everyday life situations and transitions in daily living that they are part of.

By focusing on the everyday living across contexts I gain insight into how these children take part in ordinary everyday life activities and routines from their somewhat extraordinary life situations. Hence, an important aim of the book is to analyse what is suitable for transcending 'the dichotomy between what is labelled the "common" and the "uncommon", or the "ordinary" and the "extraordinary"' (Hedegaard, Aronsson, Højholt & Ulvik, 2012, p. viii). The analysis of children dealing with extraordinary conditions in their everyday lives offers resources for general knowledge about processes of agency in relation to young children. I foreground how children actively orientate in daily transitions but nevertheless focus on both the transitioning person and the everyday life contexts (e.g. family and day care) in which the transitioning is situated. Systematically including the everyday life situations in the analysis, including relationships to peers and caregivers, will make it possible not only to address the subjective meanings of common life conditions embedded in the everyday living of the five children, but also to relate these findings to discussions of general life conditions for children's development – for instance, cultural, political and societal conditions, and how these conditions are present in microgenetic events in everyday living.

Notwithstanding that the Scandinavian welfare state is the cultural and societal context for the empirical examples, my ambition is to describe insights that may be more generally crosscutting. One example of this is that all children make transitions during their everyday lives, and by focusing on the children's micromovements within and between contexts, the book will contribute to understanding young children as active, agentic subjects as well as to how agency can be understood in the early years. Another example of insights of international relevance involves the issue of shared care arrangement. Children's compound lives highlight the importance of understanding parental tasks as embedded in their collaboration with professionals (Kousholt, 2011). This is more common, however, in Scandinavia compared to other countries (Oberhuemer & Schreyer, 2018). Even though the various configurations of children's compound lives differ, it is a common condition for children to transition between various social situations, and in this way, the discussions in the book are internationally relevant – especially since ECEC programmes have become the new normal among many families with young children around the world. In the United States, for example, approximately 60 per cent of children under the age of five, or 12.5 million children, are in some type of childcare, such as family/relative care, in-home care or centre-based childcare (Laughlin, 2010). Among those children, one out of four is in centre-based early childhood care, which means they make daily transitions from home to a childcare environment. In the Netherlands, this is the case for 46 per cent of children below age three, and in Sweden it is 64 per cent. In Denmark, the number is more than 90 per cent (Juhl, 2018). Lastly, in any society young children are part of multiple relationships, situations and transitions in this particular context, and they orientate and explore these situations as part of a compound life. Also, the subject of how to include the perspectives of young children enrolled in early childhood interventions is of international relevance. For instance, as stated by Burman (2020, p. 100), it is necessary to develop knowledge and approaches that can work against what she terms a tendency in the UK to instrumentalize children and their well-being/distress.

Structure of the Book

The children's compound everyday lives in a Scandinavian context are used as a structure for the sequencing of the chapters. This is the reason why a key chapter is allocated to the children's everyday lives in ECEC, followed by another central chapter on their daily transitioning between contexts and a significant chapter that provides accounts from the children's family lives. Creating a focus on the same five particular children throughout the book gives the reader the opportunity to gain a sense of their development. I will use these specific children's everyday activities as the basis for discussing more general aspects of how transitioning is part of their developmental conditions and how agency can be analysed and conceptualized.

The second chapter outlines how agency, in relation to daily processes of transitions, has been conceptualized within different strands of research. Readers who wish to move directly to the core chapters may want to just skim this chapter, which provides an overview of how the topic of the book relates to the current research situation.

The third chapter outlines the key theoretical concepts developed and employed in the analysis. The concepts are developed within the theoretical frameworks of cultural-historical theory (e.g. Chaiklin et al., 1999; Hedegaard, 2014; Rogoff, 2003) and psychology from the standpoint of the subject (Dreier, 2008; Holzkamp, 2013a,b, c; Tolman, 2009).

Chapter 4 focuses on children's everyday life in ECEC, highlighting how children are engaged with each other in organizing activities. On the one hand, I analyse the Danish ECEC context as a social practice focusing on the societally and historically developed aims and scopes. On the other hand, I focus on children's internal micromovements within the ECEC centre, between activities, relationships and situations as well as on how the people who inhabit the institution (children, ECEC staff) are active participants with different interests, engagement and tasks in relation to day care.

Chapter 5, which explores children's perspectives on moving between contexts and relationships, illustrates the complexity related to living a compound everyday life and how this complexity of everyday life comprises the developmental conditions for children (Haavind, 2006, 2011). The concept microgenetic makes it possible to highlight the developmental relevance of the numerous transitions that children make as part of their everyday lives across different institutions (Hedegaard & Fleer, 2019, p. 15). In the chapter, I specifically discuss how children contribute to the processes of shaping their own life conditions and also how they contribute to shaping other co-participants' action possibilities. Hence, agency and children's intentions are analytical tools for understanding the individual's perspective during transitions (Hedegaard & Fleer, 2019). I will also draw on the analyses from the previous chapter to illustrate what children are transitioning from.

In Chapter 6, I focus on children's everyday life in relation to their family contexts but also on how children move between their birth family and other family settings, for example respite families. I draw on the insights from Chapters 4 and 5 to illustrate how family life is shaped by not only what happens when parents and children are together but also their everyday lives elsewhere. I target how children orientate themselves in relation to the various ways family life is arranged and the assorted routines. I specifically focus on the ways in which children explore action possibilities in a variety of contexts, how they create coherence and how they contribute to their own transitioning and to the possibilities their parents have for supporting this compound everyday life (Westerling & Juhl, 2021). In family life, I focus on how parents process instructions from professionals from the child protection services that cover, for example, how to attend to their child's health, nutrition, care and development, as well as how to organize daily routines. I explicitly examine how parents create conditions for their children's development and how children participate and contribute to shaping everyday family life (Kousholt, 2012; Juhl, 2016).

In Chapter 7, I explore parental perspectives on the shared task of taking care of children in collaboration with other caregivers. A distinct focus is societal values about what is considered to be a good life for children according to various adults (parents and professionals), which I analysed in relation to how parents experience the possibilities they have for organizing family life and in relation to what this organization of family life means for children. A key point is that young children's agency is shaped (but not determined), and various caregivers, including the parents, play a vital role in organizing everyday life situations for children that support their development of agency in terms of experiencing that they have influence. The encounters between welfare professionals and parents are important since these encounters mediate certain understandings and values about the tasks of parenthood.

The last chapter discusses how embodied orientation, as an analytical focus, provided insights about children as active co-creators of their own life conditions, and also on how parents' and children's agency is interrelated through the processes of transitions as part of the conduct of everyday life. The chapter more specifically discusses what kind of knowledge contributions can be gained. Finally, the chapter discusses the analytical opportunities that arise from applying the analytical concepts that were presented, and how these can contribute to inspiring professional practice and the involvement of young children's perspectives and support young children as well as their parents in developing agency.

2

Children's Agency – a Topic in a Diverse Research Field

This chapter outlines different research traditions that focus on young children's development and young children's agency. What I term 'young children' is referred to in different terms. Gottlieb (2004) argues that infancy within developmental psychology is usually defined as the time between birth and two years of age, when toddlerhood starts. Others define infancy as the period between birth and eighteen months (Burman, 1994, p. 23; Sumision & Goodfellow, 2012), while Løkken (2004, p. 16) argues that toddler refers to a one- or two-year-old child. Orrmalm (2020a,b) uses the term baby or babyhood. Based on the terminology in the research field, I refer to the children as 'young children'. This term includes the entire age group zero to five years. I sometimes refer to children who have not yet developed spoken language as 'preverbal', which is only the case when the mode of communication is deemed important.

My aim with this chapter is not to provide a complete overview but rather to point out how the topic of agency has been addressed – and not addressed – in a quite diverse field of knowledge. Consequently, the chapter brings together contributions from various research traditions such as experimental research within infant psychology, resilience and early childhood intervention research, sociocultural developmental psychology and childhood studies.

A key point in the chapter is that agency has only sparsely been an explicit research topic regarding infants and children below age three. In the first part of the chapter, I will describe how research on this age group is mainly experimental and examines the development of isolated, psychological functions – for instance, in the tradition of infant research. Another strand of research on young children below age three is quasi-experimental attachment theory research. In infant research as well as attachment theory research the topic of agency is not addressed. This is different in the strands of resilience research and early childhood interventions research in which the topic of agency, I argue, is approached indirectly through a focus on how to support young children's acquirement of competences and strengthening children's individual psychological functions since these functions and capabilities are linked to expanding children's future life chances. A shared feature of the strands of resilience research and early childhood intervention research, hence, is the belief that it is possible to make young children more robust, for instance by enhancing early learning activities to optimize young children's potential life chances. However, I argue that the mentioned research traditions fail to see young children, while still in need of adult care and protection, as agentic beings that also have a need to be taken seriously as subjects engaged in the world contributing to their own development as well as the development of the contexts they take part in. This calls for knowledge about how the youngest group of children (zero to five) acts as agentic subjects in their everyday living.

In the second part of the chapter, I will therefore turn my attention towards ethnographic and anthropological contributions to childhood studies and the tradition of sociocultural developmental psychology which provides the main inspiration for this book. These research contributions approach agency in young children as a matter of having influence in a social world. I will emphasize the growing research interest in studying young children's everyday lives by the use of ethnographic designs within the last decade. As already touched upon, the existing studies that explicitly explore the topic of agency mainly include children above age three. However, I will show that an emerging field of ethnographic research examines the youngest group of children and their active relationship with the world. In relation hereto I will end the chapter by briefly touching upon how various strands of research aim at including the perspectives of young children in research. Initially, though, I delve into infant research and experimental designs, before moving on to the areas of attachment theory, resilience and early childhood intervention research.

Infant Psychology Research

Infant psychology, which studies infants and their psychological functions and behaviour, has contributed with insights into the skills and functions of human beings from the beginning of life by developing a variety of designs and technologies aimed at describing and explaining infant behaviour in experimental and quasi-experimental settings. Examples of technological advances include, for instance, eye trackers for recording eye movements (Sonne, Kingo & Krøjgaard, 2016) and video recordings of head movements and pointing gestures (Mumford & Kita, 2016). The aim of these strands of research is, for example, to interpret children's behaviour and to describe their cognitive capacities (Legerstee, 1992; Sirois & Mareschal, 2002). Computational models, an example of a tool for assessing cognitive capacities, are used to interpret infant behaviour in relation to habituation, for instance by measuring looking time on known and new objects to gauge whether infants possess innate conceptual understandings (Sirois & Mareschal, 2002). In this way, descriptions of the activities of infants and toddlers are associated with the development of various functions in children regarding, for example, associations between variables like behaviour (pointing gestures) and language development (Mumford & Kita, 2016). Infant research has contributed to shed light on early skills, providing important stepping stones for designing studies, such as my own, based on the assumption that children are capable of actively engaging in relationships with (various) other people in the earliest stages of life, an assertion multiple studies document (Reddy & Trevarthen, 2004; Selby & Bradley, 2003; Stern, 2000).

Like the traditions of infant research, I share an overall interest in understanding young children. Nevertheless, as already accounted for in Chapter 1, I approach the question of how to understand young children as related to their participation in everyday life across time and space since this approach enables me to explore young children as situated in a complex everyday life. I do not – like infant research – aim to study certain isolated psychological functions in children, since it, in my view, objectifies children. Instead, I approach young children as acting, intentional and agentic subjects developing in a dialectical relationship with specific everyday life contexts. I will elaborate this argument in Chapter 3.

In the next section, I will move on to another research tradition, which includes the youngest group of children, namely the attachment theory research.

Vulnerability and Attachment – the Young Child as Exposed

According to attachment theory, which deals with children below age three, infants form internal working models early in life based on the degree to which their caregivers are available and provide support in times of distress (Ainsworth, 1978; Bowlby, 1998; Fearon et al., 2010; Grienenberg et al., 2015;

Groh et al., 2012). Internal working models are viewed, theoretically, as fairly stable mental representations of self and close relationships. Based on the behaviour of infants in an experimental design (the so-called strange situations), Ainsworth (1978) originally identified three different styles of attachment: secure, insecure-avoidant and insecure-ambivalent. It is argued that infants with secure attachment style view their caregivers as available and responsive when needed.

Building on Ainsworth's studies, scholars within this research tradition have developed these styles into several new combinations and sub-styles of which the disorganized attachment style seems to be the most commonly used in the recent literature (e.g., Fearon et al., 2010). The main argument in this research tradition is that maternal sensitivity and maternal mentalization are pivotal for securing attachment between mother and child and the future mental health of the child (Chay et al., 2018; Grienenberg et al., 2015; Slade, Grienenberger, Bernbach, Levy & Locker, 2005), leading to the development of several attachment-based programmes aimed at ensuring young children's early attachment security. Grienenberg and colleagues (2015) state: 'Literally hundreds of studies have shown attachment to be a critical variable that has been linked to multiple measures of social and emotional functioning, psychopathology, and resiliency across the lifespan' (p. 450). Consequently, I stress that a dominant understanding created in the literature within this strand of research is that of young children as vulnerable creatures with emotional needs that must be fulfilled in certain ways (by the adult caregiver) to ensure secure attachment and prevent externalized behaviour and deviant development in the future (Fabian & Dunlop, 2002, 2007; Fearon et al., 2010). For instance, Fearon and colleagues (2010) argue that attachment theory 'created a conceptual framework for developing testable hypotheses about causal influences, developmental processes and expected long term consequences of attachment for mental health' (p. 435). I argue that this understanding depicts the young child as rather passively determined by the caregiver's emotional responses. A related problem is that young children's developmental conditions and social life are reduced to the emotional relationship with the parents or other primary caregivers. This picture does not align with the everyday lives of the majority of children in the West who, as already accounted for, from age one are enrolled in ECEC. Nevertheless, attachment theory research is the backdrop in quasi-experiments that focus on the negative effect of separation from primary caregivers when children begin attending ECEC centres (Ahnert et al., 2004; Klein et al., 2010; Xu, 2006). One specific example is a study of 'painful transitions' (Klette & Killen, 2019) which shows how infants react to separation from and reunion with their mothers after one month in day care and how this affects the attachment. In this way, attachment theory research contributes to identify factors that lead to elevated developmental risks. In the subsequent section, I will discuss how other strands of research take up risk factors, including the consequences of attachment for mental health.

Another example of research that focuses on day-care-related developmental risks for young children is studies focusing on day care's impact on young children's apparently biological equilibrium such as sleeping routines (Staton et al., 2020) or eating routines (Grummer-Strawn et al., 2008; Heller et al., 2019). These studies primarily approach young children and their daily transitions as a question of how transitions impact (negatively) *on* children and not on young children actively relate to changes and transitions in care practice across contexts and in relation to various caregivers. Consequently, how young children act and actively relate to their life conditions seems to be a blind spot. One reason for this blind spot is that the focus mainly is on caregivers' actions, emotional responses and care contributions and not on what the children do and how children relate to their conditions. Another critique is that the research situations in terms of the strange situation do not seem to share a lot of features with the everyday life situations or care practices that most young children know. This is reflected in Bronfenbrenner's (1979) critique of attachment research for being 'the science of *the strange behavior of children in strange situations with strange adults for the briefest possible periods of time*' (pp. 18–19, original italics). What is implicit in this quote is also a lack of what Bronfenbrenner (1979) terms 'ecological validity'. This term refers to 'the extent to which the environment experienced by the subjects in a scientific investigation has the properties it is supposed or assumed to have by the investigator' (p. 29). In this way, the subjective experience of the child (the research object) should be put in the centre when evaluating the validity of an experiment. Relatedly, the strange-situation-design has also been criticized for being universalistic and neglecting cross-cultural differences in caregiving practices (Norman & LeVine, 2008).

Despite agreeing with this criticism, my ambition is not to reject the need for understanding more about what young children need in order to prevent distress. Rather my point is that in order to achieve this, there is a need for situated knowledge about how concrete children experience their concrete everyday life conditions located in concrete social, historical and cultural contexts. In other words, there is a need for exploring the complexity of young children's everyday lives across contexts and together in relation to various others, as this is what comprises young children's developmental conditions.

In the next section, I will present another dominant strand of research that takes young children's life conditions into consideration in terms of identifying risk factors. In this way, this strand of research expands the focus by including more than the emotional relation between parents and children as important. However, the subjective meanings of the various risk factors are not explored in relation to what they mean in different configurations of children's everyday lives.

Agency as Acquisition of Competences and Reducing Risk Factors – the Child as a Variable

Sociology has studied adversities in children's lives as a consequence of intergenerational transmission (Bird, 2007), or as a result of risk factors related to the parents' s life situations (Love et al., 2002; Luthar, Cicchetti & Becker, 2000; Rutter, 2000). Risk factors might involve circumstances related to, e.g., being young parents, no family network, poverty or illness. As already outlined in the previous section, the field of psychology has linked young children's distress and deviant behaviour to psychological risk factors such as maternal postpartum depression or parents' personal life stories of experiencing neglect as children. One study, for example, examined the association between reduced gaze activity in infants, maternal postpartum depression and long-term negative consequences for future development (Væver, Krogh, Smith-Nielsen, Christensen & Tharner, 2015). The studies then suggest various preventive interventions to combat the negative consequences of these risk factors.

In early childhood intervention studies children are approached as mouldable beings that can be shaped towards better future life chances through stimulation from adults – not just emotional responses from parents as argued in attachment theory but primarily through educational activities. Scholars within this strand of research argue that early childhood interventions are the most efficient approach to avoiding negative future consequences of risks factors since investing in early childhood interventions provides the greatest economic return (Heckman, 2006), also maintaining that enhancing, for example, literacy and concept formation very early in life is the best way to improve later school performance and that didactics should play a larger role in ECEC starting in the early years (La Paro & Pianta, 2000). Academic learning before the age of one is considered especially valuable, leading to the designation of parents as important educators for young children. Consequently, the home as a learning environment for the youngest children below age three has been brought into focus in recent years, not only in the United States and the UK but also in Scandinavia (Westerling & Juhl, 2021). International research associating school performance with early learning and skills training, especially regarding disadvantaged children (Heckman & Masterov, 2007), has led to the prevalence of evidence-based methods and programmes intended to enhance learning in early childhood throughout Scandinavian ECEC systems (Bjørnestad & Os, 2018; Bjørnestad & Samuelson, 2012).

This focus on enhancing early learning, hence, is considered a means to the development of agency later in life. However, the young child is still approached as rather passive and even as a variable that can be affected through inputs (good or bad), resulting in a certain and predictable outcome (good or bad), hence disregarding the differences in the ways young children subjectively orientate in and relate to and act in their complex everyday lives. In this way, I argue that the focus on agency is taken up primarily in terms of an instrument to future academic outcome rather than as an approach to young children actively and intentionally contributing to shaping their life conditions.

Resilience – Agency in Terms of Being Robust and Independent

Resilience research, a related research strand including the youngest age groups, approaches children as robust and resilient agents if they are able to develop towards acting freely and independently, despite the adversities they may experience. A meta study identified studies which classified children as resilient if they showed positive outcomes (for instance, mental health or academic achievement) despite adversities (Gartland et al., 2019). Individual factors, such as cognitive skills, emotion regulation and academic engagement were most commonly investigated but also early attachment security in the relation to caregiver (Charest et al., 2019). This strand of research particularly emphasizes agency as a matter of how young children are capable of adjusting to new demands. In this way, the impact of transitions on children's social competences and adjustment-related behaviour is a widespread research topic (e.g. Beers, 2021; Field, Vega-Lahr & Jagadish, 1984). For instance, studies have explored children's gradual development of self-regulation and bodily control and awareness of their bodies in relation to their surroundings (Feng, Hooper & Jia, 2017; Jennings, DeMauro & Mischenko, 2019), and how this affects young children's regulation, impulse control and promotes self-agency (Grienenberg et al., 2015). In this research strand, the understanding of agency concerns mental processes of self-regulation which, it is argued, makes the child robust. Another study defines young children's agency as their ability to influence what and how something is learned (Adair, 2014). Others, relatedly, define agency as a matter of freedom (Visak, 2016) and a question of the child's individual ability to act independently: 'Agency combines two different aspects: The ability to act independently from others – comparable to the process aspect of freedom […] and the ability to choose from different opportunities – denoted as the opportunity aspect' (Steckermeier, 2019, p. 31). In this way, young children's agency is understood as a question of individual agents developing towards acting independently and freely. This book takes a different approach to the exploration of agency as a social process. I will elaborate this theoretical point of departure in the next chapter.

A shared feature of the stands of research I have touched upon so far is the belief that it is possible to make young children more robust, for instance by enhancing early learning to optimize their potential life chances. However, these ways of understandings fail to see young children, while still in need of adult care and protection, as agentic beings that also have a need to be taken seriously as subjects engaged in the world contributing to their own development as well as the development of the contexts, they take part in. This calls for knowledge about how the youngest group of children (zero to five) acts as agentic subjects in their everyday living. Prevailing conceptualizations of agency, however, are not sufficient for the exploration of the youngest children's contribution to the world and how they make the world respond to their actions. For this reason, the rest of the chapter will turn the attention to research contributions that cover the topic of agency in young children as linked to participating in a complex everyday life. I particularly focus on the meanings of transitions in daily living in relation to young children's development of agency. In Chapter 3 I will elaborate in more detail how I consider transitions a microgenetic event fruitful for exploring how the children orientate in new situations as a stepping stone for their agentic contributions to the development of these situations. In particular, the rest of this chapter will emphasize research contributions that can productively help shed light on the youngest children's transitioning as processes of embodied orientation in the world and how this focus contributes to a more precise understanding of young children's agency. Since the existing research on agency mainly focuses on older children I will also include empirical studies with children under the age of three that address young children's agency in more indirect ways.

Transitions and Everyday Living

According to Vogler et al. (2008), transitions can generically be defined as:

> key event and/or processes occurring at specific periods or turning points during the life course. They are generally linked to changes in a person's appearance, activity, status, roles and relationships, as well as associated with changes in use of physical and social space, and/or changing contact with cultural beliefs, discourses and practices, especially where these are linked to changes of setting.
>
> (p. 1)

The three aforementioned authors differentiate between vertical and horizontal transitions, the former defined as 'key changes from one state or status to another often associated with "upwards" shifts' (p. 2) which involves a movement from one social status to another, e.g. from pre-school to primary school pupil (p. 22). Vogler et al. (2008) define horizontal transitions as transitions that occur on 'an everyday basis' (p. 2), referring to the movements children 'routinely make between various spheres or domains of their lives' (p. 2). An example is when parents pick up the youngest children in ECEC contexts and walking, bicycling or driving home by car or bus. These daily events of transitioning between places and shifts in relationships entail notable events for children's orientation processes related to moving between places in everyday living, which I find crucial for the exploration and conceptualization of young children's agency, as will become clear throughout the book.

The importance of vertical transitions is reflected in the body of literature focused on children's transitions from ECEC to school (Bender, Pham & Carlson, 2011; Kagan & Neuman, 1998; Winter & Kelley, 2008; Yeboah, 2002). Vertical transitions are deemed especially difficult in the existing literature for children who are defined as being in marginalized positions in terms of adversities. One reason for this is the widespread understanding in the literature that growing up in disadvantaged families facing social and structural problems like poverty or inequality generally can be related to decreased future life chances due to children's poor academic performance (Love et al., 2002; Rutter, 2000). Consequently, as a means to fight inequality and marginalization, a huge focus has been put on enhancing academic skills in the early years to prepare children better for the transition from ECEC to school. Thus, children's readiness to make a successful transition has been designated as a key task for ECECs all over the Western world (Arnold, Bartlett, Gowani & Merali, 2007; Heckman, 2006; Scott-Little, Kagan & Freelow, 2006).

Less attention has been given to the informal changes in children's lives and routines that occur outside the formal educational system (Kagan & Neuman, 1998, p. 2). Nonetheless, these transitions in informal settings may crucially shape children's experiences and pathways and be central to their well-being (Johansson, 2007; Kagan & Neuman, 1998). An example of this is children meeting their peers on the local playground, or children moving between various play activities and children's communities. These daily situations, which entail processes of exclusion and successes, are significant for the children's development of self-understanding and for how they experience being able to exert influence (Højholt & Kousholt, 2018; Munck, 2018; Røn Larsen, 2015).

Horizontal Transitions

Vogler et al. (2008) stress that less attention has been paid to horizontal transitions because they are often less distinctive than vertical ones. However, within recent years scholars have stressed that vertical transitions must be explored as embedded in horizontal transitions (Kousholt, 2019, p. 146; Lam & Pollard, 2006; Winther-Lindqvist, 2019). Even though horizontal transitions turn our focus towards the daily reoccurring transitions in children's everyday lives, I do not find that transitions *within* a particular institutional setting are highlighted sufficiently in the terms of horizontal transitions. This is why I include the concept of micromovements (Murray & Cortés-Morales, 2019, p. 98) as a key focus, also because it aligns with what Hedegaard (2019) inspired by Vygotsky terms microgenetic transitions. According to Murray and Cortés-Morales (2019), the fact that babies often stay within the same context or only move between a few (home or nursery) there has been a tendency to approach them as immobile beings (p. 98). This is enhanced by the fact that babies do not move between places by themselves; they depend on adults to make the actual movement for them. However, throughout the book, I will emphasize that this does not mean that young children do not impact or shape the activities and the way transitions unfold. Even the youngest children contribute to creating the conditions for adults during transitions and other everyday life situations. Murray and Cortés-Morales (2019) argue that children's movement can be 'performed through the changing positions of the body in the relation between them and in their attachment to other bodies and spaces or being carried by another body or artefact without necessarily moving themselves' (p. 96). As will become clear in the coming chapters, this approach has inspired my focus on how young children influence the situations they are part of.

In the literature, transitions within the same context are a neglected research area (Fincham & Fellner, 2016). Even though the mentioned studies are part of a growing body of research exploring horizontal transitions, or micromovements from the perspectives of very young children (below age three), most studies on children's transitional experiences focus on children (over age three) making the formal transition from day care centre to preschool (Ahtola et al., 2016; Hugo et al., 2018; Kienig, 2002; Rimm-Kaufman & Pianta, 2000), mainly focusing on children's readiness for school and for making the transitions smooth to support children's future academic success. In this book, however, I will focus on the horizontal transitions as part of daily living and I will pay a lot of attention to what Recchia and Dvorakova (2012) term as 'internal transitions' which covers transitions within the same contexts. Recchia and Dvorakova (2012) highlighted the variability in toddlers' experiences as shaped by the social activities of the classroom. They found that toddlers transitioning together used their friendships as a 'secure base' (p. 196), which relieved transition-related stress.

In an ethnographic study of the participation and engagements of babies with everyday materiality Orrmalm (2020a,b) does not implicitly address the topic of transition. However, Orrmalm empirically explored the micromovements and engagements of babies with things (socks) across various rooms and situations in the home space. This focus helps unpack how babies constantly engage with the world and its materiality, as well as how babies use things to connect various situations during the day, regardless of adult support, just as their engagements also co-produce material and social contexts for themselves and others, e.g. caregivers. Hence this study approach babies as agentic (Orrmalm, 2020a) and, I would add, it also provides insights about how babies use things to orientate themselves in relation to transitions in everyday living, for instance by returning to and use the same spaces and things or engage in the same activities at different times during the day.

Agency as Situated and Social Processes

As already touched upon, within childhood studies children under three have received relatively little attention compared to older children (Brownlie & Leith, 2011; Gottlieb, 2000; McNamee & Seymore, 2012; Thorne, 2008). An increasing number of studies in recent years, though, have begun to include the perspectives of very young children (Clarke, 2003; Clarke & Moss, 2001; Elwick et al., 2014a; Røn Larsen & Stanek, 2015) and some scholars even argue that 'babyhood studies' will become an emerging field (e.g. Tebet and Abramowicz, 2019; Orrmalm, 2020a,b).

Childhood studies and childhood sociology (Corsaro, 2005; James, Jenks & Prout, 1998) have explicitly designed studies fruitful for exploring older children's agency. This research topic emerged in the 1970s and 1980s as a critique against how children and childhood were viewed within existing disciplines, such as developmental psychology. Several waves of research have nonetheless foregrounded slightly different aspects of children's lives. I will refrain from taking up each of these waves but only mention that in the first one, it was argued that a reconceptualization of childhood was needed that, instead of focusing on children as human becomings (on their journey towards adult beings), the focus was on children and childhood as important in themselves and not just as a preparation for the future (Lee, 2001). Recent contributions within the field, though, maintain (as a later wave) that the focus should include children as both beings and becomings (e.g. Lee, 1998). The main focus is on emphasizing children as social agentic actors. The mainly ethnographic research contributions within this strand emphasize the importance of peer cultures and how they shape individual children's understanding of the world (Brooker, 2006; Pratt & George, 2005). Corsaro and Molinari (2005) showed how children, together with other children, prepare for transitions from pre-school to elementary school. With regards to children beyond the age of three, there is a growing body of studies on children's contributions to their social life, for example on how children and adults engage in mutual negotiations involving elements of mutual apprenticeship (Pontecorvo, Fasulo & Sterponi, 2001; Rogoff, 2003). These studies relate to studies on children as participants (Hedegaard, 2002; Hedegaard et al., 2012; Højholt, 2012). Children as participants is a key theoretical analytical focus in this strand of mainly ethnographic and ethnomethodological research aimed at exploring children's perspectives. As a result, the book draws on studies of how children take part in social activities and how children orientate themselves in relation to other participants (Edwards, 2020; Edwards, Chan & Tan, 2019; Hedegaard, 2014; Hedegaard et al., 2012). I will elaborate this in Chapter 3.

One possible explanation as to why the youngest children previously have been excluded from the research, according to Murray and Cortés-Morales (2019), is that the youngest group of children who have not yet developed a verbal language (toddlers, babies, infants) are described as not having a life of their own outside the family context. In this way, I would argue – along with Orrmalm (2020a,b) – that the lack of attention paid to micromovements has led to a problematic understanding of young children as immobile beings and, I would add, an understatement of children's agency when below the age of three. Within the last decade, toddlers' experiences of everyday transitions, though, have gradually become a subject of research; (Elicker, Ruprecht & Anderson, 2014; Elwick et al., 2014a; Elwick, Bradley & Sumsion, 2014a,b; Howes, 2011; Sumsion & Goodfellow, 2012; Sumsion, Harrison & Stapleton, 2018; Sumsion, Stratigos & Bradley, 2014). Many of these studies approach young children as agentic participants that contribute to the situations in which they take part within institutional contexts, for instance how they actively create 'toddlers' s culture' and peer groups (Løkken, 2000, 2004, 2008).

McDevitt and Recchia (2020) examined the perspectives of toddlers in terms of their daily experiences of transitions into childcare by looking at their behaviour, movements and speech. The authors emphasized the variation in how the toddlers navigated and dealt with the transition process and focused on how the children became members of the toddler community in terms of their sense of 'where and with whom you belong' (p. 4). They concluded that 'individual children's experiences can be quite varied even within the same classroom. This speaks to the importance of continuing of examine everyday practices qualitatively to gain new insights on early care and education as a means of supporting young children's being, becoming, and belonging holistically within all of the worlds they inhabit' (McDevitt & Recchia, 2020, p. 16). The authors emphasized children's agentic ways of navigating the context of childcare but also underline the importance of adults not interfering in the children's communities and letting them 'be free to explore, engage, and discover with little adult interference' (p. 2). I would nonetheless argue that participants and co-participants (adults as well as peers) not only constrain but also very much enable one another's possibilities for participating and for developing a sense of belonging to a community. I provide examples of this in the empirical cases throughout the book. Howers (2011) presented a similar finding in a study on variability in toddlers' experiences of transitions, and a key finding was that caregivers and ECEC professionals are important mediators in the processes in which peers get to know each another and become active members of the toddler community. In the wake of the growing number of infants and toddlers attending ECEC centres in the Western world, daily transitioning has become an increasingly common event in young children's lives (McDevitt & Recchia, 2020). Few studies have addressed the question of how toddlers and infants support one another in challenging situations and the meaning of peer relationships in relation to transitioning (Recchia, 2012). Recchia and Dvorakova (2012) qualitatively explored the experiences of three toddlers when transitioning from an infant to toddler setting and found that their experiences varied and that the children used their peers as 'a secure base'. Sumsion, Harrison and Stappleton (2018), who examined young children's sense of belonging, focused on individual children's experiences and how they formed relationships with peers and ECEC professionals, in addition to how they became involved in peer activities and became a member of the toddler community. They concluded that 'early years' settings are complex, relational and dynamic sites in which belonging, in turn, must be understood as a complex, relational, and dynamic phenomenon' (p. 28). I am inspired by these research contributions and their focus on young children's well-being as related to a complex everyday life in various relation and in peer communities. Moreover, I am inspired by the work of Murray and Cortés-Morales (2019) as their concept of micromovements, in my view, allows me to focus on the multiple efforts even very young children put into orientating and dealing with the many transitions in their daily living. In Chapter 3 I will discuss how I conceptualize and explore these complex processes of young children's lives situated in the social complexity of the everyday living.

Fincham and Fellner (2016) explored how young children develop their identities in relation to the new context they transition to, while Traum and Moran (2016) focused on transitions as a continual process that is part of everyday living. From all of these contributions to the literature on young children and their transitioning processes, it can be concluded that transitioning processes are social and that the children use their peers in processes of orientation in new situations as a way to explore what the ECEC context is about and how to take part.

Røn Larsen and Stanek (2015) explored how children transition from being at home with a parent on parental leave to attending a nursery and how the children are active contributors to this transition. Munck (2018) studied how young children in nurseries participate in the children's communities, which involves moving across various activities. As the studies included in this section illustrate daily horizontal transitions comprise important parts of children's everyday lives and thus also their developmental conditions. These transitions, hence, are crucial sources of knowledge about how children orientate and change their participation, as well as actively contribute to the change of surroundings, in other words develop agency. For this reason, the book will discuss in more detail how young children make transitions in everyday living and how these transitioning processes become resources for the development of agency.

In the next and last section of this chapter, I will present studies which methodologically include young children in research. Even though the topic of agency is not an explicit epistemological ambition in all the mentioned studies, the methodological efforts contribute to highlight young children as active subjects whose perspectives need to be taken into consideration. For this reason, I will end this chapter by presenting some of the methodological efforts being put into including young children in research as intentional subjects acting and experiencing from their subjective standpoint. When I, in the subsequent chapters, use the term 'children's perspective' it does not refer to children's voices but to a certain, decentred location for exploring children as situated in the world (Dreier, 2008; Højholt, 2018; Juhl, 2019). In Chapter 3 I will discuss how I have approached the children's perspective analytically.

Including Young Children in Research

Participatory methods are widely used in the ethnographically inspired childhood studies mentioned earlier to allow the research to encompass the children's contributions (James, et al.,1998). As various studies have pointed out, studies that endeavour to include children in participatory research mainly involve children over the age of three in order to be able to include children's voices (Elwick, et al., 2014b). In this section I will only briefly highlight that in several of the studies with children below the age of three, researchers put a substantial amount of effort into developing methods capable of including multimodalities in the attempt to listen to children in various ways as a means to include children's voices. For instance, Clarke and Moss (2001) emphasize that 'listening must not wait until children are able to join in adult conversations' (p. 41). Such efforts have made approaches more diverse and contributed to the development of research designs appropriate for young children. Meanwhile, these efforts mainly focused on developing techniques capable of accessing and revealing children's experiences and perspectives (Hultgren & Johansson, 2013; Johansson & Emilson, 2010; Johansson & Hultgren, 2015; Waller & Bitou, 2011). Elwick et al. (2014b) put forward the assessment that, even though including infants in research is pivotal, it is a pitfall when researchers (a) position infants 'epistemologically as entities knowable through the study of their non-verbal expressions and behavior' (p. 197) and (b) subordinate the experiences and behaviour of infants into adult categories of understanding (p. 206). I maintain that it is crucial for psychological research to find ways to share subjectivity, which is why I argue that, rather than focusing on techniques, there is a need to continue carrying out conceptual work to develop and refine concepts for supporting the process of engaging collaboratively with young (and preverbal) children. Designing studies capable of exploring the everyday lives of young children is a crucial means to this end.

Summary

Even though a growing body of literature is evolving in the field of young children below the age of three (and even babyhood) the majority of studies on children's agency and everyday transitions still concerns children above the age of three. Most research on the youngest children is experimental or quasi-experimental and focuses primarily on individual development and mainly in the field of psychology. Moreover, much research with young children centres on what could go wrong and jeopardize the children developing soundly. Consequently, research about vulnerability, adversities or deviances in children's lives is predominant. In the field of sociology, the topic of adversities has been seen as the result of intergenerational transmission, while in psychology it has been seen as a result of risk factors such as maternal postpartum depression or the parents' personal life story of experiencing neglect as children. In this way, children's behavioural problems and deviant behaviour have been linked to circumstances in the family and parents' apparent lack of emotional attachment. These approaches are dominant in research focusing on assessing problems in children's lives, for instance by associating variables such as child behaviour and parental resources/deficits to a prospective outcome. The predominant research on young children, hence, contributes with understandings of young children as vulnerable creatures in risk of lopsided development if attachment to their parents does not evolve correctly. Relatedly, research about what can go wrong in terms of the risks young children face is growing, as is research on the resilience of children, while another strand of research sees children as mouldable. A shared feature of these stands of research is the belief that it is possible to make young children more robust, for instance by enhancing early learning to optimize their potential life chances. However, these ways of understandings fail to see young children, while still in need of adult care and protection, as agentic beings that also have a need to be taken seriously as subjects engaged in the world contributing to their own development as well as the development of the contexts, they take part in. This calls for knowledge about how the youngest group of children (zero to five) acts as agentic subjects in their everyday living. Prevailing conceptualizations of agency, however, are not sufficient for the exploration of the youngest children's contribution to the world and how they make the world respond to their actions. Consequently, I will discuss and develop these conceptualizations further in the next chapter, not only as a theoretical issue but also as a methodological one. Throughout the book I will examine the issue of agency as inherently embedded in the social processes in which young children orientate themselves and utilize their material surroundings in those processes.

3

Theorizing Young Children's Agency in Everyday Living

This chapter introduces the theoretical concepts that I find productive in the analysis of how young children develop agency. My approach to agency is in terms of how young children, through their intentional actions, contribute to influence the contexts comprising their developmental conditions. This approach to agency, I argue, is crucial for exploring the active and dialectic relation between young children and the social life they are part of and, consequently, it helps transcending individualized understandings of young children's development. In this way, this book is inspired of the work of others approaching agency as a social process rather than a matter of an individual property or capacity (Hopwood, Elliot & Pointon, 2021; Sannino, 2022). However, I argue for the importance of approaching agency as a dialectic process at the nexus of the individual and the social. This ambition is particularly inspired by Stetsenko (2020) who offers a notion of 'collectividual' underlining the importance of individual contributions to the transformation of the social world without losing sight of the social contingency of the individual actions (p. 10). In this way, I share Stetsenko's ambition to explore what enables individual human beings to transform their life conditions, hence, to conceptualize 'human agency yet not slip into the pitfalls of traditional approaches premised on assumptions about agency as an autonomous, solipsistic achievement of isolated individuals' (Stetsenko, 2020, p. 5).

As illustrated in Chapter 2 most of the research on children's agency in terms of influencing their lives involves children above the age of three. I argue, however, in line with other scholars contributing to the field of young children (e.g. Chimirri, 2013; Hedegaard, 2013; McDevitt & Recchia, 2020; Munck, 2018; Murray & Cortéz-Morales, 2019; Stanek & Røn Larsen, 2015; Sumsion & Goodfellow, 2012) that it is crucial to develop a clearer understanding of young children as agentic beings. In this chapter I draw on the work of these scholars, but I aim to go further by refining the concept of agency in relation to young children by emphasizing the processes of orientation as an important aspect of how they act as exerting influence on their living conditions. For this reason, the analytical concepts I will discuss enable me to develop better understandings of young children's active and transformative relation to their concrete everyday life conditions. I will discuss how these social processes can be explored and how the key concepts embodied orientation and the conduct of everyday life are a means to this end.

Methodological Issues as Analytical Cues

My interest in young children's agency and developing analytical tools suitable for this purpose has emerged over the years in various empirical studies including methodological considerations related to designing studies of everyday living from young children's perspectives. Drawing on Højholt (2018), the definition of children's perspective that I adopt for this purpose involves doing participant observations that look *with* the child rather than *at* the child. This involves positioning myself as a researcher in ways that allow me to learn about what kind of situations the children are part of across contexts and over a period of time (Kousholt, 2012). Moreover, it involves a dual focus on what the child is doing, and a focus on the contexts (e.g. ECEC and family life) in which these actions are located. This dual focus helps avoid an individualized and isolated understanding of the child, making it possible to focus on the child as acting in relation to conditions situated in everyday living.

In my empirical work with young children, it has become obvious to me that social processes of embodied orientation are a pivotal aspect of developing agency. Moreover, I identified daily transitions as a productive empirical focus for exploring these social processes of embodied orientation situated in the conduct of everyday life (I will present this concept in more detail later). Consequently, the empirical examples serve as resources for refining the conceptualization of agency in more adequate and precise ways when including young children. In this way, the chapter addresses some of the challenges outlined in Chapter 2, where I illustrated how young children are mainly pictured in three ways, as either: (1) vulnerable and exposed to their life conditions, (2) resilient, robust and autonomous agents or (3) mouldable variables whose developmental outcome can be ensured by the right stimulation (e.g. early learning activities). None of these understandings acknowledge young children as active, intentional subjects who contribute to the transformation and development of the life conditions under which they develop. The ambition to expand the understandings of young children calls for a conceptualization of agency that can explore how young children make influential contributions to the world. That is how young children make the world respond while simultaneously maintaining an understanding of young children as someone taking part in the world from a different position than adults. It is important, then, to keep in mind that adults have overall responsibility for providing care and protection, as well as for organizing the children's life conditions in ways that provide opportunities for developing agency. Young children, then, need to be taken seriously as individuals who are in need of not only protection and care but also as someone who is intentional and engaged in the world from their subjective perspectives. For this reason, I draw on scholars who have studied children (below and above the age of five) as active, intentional subjects situated in their everyday lives (e.g. Andenæs, 2011; Chimirri, 2013; Gulbrandsen, 2012; Hedegaard, 2019; Hedegaard, Fleer, Bang & Hviid, 2008; Højholt, 2018; Højholt & Kousolt, 2018; Kousholt, 2012; Røn Larsen & Stanek, 2015; Sumsion & Goodfellow, 2012; Ulvik, 2007; Valsiner, 1997). Anchored in a variety of disciplines (e.g. developmental psychology, childhood studies, sociology, social psychology, pedagogy and anthropology), these scholars employ assorted theoretical traditions (e.g. cultural psychology, social constructionism, cultural-historical theory, psychology from the standpoint of the subject and ecological psychology).

Scholars studying the child in the world employ concepts such as context, activity, action, belonging, negotiations and doings (Leggett & Ford, 2016). As a productive way to explore the youngest group of children and their development of agency, I suggest the concept of embodied orientation, which is my translation of the German term *Befindlichkeit* that Osterkamp (1991) and Schraube and Osterkamp (2013) developed in the theoretical framework of psychology from the standpoint of the subject. I will elaborate this concept later in the chapter. Besides drawing on the theoretical tradition of psychology from the standpoint of the subject (e.g. Dreier, 2008; Holzkamp, 2013a,b,c; Højholt & Koushold, 2018; Tolman, 2009), I also draw on inspiration from cultural-historical theory (e.g. Hedegaard, 2008a, Hedegaard, 2014, 2019; Stetsenko, 2008, 2020; Vygotsky, 1988). Both of these theoretical traditions have their philosophical roots in Marx's historical dialectic-materialism, where individuals are understood as societal beings co-constituting the world that they also are constituted by. I will employ analytical concepts from these traditions as one coherent analytical framework. The reason for including analytical concepts from both traditions is that cultural-historical theory offers a strong focus on cultural understandings, values and traditions in historically developed social practices which comprise the living conditions of young children and their parents. Psychology from the standpoint of the subject offers a strong focus on the subject which is pivotal in order to explore the subjective meanings of the living conditions.

A basic assumption across these theoretical traditions is that the human-world relationship is interrelated, which implies that psychological phenomena such as emotions, thoughts, intentions and actions are understood as situated in concrete socially and historically developed contexts and within specific social relationships (Dreier, 2008). The interrelatedness means that people and the world mutually shape and transform one another through the individual's actions in the world (e.g. Holzkamp, 2013a; Mørch & Hunniche, 2006; Kousholt & Thomsen, 2013). According to Holzkamp (2013a), 'human beings not only live under conditions, but also need to control the conditions of their lives. Producing the conditions under which we live means that every single individual is, in one way or another, participating in the production, transformation, affirmation, and reproduction of the circumstances under which we live' (p. 20). The methodological consequences of this are that children's actions must be explored as related to the concrete situation, conflicts, relations and activities that these actions relate to.

Young Children's Agency as Orientating and Transformative Actions

The participant observations I conducted focused on young children's gazes, (micro)movements, their way of using materiality and spaces, verbal sounds and facial and emotional expressions. Drawing on Hedegaard (2008a), I focus on actions as young children's 'intentional orientation' in the world (p. 19). Consequently, I understand intentions as children's purposeful actions and ways of orientating themselves in situations as their exploration of what is at stake in the various situations they enter into, and how to become part of the shared activities and social dynamics they encounter. Based on Bruner, Hedegaard states that 'from the very first moments of an infant's development, the child is intentionally oriented to its surrounding and from this orientation springs further development of the child's dynamic and cognitive orientation to the world' (Hedegaard, 2008a, p. 19). Hence my ambition is to understand children in the world, and their embodied and intentional orientations are key to understanding how children experience the situations they are part of and how they actively relate to the world from their location in social practice.

As already touched upon, I find daily transitions a fruitful focus when exploring how even very young children act in agentic ways and which processes this involves. Whenever children enter into and move between various activities and situations, they actively orientate themselves. For this reason, transitions in daily living represent a key empirical event for studying the processes of agency. Schraube and Osterkamp (2013) describe agency as striving to gain control over ones' living conditions and that this process involves orientation as an existential way of being in the world. The authors also elaborate on the subjective quality of this orientation process as the 'subjective aspect of the type and degree of her/his agency – that is, opportunities to act and constraints on those opportunities' (2013, p. 20). Hence, agency is more than a capacity to consciously relate to oneself, others and the world; agency involves the ability to change the world. Young children deal with multiple transitions on a daily basis, and transitions involve processes that can lead to conflicts. Also, transitions can be resources for the development of new action possibilities and transformations. I focus on how young children, when pursuing their engagements in terms of what matters to them in a particular situation, also persist and insist on transforming and co-authoring the situation. This brings into focus the children's actions as transformative contributions to social practice, which Stetsenko's (2019) activist stance reflects:

> The primary emphasis is on people encountering, confronting, and overcoming the circumstances and conditions that are not so much given as taken up by people within the processes of actively grappling with them and their contradictions and thus, realising and bringing them forth, in striving to change and transcend them [...] It is directly through and within the dynamic process of transforming and cocreating their social world that people simultaneously come to be, to know and to act, as active agents of their own lives and society, that is, as agentive actors of social practices.
>
> (p. 257)

Drawing on Stetsenko I use the children's intentional actions situated in everyday living and how children orientate in the world through these actions as a way to understand and explore agency. This calls for a focus on the relationship between young children's actions and the conditions they act in relation to. Studying how children move, orientate, act, deal with and transform their everyday life conditions, then, becomes an opportunity to understand the processes of micromovements through which young children contribute to change, develop and create the situations as part of the life conditions under which they live. This analytical focus is fruitful for the exploration of children, not as being passively exposed to their life conditions, but as actively relating to those conditions in situated ways stemming from specific locations in everyday life.

Focusing on young children's micromovements required me as a researcher to learn what to focus on when I conducted the empirical study. At first, I did not know what to look for since I did not think that much was happening when observing. Often, I just sat for hours on the floor in nurseries observing how babies struggled to take their socks off, how they observed their peers or how they moved blocks around the room or tried to get hold of the other children's toys. In the beginning, honestly, I was bored since apparently nothing important happened during the observations. It took a while before I started to notice how activities, relationships, spaces and materiality were related through the children's purposeful actions and initiatives. I learned how babies moved things around and used these things (e.g. toys, boots, socks) to orientate in the routines of the day and in the social dynamics. I had to learn to acknowledge the importance of details that could easily be overlooked. These details were small bodily movements, or movements across extremely short distances, for instance, within the same room in the nursery or the family home (hence, the term micromovements). In this way, I had to adjust my adult way of understanding movement, agency and much more. After a while I became aware of how even very young children make a tremendous effort to pursue engagements. Actually, they are exceedingly persistent in their attempts to make things work, to communicate, to become part of what is going on and to contribute to the activities. Consequently, drawing on Stetsenko (2017) I argue that agency develops through concrete processes of contributing to the transformation and affirmation of the activities one takes part in, through processes of 'agentive enactment of changes that bring the world, and simultaneously their own lives, including their selves and minds into reality' (Stetsenko, 2017, p. 31), and further 'contributing to transformative communal practices' (Stetsenko, 2017, p. 34). However, my ambition is not to solely define young children as independent or autonomous. On the contrary, I find it crucial to keep in mind that adults are responsible for children, regardless of their age. Moreover, adults arrange everyday life situations for children, which means adults organize and decide on behalf of children in their everyday lives, e.g. when to be where and for how long, and when to be moved to a new place. This will be discussed in more detail later in the chapter. The point I wish to make is that young children are not passive in such processes. Inspired by Køster and Winther-Lindqvist (2018) I aim to emphasize how young children (like other people) are creative, proactive as well as responsive beings: 'although I am always already involved in the unfolding of my life, it is neither as a privileged author nor as a self-initiating agent [...] Rather I find myself *responding* to events that affect me, and that I did not initiate. As human beings, we always start from *elsewhere*; we are essentially responsive, and thus, historical, beings' (Køster & Winther-Lindqvist, 2018, p. 552, author's emphasis).

When analysing the actions and perspectives of young children and approaching them as responsive beings it becomes clear to me through multiple empirical examples that the young children spend time on observing what is going on in a given situation, and after having observed for a while, they often try to imitate older children or adults to explore how to become part of an activity. These actions (observing and imitating) do not mean that children only act in reactive ways, but, I argue, reactive actions are a means of orientating oneself in situations – especially in new, unknown situations and with activities the children have not previously experienced. My observations indicate that whenever they have become more familiar with what is going on they start to act more proactively. In this way, part of being a young child is to have fewer experiences with different activities and situations compared to older children or adults. Focusing on responsiveness is thus a productive way to help understand processes of orientation in responsive ways as a stepping stone for young children's possibilities for acting in more proactive and transformative ways. Hence, I consider responsiveness an important aspect of the development of agency.

How to Explore Agency

So far, I have presented my approach to the concept of agency in relation to young children, and I have argued that the children's intentional and orientating actions are a key analytical focus since these actions are what relate the children to the world. I found it necessary to include a focus on the body, which I argue has not been included to a great extent in the theoretical traditions that I draw on. I have discussed this in more detail previously (e.g. Juhl, 2019) but wish to briefly touch on how I expanded and clarified concepts in ways that I find productive for the purpose of analysing agency from the perspective of young children. Let me illustrate the importance of including the body as well as identifying bodily actions as part of young children's embodied orientations with an example from a one-year-old boy named Daniel in his family context one afternoon together with his older brother and his mother:

> Daniel comes into the kitchen and looks at Matt (age four), who is sitting on the counter. His mother stands next to him. Daniel grabs his highchair and hangs on one side of it, almost making it fall over. Ashley, who is making a strawberry drink for Matt, quickly steps to the highchair and grabs Daniel by the arm to pull him up into the chair. She returns to the counter and finishes the drink. 'Do you want some too?', she asks Daniel. Daniel grabs the arm of the chair with both hands and lifts himself up and lets himself fall down as he laughs, delightedly saying: 'A, a, a', which is what he says when he means yes. The chair tilts slightly off of the floor as Daniel lets himself fall into it. Ashley stands sideways to see what she's doing at the counter while simultaneously keeping an eye on Daniel in the chair. 'Yes, yes! You'll get some too,' she says to Daniel.

In this situation, Daniel uses his body to get into a position from which he can observe what is happening on the counter, which from his perspective is out of view. He also uses his body to make his mother respond to him, just as he uses his chair as a location in the room to be able to see what his brother is up to. However, focusing only on Daniel's actions is not enough to get an idea of what is at stake for him and why he is acting the way he is, or how he perceives the situation. I must also focus on what his mother and brother are doing. Moreover, I need to link this situation to other situations in the family, as well as to other everyday life contexts in Daniel's life. This entails exploring questions such as: What is at stake here? For Daniel? For his mother and brother? What kind of activities are going on? What is Daniel doing? What is he trying to achieve? How is that going? What do the others do? Is this an ordinary situation for Daniel? Or is something unusual at stake? How does this particular situation relate to other situations in the family? And how is the family one part of the complex constellation of social practices comprising Daniel's everyday life? How is this situation involving a chair taking place in the kitchen related to other similar of different situations across Daniel's everyday life contexts? In this way, I both focus on what is going on here and now while simultaneously including information about the family context as a historical and societally developed practice characterized by certain activities, routines, tasks, responsibilities, spaces and materialities, which creates possibilities as well as limitations for the participants inhabiting the social practice. I also decentre my focus from the concrete situation and link it to the constellation of other social practices that Daniel is part of, for instance his nursery context. I will return to Daniel and the analysis of the concrete example in Chapter 6. My point here is mainly to illustrate the need for concepts that enable me to turn my analytical attention towards the relationship between the (bodily) acting child and the context for these actions in order to understand what is at stake. In the nursery context, what happens in the concrete situation a child is located in relates not only to the social dynamics among the children and what the staff is doing, it also involves knowledge about how these social dynamics unfold in the social practice of the Early Childhood Education and Care (ECEC). Moreover, it also concerns how this social practice is related to other social practices. In this way, I focus on what Dreier (2019) terms interrelatedness:

> concrete situations and scenes are part of a social practice in a local social context and affected by it. They must be grasped accordingly. And these social practices in social contexts are part of the overall social practice of a society through which this society and the life of its members are re-produced and changed. Indeed, the complex practice of a society is divided into many social practices in different social contexts which hang together in that way. [...] We can, hence, not comprehend an aspect of a societal practice, context, scene, and situation as an isolated element or stimulus.
>
> (p. 183)

I will return to interrelatedness later in the chapter. First, however, I will elaborate on how I see processes of embodied orientation as an inevitable part of young children's possibilities for acting in transformative and influential ways, hence for developing agency. After that I will discuss conduct of everyday life as a key concept for understanding agency as related to everyday life and how this concept offers the analytical opportunity to emphasize how young children exert an effort to deal with differences between the contexts, situations and activities they participate in and how the daily transitions between these contexts, situations and activities are important developmental conditions for the children. In this way I will argue that the concept conduct of everyday life offers a backdrop for the analysis of children's actions in specific situations and helps turn my attention to other related situations and social practices elsewhere. But first, in the next section, I will turn my attention to the importance of including a focus on the embodied aspects of young children's intentional actions.

Necessity of Including the Body When Exploring Agency

In this section, I will discuss in more detail how the intentional actions of young children can be grasped by applying the notion of *Befindlichkeit* (Osterkamp-Holzkamp, 1991), or embodied orientation as I suggest as a more precise key concept (Juhl, 2019).

Approaching young children as agentic and intentional relates to a basic assumption about humans as subjects that always have good reasons for their actions (Holzkamp, 2013a). This is not as rationalistic as it may sound, and I use the term reasons for action as merely a philosophical assumption about human subjectivity as reasoned beings in opposition to being 'conditioned' by external stimuli, as Holzkamp (2013c) maintains when distinguishing between what he calls 'reason discourse' and 'condition discourse':

> The sole validation language for a psychology from the 'standpoint of the subject' is the reason discourse which is merely practicable and conceivable from each individual's own standpoint. […] The reason discourse distinguishes the subject science approach from the conditioning discourse in traditional variable psychology, which is not based on the subject standpoint as a first-person standpoint but on the external 'third-person standpoint'.
>
> (Holzkamp, 2013c, p. 49)

The methodological impact of this critique is that doing research with young children implies two premises: first, that the child must not be looked at from an artificially detached researcher position, and second, that the research process must be designed to make it possible to look *with* the child rather than *at* the child. Thus, children and other participants – irrespective of their age – are not research objects but co-researchers in the processes of exploring a relevant problem in relation to the concrete everyday situations in which the child participates. Research, then, must be organized as a collaborative effort on a shared issue of relevance for the involved children and the researcher (Kousholt, 2016).

Approaching young children as acting in agentic ways becomes even more essential when researching children whose development is defined as being at risk. These children, however young, and not yet having a developed spoken language, have perspectives on their lives that need to be explored and included to understand what specific life conditions and conflicts mean to different children, depending on the complexity of their everyday lives. Tolman (2009), who emphasized the importance of including people in research as participants, stated that, if the subjectivity of the subject is going to be preserved, the subject obviously cannot be treated as an object '[s]ubjectivity is not private but shared ... the aim is to have [the subjects participating in research] share with us, their subjective point of view' (Tolman, 2009, p. 157). How is it possible, however, to have very young and even preverbal children share their perspectives? How is it possible to explore and understand the situated meanings of their life conditions? How is it possible to understand children's agency in everyday transitions? Notwithstanding the fact that Holzkamp (2013b) described other feasible sources besides voiced reasons, stating that first-person perspectives 'are not to be confined to voiced reasons for action, but have to view the entirety and interrelatedness of the externalized aspects of these reasons' (p. 293), he did not specify how the term 'externalized aspects of reasons' (p. 293) can be concretized. I take the concept of reasons for actions as merely a philosophical basis and as a constant reminder that children's actions are to be understood in relation to conditions in a specific context. However, I will employ the concept of embodied orientation (Juhl, 2019) as a more adequate way of approaching young children as intentional subjects acting in reasoned ways. Hence, I find that embodied orientation is a more precise way to explore the perspectives of young children. The basis for this concept is *Befindlichkeit* which Osterkamp-Holzkamp (1991) defined as a situated emotional evaluation of how one feels in relation to the concrete situation one is participating in, stating 'emotions function as subjective evaluations of environmental possibilities for acting as they are apprehended cognitively' (p. 103). She also pointed out that an emotional reaction 'generally [is] a more or less diffuse feeling of "ease" or "unease" evoked by the complex situation' (1991, p. 105). Osterkamp-Holzkamp (1991) translated the original German notion of *Befindlichkeit* into English as subjective situation, going on to expand this translation to 'the subjective quality of our existential orientation' in Schraube and Osterkamp (2013, p. 20) in order to underline agency. I agree on the emphasis and importance of linking emotions to agency in order to understand young children's embodied actions, and hence, I will account for why I consider the concept of *Befindlichkeit* the best concept available when the aim is to include young children as subjects in their own lives. I do not find that the English translation (the subjective quality of our existential orientation) sufficiently emphasizes that it is an immediate, pre-reflective way of orientating oneself in social situations. Shotter (2011) argued that human beings have what he terms, 'orientational understanding' (p. 440), which is 'a much more immediate and unreflective, bodily way of being related to our surroundings than the ways that become conspicuous to us in our more cognitive reflections, a way of relating or orienting toward our surroundings' (p. 439). Based on this, I suggest *embodied orientation* as a more adequate translation of *Befindlichkeit* than subjective situation. Orientating, according to Osterkamp-Holzkamp (1991), is substantial in relation to sustaining one's possibilities for action; hence, the process of orientating is the nonverbal link between the acting subject and the situation. Hence, as argued in Juhl (2019) the embodied orientation expands the modalities for analysing children's bodily ways of being in the world as a way of exploring the children's perspectives in non-verbal ways (p. 62). Moreover, young children's actions must be analysed in relation to the complexity of the conduct of everyday life situated in the nexus of social practices. This kind of analysis requires an ongoing exploration of the children's perspectives across situations and in transitioning processes. For this reason, the embodied orientation is always situated in the conduct of everyday life, and this is pivotal in order to be able to address the question of how to grasp what children's diverse life conditions mean to individual children. In this way, the concept of conduct of everyday life highlights the various subjective meanings that life situations entail for the five children in my study, even though these life situations have similar aspects.

As a researcher, I must relate to the children's embodied orientation through my own embodied orientation. As already accounted for, observing young children involves paying attention to, on the one hand, what the child does (e.g. micromovements, gazes, sounds and emotional expressions) and, on the other, what is going on in the situation and what is at stake for the child. This knowledge must be linked to knowledge produced in other situations, and that knowledge provides a backdrop for understanding the particular situation. Through my ethnographic fieldwork I became familiar with the children in various situations and in their relationships with others. Based on this knowledge about their everyday situations, routines, activities and the children's engagements and interests I related to their embodied orientations through my own embodied orientation. During my fieldwork, part of my conduct of everyday life and the children's conduct of everyday life became entangled. Through the shared experiences from the social practices we participated in together (however, from various standpoints and with various interests and tasks) I acquired a basis for interpreting children's actions and thereby obtained an idea of what situations meant to them. I utilized knowledge obtained as a researcher through conducting various studies of young children and knowledge developed through my own conduct of everyday life as a mother, but also based on the experience I have obtained through years of work as a professional in ECEC and early childhood interventions. In other words, my embodied orientation was situated in my conduct of everyday life, which during the study was entangled with the children's conduct of everyday life. This situation served as the backdrop for becoming aware of the atmosphere and embodied actions in the form of, e.g. emotional expressions, movements and sounds.

I argue that the processes of embodied orientation are important to include in analysis of agency for all age groups. However, I find it particularly important in the study of young children's agency due to fact that one of the conditions in everyday life that differs from adults' transitions between various activities is that young children are literally being lifted up and put down by adults. For instance, when children are lifted up and carried to the table and placed in a highchair when it is dinner time or being lifted away from the table after the meal and placed back on the floor. They spend a great deal of time orientating themselves when their location, activities and co-participants change. Since they do not yet have an abundance of life experience, these shifts and changes involve continuously orientating and re-orientating themselves. These processes are deeply social, and the children utilize materials, sounds, people and routines to orientate and these orientation processes are social and embodied. For adults as well as older children, language is a resource that is drawn upon in the orientation processes (Juhl, 2014; Kousholt, 2012). Young children, though, chiefly communicate with their bodies.

As I will elaborate in the next section, having observed the children across contexts and taken part in their lives is what allowed me to situate the way children act and orientate themselves in the conduct of everyday life. I share this ambition of contextualizing children's actions with scholars from within various theoretical traditions (e.g. cultural psychology and poststructuralism). As already explained, my approach to contextualizing is based on Dreier (2019) and the concept of nexuses of social practice (2019). This concept provides the analytical opportunity to examine a specific situation that the child takes part in from the child's perspective located in the complexity of social practice. This helps to provide an understanding of a given situation as linked to other situations and to include differences as well as similarities across various contexts. I will further explore the concept of social practice more in the next section. First, however, I will present the concept of conduct of everyday life (Holzkamp, 2013b) since it highlights the active efforts children make every day to create links between their various contexts and the multiple activities in which they take part in their everyday lives. I will discuss how I worked with and clarified this concept in relation to young children (see Juhl, 2015).

Conduct of Everyday Life

Just as children cannot be understood as detached from the practices in which they participate, their participation in one social practice cannot, as already stated, be understood in isolation from their participation in other social practices (Dreier, 2008). For example, the child's life in an ECEC will have an impact on family life and vice versa (Højholt, Juhl & Kousholt, 2017; Kousholt, 2011). Thus, social practices must be understood as interrelated through historically developed social practice structures created, transformed and maintained by the participating persons. Due to the fact that the practices that children participate in are connected to and separated from other practices in particular ways through social practice structures, and because it is the child who moves, acts and deals with conditions across these practices in everyday life, it is necessary to be able to conceptualize the continuous, daily efforts children make in relation hereto. Holzkamp (2013b) conceptualizes such active processes of everyday living in the conduct of everyday life. This concept is thus fruitful for highlighting the exploratory, active and creative processes involved in living a complex everyday life across various contexts. Holzkamp (2013b) examines the original sociological concept of the conduct of everyday life, which primarily Dreier (e.g. 2008, 2009 and 2011) further developed in a Danish context, arguing that the conduct of everyday life involves daily efforts through which people are 'coordinating their various obligations, relations, and activities with their various co-participants in various social contexts across the day' (Dreier, 2011, p. 13). Holzkamp argues that human beings develop social self-understanding in relation to the way they conduct their everyday lives and the possibilities available to them for gaining control over their life conditions (2013b). Thus, the ways in which life conditions become subjective premises for action in everyday living shape the way children understand themselves as active participants who co-produce the conditions under which they live. The activity of exploration is not only for the researcher to engage in; on the contrary, exploring (and learning) is regarded as a fundamental part of a human being's life-sustaining activities, as argued by Kousholt: 'to live our lives we must explore our life conditions and how to develop influence on matters important to us in our different life contexts' (Kousholt, 2016, p. 246).

Inspired by the work of others (Chimirri, 2013; Dreier, 2009; Røn Larsen & Stanek, 2015; Munck, 2018) and based on my empirical work, I have developed a more complete understanding of the concept conduct of everyday life (Holzkamp, 2013b) in relation to young children (Juhl, 2014, 2019), allowing me to gain more complex and situated knowledge about their lives. Dreier (2009) calls for our understanding of conduct of everyday life to be developed further, specifically in relation to children, as their participation and engagement in contexts outside the home increases when they 'grow older' (p. 179). However, Dreier (2009) argues that the youngest children 'need not attend to the conduct of their lives and may instead conduct themselves in the carefree manner we generally associate with being childlike' (p. 177). Like Dreier, I emphasize that the processes of young children conducting their everyday lives is qualitatively different from older children and adult co-participants; young children do not have the same responsibility as adults, nor do they need to engage in the same tasks of planning and decision-making. As already explained, adults arrange and decide upon many things for children. That said, I argue that the conduct of everyday life is not something human beings attend to or not. According to Holzkamp (2013b), the conduct of everyday life is 'the elementary form of human existence: there is no human being who is not situated within a scene of everyday life conduct' (p. 314).

Although adults often transport young children by carrying, driving and picking them up to move them back and forth between places, rather than the children moving between contexts autonomously, even young children nonetheless take active part in pursuing their different engagements across contexts. Children collaborate and negotiate engagements with co-participants as part of living a shared life. Consequently, investigating young children's everyday lives across contexts shows how conducting their lives is a complex process that includes collaboration with various parties and across different activities, which children combine, and sometimes struggle to combine from a very early age. Hence, the conduct of life is a collective process (Chimirri, 2013; Højholt & Kousholt, 2018). Chimirri (2013) argues that both adults and children 'are concerned with ambivalent demands the conditions pose and are seeking possibilities to overcome dependencies' (p. 356). This quote illustrates the fact that the conduct of everyday life is an activity, children actively do and develop in collaboration with others from the moment they are born. Notwithstanding, in accordance Dreier (2009), I argue that how young children conduct their everyday lives differs from how older children and, in particular, adults do, I maintain the importance of the concept in relation to young children. Conduct of everyday life in terms of the continuous efforts made to create coherence between the multiple activities and contexts children engage in, in other words, is not just something older children or adults do but also an activity young children engage in every day. As Holzkamp (2013b) explains, the conduct of everyday life is 'not an additional concept, superimposed from the outside, but the elementary form of human existence' (p. 314). I seek to further elaborate on this understanding of conduct of everyday life as an elementary form of human existence. I argue that this is important to avoid the alienation of young children as a different 'species' that is not included in conceptualizations of the human existence. Developing the concept in relation to young children contributes by focusing attention on how children not only participate in various contexts but also contribute to developing and transforming these contexts and that they do this by drawing on experiences across contexts (Chimirri, 2013, p. 361). At the same time, however, I argue that it is important to maintain the differences in the responsibilities and power positions of adults in social practices compared to young children. In this way, I aim to transcend the risk of alienating young children and infants, and at the same time take into consideration the qualitative differences in how young children conduct their everyday lives compared to adults.

Holzkamp emphasizes that conduct of everyday life is a social and collective process since it involves making a shared life work. Consequently, conducting one's daily life is not harmonious or a final process that means that everyday life can be settled or arranged once and for all. For example, to make a shared family life work, children and parents must adjust daily routines and activities to each other's interests (Kousholt, 2011). The solution for one family member may create problems for other family members, which means the conduct of everyday life also involves prioritizing and adjusting according to conflicting conditions and differing interests (Andenæs & Sundnes, 2019). The point is that these processes are not harmonious but entangled with other co-participants' conduct of life in complex ways that constantly need to be dealt with by children as well as adults. I argue that conduct of everyday life can help unpack the processes of transitions from the decentred focus on children's everyday living. This focus highlights the interrelatedness of the compositions of everyday life as it develops across time and space, and of the actions of people as the key in creating this interrelatedness. Importantly, the concept highlights differences between the five children's everyday life situations and how apparently similar conditions entail various subjective meanings to different children, depending on the complex composition of the conduct of everyday life.

Children Situated in the Social Practices of Everyday Life

The goal to contextualize the study of children and the related ambition of conceptualizing contexts as dialectically related to the child's actions is a shared endeavour across the theoretical traditions that I draw on in this book. Dreier's (2019) notion of nexuses of social practices represents one way to conceptualize the daily contexts in children's everyday lives, for instance, their family and ECEC contexts. The concept of social practices highlights how people act together with others in specific historically and societally developed contexts about something in particular. Dreier (2008) argues that social practices exist because people, through their continuous actions, contribute to changing and reproducing practices. In relation to the subject matter of this book, this means that social practices are changeable and dynamic and shaped through the activities of children and other co-participant, while social practices also comprise dynamic conditions for the children's actions. These conditions are dynamic because they are constantly changed, developed and created through the actions of the children and other co-participants in a dialectical relationship.

The concept social practice offers the opportunity to relate a specific situation or activity located in a specific everyday context to other activities and situations in contexts elsewhere. And in this way, when observing a child acting in certain ways situated in a specific situation, I can analytically connect this to how the child acted in other situations in the same contexts or across contexts. A given situation is, then, analysed in its connections and separations to other situations. The reason that I take my point of departure in Dreier's understanding of social practice is that it offers the possibility to include various aspects of social practices in entangled ways, and to highlight differences as well as similarities across various social practices in the analysis of a specific situation. Accordingly, the concept of social practices in Dreier's understanding of it provides the analytical opportunity to maintain complexity and entanglement in the understanding of everyday life contexts as a complex composition and profoundly characterized by the hanging-togetherness that Dreier defines as:

> a nexus of a society, a social practice, a social context, etc. Other related concepts are insufficient because it is too ambiguous whether they merely stipulate that certain aspects are linked, connected, related, or that they also hang together, in the sense that they always are aspects of a nexus of social practice and cannot exist and go outside any nexus.
>
> (Dreier, 2009, p. 183)

This is pivotal since I wish to emphasize the importance of decentring the analysis of children's actions in a specific situation and relate it to other situations in a complex everyday life elsewhere. Every situation in which a child takes part in their everyday lives, hence, is part of a complex constellation – or configuration – of that specific child's everyday life. And as embodied beings, young children's well-being and development must then always be explored and assessed as interrelated with and situated in everyday life contexts. In this manner, social practice is an important concept for situating children's actions in their conduct of everyday life. Moreover, children's actions must be seen in relation to what is happening in a context in which other children and adults also participate and that the various participants may have conflicting interests (Højholt & Kousholt, 2020; Højholt & Røn Larsen, 2021). I will illustrate this with one more example from an ECEC centre.

Emily (three years old) is playing with a younger child, and Emily continuously rejects the younger child's attempts to contribute to the play. Emily says that she wants to decide what they are going to do. The play, then, is not developed as a shared venture and the younger child eventually withdraws from the play. This means that Emily has no one to play with. Emily tries to regain the younger child's interest by inviting her to shape the progression of the play. They succeed after a process involving bodily negotiations, coordination and several adjustments, and the play is continued, but on new terms for both of them. The personal interests of each of the children and their common interests are thus adjusted and transformed through a collaborative effort that includes both of their perspectives to overcome the conflict and make their play work. In this fashion, Emily's actions contribute to structuring (and restricting) not only her own but also other participants' action possibilities, transforming the conditions in a shared social practice. Or as Stetsenko explains, 'each person thereby also realizes oneself in the same process, that is, each person comes into being by coauthoring social practices through enacting, realizing and transforming them [...] thus gradually coauthoring these practices by making a difference (however small or large) in them' (2019, p. 257). Consequently, when aiming to understand children as agentic and intentional I take my point of departure in an understanding of young children's actions as not merely a reaction to other's actions or care contributions, but also how young children act as transformative agents (Stetsenko, 2008).

Stanek (2019) suggests acknowledging the fact that children contribute to the production and reproduction of society while concurrently taking into consideration that 'the individual subject does not take part everywhere. That is why some societal conditions become more significant or proximal to the subject' (Stanek, 2019, p. 851). Along these lines, Stanek proposes that the everyday life contexts that the child takes part in can be taken into consideration as children's proximal societal conditions. In Dreier's notion of nexuses of social practice these everyday life contexts – and the children's contributions to the development and transformation of them – are analysed as interrelated. Many more historical and societal conditions are significant for what is at stake in a situation than it is possible to observe in a given situation. That is why there is a need for concepts that bring the analytical attention to these conditions that are significant but not immediately visible or observable or even recognized by the children and adults inhabiting these social practices. For this reason, the analysis must account for the nexuses that a given situation is shaped by and how children and adults contribute to transforming and reproducing these while also contributing to their own development of agency through microgenetic processes.

Everyday Life as the Context for Exploring Microgenesis

A focus on everyday life aligns with Holzkamp's endeavour to make psychology more 'worldly' by making people's everyday living the focus of psychological knowledge production. Holzkamp (2013c) criticized what he terms 'traditional variable psychology', which refers especially to the traditions of behaviourism and cognitive psychology for understanding people as isolated from the world. Part of this criticism is based on the methods prevalent in traditional variable psychology, for example experiments where people are exposed to assorted stimuli in a laboratory and where subjects are considered as determined by conditions but not *as creators and shapers* of these (Holzkamp, 2013c). Researchers observe and record the effects of stimuli from what Holzkamp terms a 'third-person perspective' (2013a, p. 20). Holzkamp points out that an experimental design thus does not provide knowledge about psychological phenomena as part of the social contexts of everyday living in which these phenomena unfold, stating '[t]he personality hypostases within psychological experiments only allow personality-related theoretical interpretations *where the individuals are not conceivable as the origin of subjective-active contributions to determining the conditions of their lives, but merely as vehicles of some invariant personal "ontological determinations" allegedly allowing the "prediction" of their further behaviour from an external control standpoint*' (2013c, p. 84, original emphasis). Taking this critique into consideration, it is not possible to create knowledge about what everyday life conditions mean to young children without including their perspectives located in everyday living. This situates the exploration of psychological processes and psychological phenomena as children's experiences, emotions, well-being and development in their everyday lives (Andenæs & Haavind, 2018; Hedegaard, 2013; Højholt, 2012; Hviid, 2008; Rogoff, 2003).

Hedegaard (2013), who asserts that it is not possible to study child development directly, emphasizes that the best way is through 'interacting and engaging with the child in everyday activities' (p. 8, author's translation). In this regard, Hedegaard in line with Holzkamp (2013b) defines everyday life as the appropriate context to explore children's development through their interactions with the world. In other words, the complex composition of everyday life in and across various contexts, such as ECEC centres and family life, comprises the developmental conditions for children. Hedegaard further argues that developmental processes must be understood by focusing on the relationship between a child's intentional actions and the institutional demands (e.g. in ECEC) put on the child (Hedegaard, 2013). However, what the child is engaged in together with others and the origin of this engagement relates to more than just the present situation located in an institutional context. What goes on in the present situation also goes beyond that actual situation and must be viewed as part of the entire everyday life embedded in the nexus of social practices (Dreier, 2019). This is why I argue that a child's actions cannot be understood solely by looking at the demands put on the child in a specific context, or how the child acts in relation hereto. Instead, actions but must be analysed from the decentred and subjective standpoint of the child to understand how the child as a historical person dialectically relates to demands, changing activities, interests and conflicts in a variety of contexts. The child, then, also contributes to restructuring the situations and, hence, how the institutional demands can be carried out by drawing on their experiences from contexts and activities elsewhere.

Vygotsky (1998) emphasizes how the dialectical relationship between human development and the culture and society could be analysed. For this purpose, he proposed four domains through which the development of psychological functions can be analysed as a social process. One of these domains is what he terms microgenetic. Geneticism conceptualizes how humans form and how actions can be analysed in terms of the history of both the individual and the human species. The four genetic domains that Vygotsky (1998) proposes are phylogenetic (biological basis for human development as a species in evolution); sociocultural (development of the social, cultural and historical world in which human activity unfolds); ontogenetic (development of human beings across the individual lifespan); and microgenetic (specific momentary fragments of development). When concentrating on the lives of the five young children in my study I approach the children's activities in and across everyday life situations as an opportunity to study daily microgenetic moments. The term microgenetic puts the child's situated activities into focus and, analytically, the microgenetic domain emphasizes how societal and historical events are present in daily microgenetics moments. From this perspective, the concept microgenetic refers to children's personal developmental processes as interrelated with the development of the contexts for these processes. This approach to development means that psychological functions and self-understanding are profoundly socially developed. For instance, social and spatial dimensions are emphasized as important for understanding young children's psychological functions, as, for instance, language development (Hackett, MacLure & McMahon, 2020, p. 14). Rather than focusing on individual children's linguistic skills as a matter of vocabulary, grammar and pronunciation, and deficits in relation hereto, young children's language is 'an assemblage and the exploration of instances of language use that make sense for children' (Ahrenkiel & Holm, 2021, p. 14). In this manner, language is developed and used in specific social events in which language is linked to activities in a specific situation and hence becomes meaningful to children, for instance in ECEC. This approach to children's development turns attention towards children's meaning creation and participation in a social life together with peers and caregivers.

Transitions in Everyday Living

Hedegaard and Fleer emphasize the importance of the daily transitions between institutional contexts for understanding children's development (Hedegaard & Fleer, 2019, p. 15). Although inspired by Vygotsky, Hedegaard & Fleer (2019) argue that Vygotsky's work stops at the institutional level, e.g. home or ECEC and does not encompass the transitions across different institutions or the societal level. Consequently, Hedegaard (2009) has conceptualized a cultural-historical theory of children's development in a model that incudes the relationships between society, institutions and people, comprising three different perspectives '(a) society's perspective with traditions that implies values, norms, and discourses about child development; (b) different institutions' perspectives that include different practices; and (c) children's perspectives that include their engagements and motivations' (Hedegaard, 2009, p. 65). These interrelated aspects help unpack the notion of social practice highlighting the cultural understandings, values and traditions in historically developed social practices which comprise the living conditions of young children in which they develop agency. Hedegaard (2019) suggests 'to study children in their everyday settings as social beings, starting to orient themselves intentionally to the world in interaction with other persons from the moment they are born; and how this orientation in interactions with the demands a child meets creates conditions for his or her development' (p. 28). Drawing on these thoughts, I consider observing how children orientate in terms of what children are looking at, what they are doing, how they move, what they are headed towards, what they attempt to accomplish, the activities or things they pursue in a specific situation a key to learn about what matters to this specific child in this specific context.

Hedegaard (2019) puts strong emphasis on how historical and cultural norms form demands and a child's development is considered a result of conflicts, negotiation and compromises between opposing demands in a specific context and the child's intentions. According to Hedegaard, children develop motives based on the mediation of societal values and culture, and the children's ways of relating to these through their actions in institutional contexts. Children, however, also through their intentional activities, have demands that contribute to changing the activities. In this book, I foreground the children's subjective contributions to the transformation of situations, and I argue that the driver of such changes must be analysed from children's compound everyday lives to understand their agentic actions. In that sense I stress the meaning of the complex composition of everyday life experiences as crucial for understanding children's perspectives. In this way, I focus on what is going on around the child. As Højholt (2018) states, if we want to understand what is at stake for the child it is necessary to focus as much on what is going on around the child as on what the child does. As I will illustrate in the empirical chapters (4 to 7), individual action develop in relation to multiple interests, relations and activities pursued across contexts; hence the development of these actions is a social process in which other co-participants' interests and activities also shape the child's intentions, actions, interests and social engagements in institutional contexts as well as in non-institutionalized contexts (Mercer & Littleton, 2007) – including conflictual aspects of participating in children's communities (Kousholt, 2012; McDevitt & Recchia, 2020; Recchia & Dvorakova, 2012). As also suggested by Chrimirri and Pedersen (2019), one needs to:

> decenter [the] analytical focus from single institutionalized arrangements to seeing them as interrelated or connected to where and how human subjects were acting otherwise in their life. Thereby, the problems that the affected people who the researcher comes to meet could be decentered, seen in the light of problems elsewhere in their life, and consequently in relation to more generally present societal conditions.
>
> (p. 611)

Based on this, I argue that it is not enough to only include the current institutional context in which a child participates and acts in. Rather the child's development and well-being must always be analysed from their subjective standpoints and as situated in their conduct of everyday life. In other words, all psychological processes, feelings, experiences and problems, as Schraube (2013) asserts, always come in the first-person mode. In the next sections, I will further discuss how to explore young children's perspectives as a means to understand their intentional acting in the world.

Children's Perspective

Subjective perspectives are located in nexuses of social practices, which means that the children's perspective is more than a phenomenological exploration of experiences. Meanwhile, the notion of children's perspective is often used in the sense of children's own voices (Johansson, 2011; Thorne, 2008). Elwick et al. (2014b) questioned whether 'infants do or do not possess well-worked out "perspectives" on their experiences' (p. 204) but did not specifically define what 'well-worked out perspectives' meant, other than it implies a 'well worked out "view" that it would take more than a yawn to articulate' (Elwick et al., 2014b, p. 204). As a result, the authors presented an understanding of the first-person perspective as something that requires other kinds of communication than infants and toddlers are capable of. In accordance with Schraube (2013), I argue that it does not make sense to talk about agency without acknowledging that everyone in the world participates in the world from his or her subjective standpoint and hence has a first-person perspective, though it is not always articulated. Schraube (2013) used the term 'ontological symmetry in human relations' (p. 25) to emphasize the subject–subject relationship between the researcher and co-researchers. Further, Schraube argues that human beings need one another's insight into a given problem to develop social self-understanding and expand possibilities for action. Schraube suggests the term 'epistemic asymmetry' (Schraube, 2013, p. 25) to emphasize the fact that only I, from my first-person perspective, can know what I think, feel, experience and so forth. Accordingly, this is also the case for the other person I interact with and involves a 'symmetrical reciprocity between first-person perspectives' (Schraube, 2013, p. 25). Hence, 'the other' remains 'the other', but not in an alienating way since our lives are connected through our engagement in a shared world. For this reason, 'the other' is 'the other' in the sense of living separate but entangled lives. My goal is not to determine what other people – including infants and young children – are experiencing or to claim to have developed an epistemological solution capable of knowing how to interpret the non-verbal activities of infants and young children with certainty. This is implicit in the epistemic asymmetry. Through shared social practices, however, a person's perspective is connected to other participants' perspectives. Through a shared life anchored in social practice structures, people have the opportunity to engage in the shared exploration of each other's perspectives on how they experience and perceive a certain situation. However, since the first-person perspective is only 'mine' and I therefore, from my first-person perspective, explore 'your' perspective, I suggest that the notion of second-person perspective enables me to distinguish between the researcher's (first-person) perspective and the researched person's (first-person) perspective (Hedegaard, 2008b, p. 43). As Martiny (2017) claims, the 'second-person position is an exchange between situated individuals focusing on a specific experiential content developed from a first-person position' (p. 66). Consequently, the analysis in the children's perspective more adequately can be termed an analytically first-person perspective explored through the researcher's second-person perspective, thus emphasizing that subjective reasons for action are complex and alternating, which is why people develop their reasons by interacting with the world and the other people in it, for instance through the process of collaborative research. Holzkamp (2013b) termed the process of gaining knowledge about first-person perspectives for action as 'intersubjective understanding' (p. 287), which will be looked at more closely in the final section. First, however, I will elaborate what I consider the language problem.

The Language Problem

As discussed in Juhl (2019) communication within the tradition of psychology from the standpoint of the subject is primarily described as verbal; hence, other kinds of bodily activities and non-verbal communication are not given much attention (Teo, 2016), which is why I have suggested embodied orientation as a more adequate concept for exploring young children's agentic actions. As already touched briefly upon and as argued in more details elsewhere (Juhl, 2019) I find the prevailing conceptualization of subjective reasons for action inadequate for including very young children in research. For example, Holzkamp (2013b) argued that a conversation is the premise for getting to know anything about another person's reasons and states that 'it has to be emphasized that without communicating with the partner I will learn absolutely nothing about her/his reasons. … I will have to ask her/him and s/he will have to be willing to answer me' (Holzkamp, 2013b:287). He continues: 'We are presupposing that verbal communication between human beings always and necessarily occurs in terms of premises, interest related ("good") reasons, intentions to act and actions' (p. 289). Non-verbal activities are not given enough attention, making it necessary to consider how to support intersubjective understandings in other modalities besides language. One presupposition is that people 'must have had "good" reasons for realizing just that option chosen and no other' (Holzkamp, 2013b, p. 285). This assumption can give the impression that having reasons for an action is the same as every person being rational, but, as Holzkamp (2013b) emphasized, this is not the case as, 'the formula "reasonably" has nothing to do with "reason" in some generalized philosophical sense' (Holzkamp, 2013b, p. 287). However, the notion of subjective reasons for action might connote a rational process which contrasts the complex everyday life as the context for these actions. However, the main purpose of approaching people as 'reasoned' was to overstep the tendency to approach people as someone not being able to explore or understand their own way of acting. In this way, it was an ambition to avoid a third part (the psychologist) to make an external interpretation of people's experiences and actions. As Teo (2016) argued, the concept of subjective reasons for action, however, 'is focused on the mind' (p. 115) which is a problem since this individualizes the processes of children's intentional actions. Furthermore, the reasons behind one's own or someone else's actions are often complex and messy, developing in common processes and interactions with co-participants in their shared everyday lives, rather than being fixed and explainable. The point, then, is not to empirically identify what young children's (or other individuals') exact reasons are in this or that context, but rather, to draw attention to the fact that young children act agentic (and with reason) in relation to their life conditions (as opposed to being determined by them). Thus, it is necessary to engage in a continuous exploration of how the world is experienced and lived in everyday life and how people's actions are grounded in a given everyday life based on a given set of premises. In this way, the philosophical concept of subjective reasons for action draws attention to the fact that very young children have reasons for their actions, even though they cannot verbalize these, which consequently draws attention to the importance of a continuous co-exploration of these reasons. For this purpose, the notion of embodied orientation situated in the conduct of everyday life allows for a broader, multimodal approach to communication and intersubjective understanding.

Embodiment

The mode of intersubjective understanding calls for a broader understanding of communication, including movements, gestures and posture as a part of a person's activities. Especially, when the children I wish to communicate with do not express themselves verbally. The field of phenomenology of embodiment takes this approach, arguing that the body is 'the visible forms of our intentions' (Merleau-Ponty, 1964, p. 15). Holzkamp's conceptual work on the first-person perspective is profoundly inspired by phenomenology, and Schraube has developed this approach further by systematically analysing its foundations based on, for example, Merleau-Ponty (1964). A basic assumption in the phenomenology of embodiment is that people constantly express themselves, thereby making themselves understandable to others (Gallagher, 2005). When co-participants succeed in understanding one another, it is a result of the fact that they share intersubjective situations, and experiencing these situations provides access to understanding each other's intentions. According to phenomenology of embodiment, sharing social situations with other human beings makes it possible to access the intentions of others (Csordas, 2008). This can, on the one hand, seem obvious since human beings live together in the same world, allowing us to imagine how others experience given situations. Hence, first-person perspectives are subjective and personal, but at the same time, connected through our shared conditions and premises for action

(Schraube & Osterkamp, 2013). On the other hand, I argue that participating in a shared practice has various meanings to different participants, which is why we have diverse perspectives on the shared practices that we participate in (Juhl, 2019). Apparently, the same situation entails distinct positions for different children to take part from in social practices, and thus, also different possibilities for contributing to changing and developing a shared activity. The risk of blurring the differences by concluding that others experience the same as oneself is that we neglect to explore how shared conditions have assorted personal meanings and become premises and reasons for acting in a variety of ways. As already stated in Chapter 2, I insist on not separating emotions and subjective experiences from social situations (i.e. embedded in historically and societally developed social practices), which is exactly why I argue that the concept of embodied orientation is fruitful for the situated exploration of young children's perspectives and their development of agency.

Summary

In the chapter I have discussed analytical possibilities embedded in various theoretical concepts to explore young children's agency through the analytical concept embodied orientation situated in historically and socially developed nexuses of social practices.

I have argued that what young children are engaged in their attempts, efforts and struggles, and what they pursue relates to the concrete possibilities for action developed in specific contexts and situations. Consequently, what children try to accomplish, the interests they pursue, also develop beyond the specific situations they take part in here and now. What they are trying to accomplish in a specific situation also relates to situations they have been part of elsewhere as historical and responsive beings. As a result, when trying to understand a child's actions in a specific situation, I focus on more than just the particular situation and what the child is doing here and now. I also examine how the particular situation is interrelated with other situations in the child's compound everyday life. For this purpose, I employ the concept conduct of everyday life to focus on the various situations children participate in during their everyday lives. I use the concept conduct of everyday life to be able to highlight the situations children transition to and from. As a result, I bring together the concepts conduct of everyday life and transition.

Children take up their conditions in various and ambiguous ways. To understand the meaning of this for the child, I argue, can only be analysed from the standpoint of each child and situated in each child's unique conduct of everyday life. For this reason, I emphasize the importance of focusing on transitions not only between different contexts bus also *within* a certain context since the variety and complexity of multiple situations in a specific situation (e.g. during the day in the nursery) comprise developmental conditions in a child's conduct of everyday life (Hedegaard & Fleer, 2019).

Analysing human actions in specific contexts makes it possible to gain an understanding of their subjective ways of relating to the conditions in the specific situation as well as in the complexity of everyday life (Dreier, 2008). This is important when my aim is to avoid approaching young children, however difficult their life situation may seem, as passive recipients of what they are exposed to or causally determined by their conditions (including what from a sociologically perspective can be defined as risk factors). I instead approach young children as acting in relation to the various scopes of possibilities and difficulties they encounter as part of a social life together with multiple co-participants across various contexts. In this way, I explore children's actions as social rather than individual. Even though the actions are of course always the actions of someone in particular, actions invariably carry a sociality as they are directed at something in a specific practice that is socially and historically developed. As argued by Schatzki (1996) '[a]n action is the action it is as part of a practice' (p. 97). In this way, the phenomena I have studied in my empirical work – young children's embodied orientation and intentional actions as a key to understand agency – only exist in a specific context and must be analysed accordingly. Hedegaard states that in order to analyse the child's perspective actions must be understood as part of a process in which 'the child's prior activity is understood in the light of the following, and the following in the light of the preceding' (Hedegaard, 2013, p. 66, author's translation). Moreover, as will become clear in Chapters 4, 5 and 6 the children's actions most often also represent the attempt to become part of a social activity together with others and can therefore also often be viewed as a response to other's actions.

I have elaborated how psychology from the standpoint of the subject strongly focuses on communication as a means to collaborate with children in order to gain insights about their perspectives. However, as argued, there is a need for developing concepts that include verbal and non-verbal modes of communication to make it possible to conceptualize children's reasons for action and to understand the subjective meanings of situations from the children's perspectives. For this reason, I emphasized the bodily aspects of acting since they are predominant when observing the youngest children. I propose employing the concept of embodied orientation to be able to include young children's bodily way of acting in the world and as a fruitful concept for foregrounding subjective orientation as related to not only the experiences children gain across contexts but also their efforts and engagements pursued across contexts.

Part Two

4

Children's Everyday Life in ECEC Contexts

In this chapter, I focus on the part of children's everyday lives unfolding in early childhood education and care (ECEC) contexts. Their everyday lives in ECEC contexts are generally filled with a multitude of children and various adults compared to the children's family contexts. In some ECECs, however, children are in a small group with only one caregiver. Regardless of what form the ECEC takes the daily routines and activities differ from the family contexts and involve numerous shifts and transitions for children. The detailed analysis of the myriads of internal transitions (Recchia & Dvorakova, 2012) and micro movements (Murray & Cortéz-Morales, 2019) that even very young children make on a daily basis contributes to developing clearer theoretical understandings of young children's agency – and also to shedding light on the difficulties these children experience in everyday transitions. Hence, a key point in this chapter is to highlight the children's movements, initiatives, creativity, orientation processes, negotiations and efforts. In this way, the chapter also contributes to studies aimed at transcending the dominant understanding of babies as being rather immobile. Even though the analysis is situated in a Danish context, theorizing the agency of young children in relation to daily transitions is of international relevance. I will focus on how the children develop agency through their transformative contributions to the social practice of ECEC. I will do this by (1) emphasizing the children's ways of making micro-movements as part of their conduct of everyday life and by (2) analysing the personal aspects and efforts related to the multiple and complex internal transitioning processes.

I will give a quick introduction to how the ECEC system is organized in Denmark, this particular institutional context serving as the backdrop for exploring children's activities and my analysis. This is important since the three kinds of ECEC centres presented offer quite varied conditions for the children's development and the support they get from caregivers. I will also present some of the discussions of the tasks and responsibilities assigned to the ECEC system as these are currently changing. The tasks and responsibilities are important for understanding the conditions in the social practice of ECEC.

Historically, the ECEC system in Denmark dates back to the beginning of the last century, and since the 1980s the number of ECEC centres has multiplied. In 2019 approximately 90 per cent of one-to-two-year olds and 98 per cent of three-to-five year olds were enrolled in public day care in Denmark[1]. Only a small percentage of children are enrolled in private day care. The three most common forms of ECEC contexts are public nurseries, public family nurseries and public day care centres. In public nurseries, approximately two professional nursery caregivers and one untrained assistant are assigned to twelve children (0–3 years). In public family nurseries, one caregiver with limited training is responsible for three to five children (0–3 years) in the private home of the caregiver, with opening hours varying but usually between 7:00 am and 4:30 pm. In public day care, approximately three professional caregivers and one untrained assistant are assigned to twenty-four children (3–6 years). In public nurseries and day care centres the opening hours also vary but are normally 6:30 am to 5:00 pm. The financing is heavily subsided by the state, and low-income parents can apply for a free place (Juhl, 2018).

ECEC in Denmark has traditionally been child-centred, valuing and respecting children's democratic rights and their right to play (Jensen, 2009; Winther-Lindquist, 2017). In recent years, political interest in ECEC as a context for learning and preparation for school has challenged these traditions. This change in political interest grew in the wake of several transnational comparative studies and assessments of children's school performance in the late 1990s and in the 2000s, e.g. the Programme for International Student Assessment, or PISA. These assessments indicated that Danish children were falling behind academically compared to other European countries (Egelund & Mejding, 2004). Subsequent research findings focused on ECEC (initially day care centres and later nurseries) as a potential resource for enhancing children's learning skills to ensure a higher level of school readiness (Benders, Pham & Carlson, 2011; Ramey & Ramey, 2004; Winther & Kelly, 2008). Consequently, during the late 1990s, the Danish Daycare Act explicitly underlined that one of the main purposes of ECEC was to support the development of certain skills, e.g. language and early understanding of natural phenomenon. Scholars described this change in focus as a transformation from the core task of care to what they term educare (Broström & Hansen, 2010). During the 2000s this trend was reinforced in 2004 when national education curriculum comprising six areas of learning was implemented. The learning areas were revised in

2018, further emphasizing that a core pedagogical task is to create high-quality learning environments and to evaluate and reflect on learning indicators. In addition, play and children's self-organized activities are stressed as equally important (Ministry for Children, Education and Gender Equality, 2016). Some Nordic studies reject these arguments, emphasizing that the best way to support child learning in school is to prioritize children's self-organized play in ECEC (Pellegrini, 2009; Sommer, Samuelsson & Hundeide, 2010). Winther-Lindqvist (2017, p. 111) argues, for instance, that children's self-organized play activities have significant importance in the personal and social development of children. The result is that ambiguous interests and demands are put on the professional caregivers who are responsible for implementing and conducting these changing and highly politically influenced tasks (Winther-Lindqvist, 2021). One task that ECEC professionals are assigned with is related to the fact that ECEC is considered a resource for fighting social inequality (Jensen, 2009). The prevailing academic debate reflects major political interests, and despite the conflicting perspectives in research on how to best support children, the focus on improving early academic learning unambiguously dominates the current political agenda on ECEC in Denmark (Dannesboe, Westerling & Juhl, 2021; Juhl, 2016; 2018; Westerling & Juhl, 2021). Public family nurseries, however, still focus less on enhancing children's early learning compared to public nurseries, and especially compared to public day care centres, where there is an intensified focus on children's transition to school and especially on making children ready for this transition.

Everyday Life in ECEC

The analysis of children's everyday life in ECEC underscores how young children are engaged with each other in organizing children's communities and how children continuously are in the midst of transitioning between different situations and activities. Thus, it is also in relation to these processes of finding their way in a myriad of activities and orientating themselves in these processes of becoming a part of activities that children often experience conflicts. These struggles and obstacles can lead to the development of new possibilities for participating and, hence, also for the child to contribute to creating and transforming the practices in new ways (Hedegaard, 2014). Meanwhile, conflicts can also lead to exclusion, which influences their social self-understanding (Kousholt, 2019). This chapter analyses these social processes in relation to children's daily life in ECEC as an institutional context entailing societal values, norms and culturally and historically developed societal tasks that create certain conditions for children's participation. Consequently, on the one hand, I analyse the ECEC context as a social practice focusing on the societal and historically developed aims and scopes that characterizes the various ECEC contexts. On the other, I centre on how the people who inhabit the institution (children, ECEC professionals) are active participants with different interests, engagements and tasks in relation to day care. A couple of examples of aims and scopes will illustrate the already introduced mandatory curriculum promoting school readiness and language stimulation. Moreover, the aims and scopes are also shaped by the political identification of ECEC as an important site for early childhood interventions and, in particular preventive interventions. These aims and scopes comprise conditions for children's intentional actions and interactions in ECEC contexts and for the ECEC professionals' possibilities for supporting these interactions. Yet, the tradition of a child-centred framework and the emphasis on play and the children's own activities are also important values characterizing the professionals' approach to children. In public family nurseries, the routines and daily activities are organized in a way that is compatible with only one caregiver and three to four children. In this way, ECEC is a complex practice with contradictory aims, conditions and values that guide the professional work and comprise quite different developmental conditions for children, as well as for the various caregivers.

A Glimpse of Everyday Living in a Public Family Nursery – Daniel

In this section, I introduce Daniel, who has been enrolled in a public family nursery five days a week (Monday–Friday 7am to 4pm) since he was five months old. I started observing Daniel in his everyday life contexts when he was fifteen months old, ending observations when he was twenty-seven months. Daniel lives with his mother Jennifer (nineteen years) and his older brother Chris (four years). The family has no network since Jennifer grew up in foster care and she currently has no contact with her birth family. The fathers of the two boys are only sporadically involved in the parental responsibility and care. Jennifer has no education besides basic schooling and is unemployed. The municipal professionals assigned with the task of providing early interventions are concerned about whether the task of taking care of two young boys is too much to handle for the mother. The concern is not related to a specific problem with the children but to circumstances related to Jennifer. Very young (average age of first-time mothers in Denmark is 29.3 years) unemployed and/or uneducated mothers like Jennifer with no family network and a previous history of abuse or psychological problems are considered at-risk parents. Thus, Jennifer's life circumstances are the reason that the family was enrolled in preventive intervention when Daniel was born. The intervention comprises extra visits from a health visitor, assignment to a municipal group for marginalized mothers and an early start and a free place for Daniel in a public family nursery.

The family nursery is in the private home of a caregiver named Ann. She takes care of Daniel and two other children: Kelly, twenty-two months old, and Liam, ten months. In the subsequent excerpt, which is one among countless examples, I illustrate how a typical morning unfolds and what the children are doing:

> Daniel, 15 months, sits on the floor and is busy pulling off his socks. Once the socks have come off, he smiles and looks at Ann, who comments: 'Well, have you taken off your socks, Daniel?' Kelly looks at Daniel's bare feet. She sits down and pulls her own socks off as well. Daniel laughs. He gets up and pours a plastic box full of toys out on the floor. Kelly walks over to him and reaches for a toy Daniel has in his hand. Daniel bites Kelly in the arm. She cries. Ann gets up and heads for Daniel and Kelly: 'No, no, Daniel! Don't do that!' Ann lifts Kelly up and comforts her. Daniel sits down and looks down, holding on to his bare feet.

Despite its seeming insignificance, this episode shows the essence of what is at stake for Daniel in the family nursery, illustrating several key issues that come into play for him while there. Kelly and Daniel are exploring what they can do together, orientating themselves in relation to what activities they find exciting. For instance, what playthings do they each consider exciting, adding to the allure of the objects. They often pursue the same toy and spend a large amount of time observing and imitating each other. They respond to each other's actions, ostensibly communicating and coordinating their embodied actions in relation to one another, hence using each other as resources for orientation processes in relation to transitioning between different activities and situations in the nursery. At the same time, their mutual interest in one another leads to multiple conflicts, e.g. pursuing and then fighting about the same toy. Most often, the toy itself does not appear to be of importance since they lose interest in it when the other abandons it. In this way, their relationship is of great importance to both of them but also leads to conflicts, which at first glance appear to be just one of many trivial daily tussles. I argue that the importance of the episode in the above excerpt involves details that can easily be overlooked but that nonetheless remain key to understanding the daily lives of young children and their processes of agency in relation to transitions. For example, Daniel tries something and finally succeeds, i.e. manages to take off his socks. He takes the initiative and proactively acts in ways that other children can relate and respond to. These young children provide us with an idea of what conducting everyday life looks like for toddlers. Their lives encompasses exploring the opportunities different situations offer and how their actions comprise a social meaning that other children and adults relate to, respond to and act on. Hence they gain experiences about how what one does contributes to changing the situation for everyone involved. When Daniel takes off his socks, Kelly does the same. And when he pours toys onto the floor, Kelly moves towards him and wants to join in. In addition, they learn orientate in the possibilities to interact in various ways depending on how various situations unfold during the day. Daniel explores how his actions have various meanings, and he experiences opportunities, conflicts across various situations and activities and how he can contribute to creating, reproducing and developing his surroundings.

The episode in the above excerpt illustrates one of the many types of daily conflicts that occur in ECECs, oftentimes when the children struggle about the right to a certain toy. It also demonstrates how Daniel seeks to deal with the conflict by biting Kelly, which leads to a new conflict that requires the caregiver to step in. Thus, life in the nursery for young children highly involves trying to deal with and explore how to make a common everyday life work together with other co-participants. The communication and interrelations between the children are expressed bodily, for example when they move towards something, looking, pointing, hitting, biting, hugging, reaching out and giving and taking things from one another. The children frequently make an effort to explore how they can be together, mutually shaping opportunities and limitations based on their actions. In other words, they develop their being in the world together by acting together, and through their embodied orientation they relate to each other and coordinate their actions. Sometimes the shared activities lead to them having a great deal of fun and sometimes to disputes. Overall Kelly and Daniel expand and develop their experience in terms of being part of a social world. Moreover, they contribute to one another's and their own development when transitioning between various activities. Accordingly, the situations they take part in constantly develop and change, putting new demands on themselves and each other.

In the following analyses of the lives of toddlers in public family nurseries and public nurseries, I mainly focus on the children's embodied orientation in order to gain a stronger idea about what the situations Daniel and the other children are part of mean to each of them. I combine this situated knowledge with the insights obtained while I was part of the children's lives in and across various everyday life contexts. These insights provide information about the daily routines, actions, changing interests and personal preferences of the children. Later in the chapter, when I present the older children (3–4 years) enrolled in day care centre, the empirical examples include spoken language, which plays a larger part in the children's interactions and negotiations.

Conflicts and Mutual Interest

During the day at the nursery, Daniel eats breakfast, lunch and snacks, and takes a daily nap after lunch. Kelly and Daniel constantly spend time observing each other's actions and imitating each other, but they also struggle with each other and clash about who decides and who should have the toys. Once Ann intervened to stop Daniel from biting Kelly, the situation continued as follows:

> Ann says it's time to have some fruit. Daniel runs to the table and leans over his chair to get up. Kelly, who has stopped crying, pulls out her chair and sits down. Ann helps Daniel into the chair and gives each child a sliced apple that was prepared in advance. Kelly and Daniel repeatedly look at each other while eating. For example, Kelly watches Daniel take a bite of the peeled side of the apple slice first, after which she then turns her own apple to bite it from the peeled side. Ann pours milk into two cups on the windowsill. When the children have finished their apples, Ann offers them a cup of milk and they both drink.

The kerfuffle in the previous excerpt gives way to a new way of interacting that is mediated by Ann, who introduces their routine morning snack. This new situation provides a change of dynamics that allows the children to show interest in one another in a different way compared to the previous situation. Ann helps Kelly and Daniel extricate themselves from the conflict behind by aiding them in moving on together into another situation (morning snack), furnishing them with a way to be together on different terms. The children sit down, look at each other and watch how the other person eats, and they imitate each other. As a result, they orientate themselves in relation to what the other one is doing. This situation creates various opportunities for the children to relate to each other compared to situations where they fight about toys. In the eating situation the children sit on their own chairs and are not permitted to move around, providing them predictable parameters that allow them to observe each other without having to chase or touch each other. In this particular situation being stationary creates a different experience, helping them to adjust to each other's contributions in another way.

In addition to the concrete interaction between the children and Ann's support, the situation also highlights what kind of practices occurs in a family nursery, and how this particular context entails certain possibilities for the children's interactions.

The Family Nursery as a Social Practice

The morning snack is an example of a daily routine in the family nursery, with meals and naps largely structuring a typical day. The children who arrive early in the morning are given breakfast. When all the children have arrived by about 9:00 am, they are given a piece of fruit and a glass of milk or water before engaging in a planned activity such as a walk, a creative activity or just playing until lunch. Once or twice a week, the caregiver and children meet with other caregivers and their children at a playroom provided by the local authorities.

Family nurseries differ from the public nursery in that the children are taken care of in the caregiver's own home. In public nurseries, children are taken care of in publicly owned facilities. Moreover, in family nurseries, only one adult cares for the children and is responsible for executing practical tasks and collaborating with parents. To ensure that the day goes smoothly, planning and preparing the practical tasks beforehand is necessary. Before the children arrive in the morning, for example, the day is planned based on routines in relation to meals, changing diapers, naps and activities. Early in the morning before the children arrive, the caregiver prepares lunch and puts it in the refrigerator on a plate so it is conveniently ready to serve when the children are hungry. Ann had, for example already cut the apple, putting it in a bowl of water to keep it fresh for the morning snack. Similarly, prams and beds for naptime are also readied ahead of time. Even bibs are washed and placed in a pile within easy reach. All these practical measures let Ann quickly step in when conflicts arise, allowing rapid adjustment of the situation, even when carrying a crying child on one arm. To reiterate, the practical tasks are completed at times when the children are not present. The underlying aim of presenting these details is not to focus on the organization per se but to demonstrate that the preparations and prioritizations represent an important means for understanding the family nursery as a social practice and how this context establishes the conditions for the caregiver and the children.

For the children, the predictable structure and Ann's meticulous preparations do not leave much room for them to circumvent what happens, reducing the opportunities available to them to negotiate how the day is structured. For example, Ann always sits at the table to ensure that no one plays with their food or leaves the table early. Even the slightest attempts cause Ann to employ measures to stop the children, for instance by taking away their cup. The foreseeability of the morning snack routine, however, does give the children an opportunity to safely relate to each other in other ways than when they organize activities on their own.

Snack time is quite a structured affair, with the children only given a new slice of apple or a drink of milk once they have eaten the slice they have. Likewise, when out for a walk, they must hold onto the side of the stroller, but if they let go and try to wander away they must sit in the stroller. Ann's systematic approach allows her to take care of several children on her own. Meal prep and strategically placing cups, wet wipes and other items within arm's reach of the table enables her to stay close to the children as much as possible. Staying one step ahead of the children is a common practice among caregivers who work alone (Sumsion & Goodfellow, 2012). Ann knows the children well, making her familiar with what preoccupies them and what situations trigger conflicts, which means she is aware of when she must pay special attention. The structured setup is somewhat constraining but provides the children with the opportunity to easily orientate themselves in relation to the well-known routines. Knowing what will happen next seems to make the transition between activities and situations easier for the children. Even though also limiting the children's possibilities for action, the fixed routines at the same time leave more room to negotiate because they do not have to spend a lot of energy on constantly navigating in unknown situations, leading to the children having more resources to spend on exploring new possibilities. This is the case in the next example.

Agentic Contributions

As mentioned, Ann plans most of what happens, when and how, during the day, which means the children are not often invited to influence the daily routines and plan for the day. They nonetheless continuously negotiate and sometimes succeed in changing the plans. In the next example, Daniel indicates that he would prefer to not do what was planned and is then given the opportunity to pursue what he was engaged in. Daniel asserts himself in various ways and is provided with an opportunity to experience that he is capable of influencing what happens. The empirical data derived from observing Daniel in the family nursery contains many episodes like this one, where he actively draws attention to what he wants and tries to get Ann and his peers involved. What I want to emphasize is that Daniel's proactive actions not only influence his own possibilities for acting but also contribute to transform the situation for Ann and his peers.

It is morning, and Kelly and Daniel will be the only children at the nursery. Ann has scheduled indoor play because it is raining. She would like the children to play in the living room and the kitchen with new blocks that she recently purchased. Daniel has just finished eating his oatmeal, and Kelly is playing with the new blocks on the floor. After Ann mentions the pouring rain, Daniel looks at her and then looks out the window before heading to the coat room:

> Daniel (20 months) picks up one of his boots and carries it into the kitchen. He sits down and struggles a bit before finally getting it on. He gets up and walks further into the room with the boot on one foot. Ann stops him, takes off the boot and kindly, but determinedly, says: 'We don't wear boots inside'. She carries the boot back into the hallway and then returns to the kitchen. Daniel goes back to the hallway and picks up the boot again. Ann takes it from him once more and puts it back. Daniel picks it up a third time; Ann laughs and asks Daniel if he wants to go for a walk. He gets up and runs around while squealing and sounds very happy. He runs to Kelly, grabs her hands and tries to pull her up off the floor. She gets up and also starts running around and squealing. Ann laughs and directs the children into the hallway to help them put on their jackets and boots.

In this episode, Ann mentioning the rain outside gives Daniel an idea. When he was on his way to the nursery with his mother and brother, they stopped to jump in puddles in the rain. Later at the nursery he draws on this experience and fetches his rainboots, not his shoes, which I recall he normally prefers to wear. He evidently knows that boots are appropriate footwear for a rainy day and are the same ones he used to jump in puddles earlier. Daniel's various experiences in the rain become a resource that pushes him to pursue his interests. He also draws on similar previous experiences with rain and the boots and with how to succeed in communication with the caregiver. In this way, the materiality seems to provide resources for Daniel in order to communicate his intentions to the caregiver and to Kelly.

His embodied actions, persistently fetching his boots and putting them on again and again, communicate his intentions. Initially Ann takes off his boot, telling him that boots are not allowed indoors. But Daniel is persistent, and after his third attempt, Ann agrees to go for a walk. Daniel is aware of the necessity of persuading Ann to change her plans if he is to succeed in his attempts to go outside. He is simultaneously reactive and proactive when responding to Ann's refusal, and he is proactive when he perseveres and pursues a wish based on previous experiences. Daniel does not change his wish in relation to Ann's plan.

When Daniel realizes that they are going to go outside he becomes elated and he tries to get Kelly excited as well. This episode illustrates the amount of effort Daniel makes to pursue his wish and to get other co-participants involved. When opportunities become available for Daniel to influence the situation and activities, he is able to experience that his actions do not have to resort to biting to get his way. Analysed from Daniel's perspective, relevant care involves supporting him in contributing to the situations he participates in. For Ann to be able to provide this type of care she needs to include his perspective in terms of what he finds relevant and what he is trying to communicate, just as she needs to be flexible about her plans for the day.

Hedegaard (2008b) argues that the institutional perspective is important because children's everyday lives are compound and include daily transitions between institutional contexts, such as the home and day care. In each of these contexts the child meets different demands. Transitioning and meeting new demands in institutional settings, according to Hedegaard, may lead to a crisis because children's way of relating to their surroundings, orientating themselves and acting do not always fit with the new demands. Hedegaard and Fleer (2019, p. 8) argue that this leads to a restructuring of the child's motives. Consequently, the various institutional demands, they assert, are pivotal for understanding the child's intentional actions and motive orientation. I agree with this but would add that the example with Daniel is a resource for understanding how children coordinate their interests and engagements in relation to the institutional demands, though not always in ways that lead to children changing their motivation or interests. Sometimes, the differences lead to conflicts between children and their surroundings, and at other times children – like Daniel – succeed in changing the surroundings by aligning the institutional demands with their intentions. A related point is that the demands in a specific situation or context entail different meanings to different children. For this reason, I argue that it is difficult to conclude that demands in an institutional context (in this example mediated by the caregiver's initial rejection of Daniel's attempts to go outside) generally lead to a restructuring of children's motives if their actions and orientation do not fit with the institutional demands. Whether children change their intentional actions in accordance with the demands they encounter, I contend, depends on the possibilities for action in the situation and what other activities are occurring. This differs heavily in a group of children, and the concept of social practice can help illuminate how children participate in the same situation from different standpoints and locations in this practice. Thus, the same situation comprises multiple meanings for different children depending on what the specific situations are part of in a compound everyday life in which children not only in transition between different institutional contexts but also in transition across multiple complex situations within each of these contexts. The many situations a child takes part in during the day in ECEC contexts comprise a complex nexus of interests, engagements, motives, orientation processes, possibilities, limitations and conflicts, the subjective meanings of which must be explored from each of the children's first-person perspectives.

In the next section, I show how a conflict between Kelly and Daniel illustrates how the conflict emerges in relation to them relating to each other in new ways. The conflict involves their mutual interest in one another but also how their interests are simultaneously contradictory.

Changed Dynamics in the Children's Community

Kelly and Daniel have had many conflicts for a while. Often the conflicts end with Daniel biting Kelly. Ann explains that an older child has recently stopped in the family nursery and that it is highly common for conflicts to occur and escalate when the dynamic in the group of children changes. Ann's experience is that these kinds of conflicts usually gradually diminish if the children are supported in figuring out how to relate to each other in new ways. From Ann's viewpoint, Daniel's act (biting) relates to an ordinary situation in the family nursery, where biting is considered a common reaction when children without spoken language try to assert themselves among children with more developed language skills. What is described here as a common and, importantly, a social problem is, nonetheless, interpreted as Daniel's individual problem. To understand the reason for this, we must leave the family nursery for a moment and turn our attention towards a meeting between the various professionals involved in Daniel's life. Due to concerns about Daniel's well-being, various professionals are involved in his life. Daniel's social worker does not know Daniel personally, but she has the authority to make important decisions in the boy's life. The social worker must be kept informed about Daniel's well-being to determine what interventions should be initiated. She primarily receives information at meetings in reports from Ann, the health visitor, a psychologist and the manager of the family nursery department.

I observe the meeting where the issue of Daniel biting while at the nursery is being discussed. It begins with the assorted parties presenting how Daniel is thriving in the various contexts. The caregiver says that it is a somewhat difficult period for Daniel in the family nursery since there has been a change in the group of children. He is currently adjusting to the new situation together with another child, Kelly. The pair, who not earlier used to play together, is now adjusting to the new situation, often leading to conflicts where Daniel bites. The health visitor, however, says that she believes that the biting is due to his need for adult contact, which is not being met sufficiently by his mother. The main concern about Daniel's well-being is related to his mother's rather young age (nineteen) and to her living alone with Daniel and his older brother. The health visitor who monitors Daniel's weight and nutrition believes that the mother puts him to bed every evening alone with a bottle of milk and lets him fall asleep with it. She has advised the mother to have quiet time alone with Daniel and introduce him to a structured, peaceful evening routine by either singing or reading to him. Several of the professionals attending the meeting have doubts about whether the mother can independently handle her role as a parent on her own.

Several of the professionals argue that there is a need for increased adult contact in response to the difficulties Daniel experiences in the family nursery as they think that this will prevent him from biting. The nursery manager suggests that Ann gives Daniel a daily massage to provide a quiet moment where he receives individual attention. The idea is to provide a space where he does not have to fight with the other children for Ann's attention. The professionals have different understandings of why he bites. Ann sees it as Daniel's way of handling a social problem related to a change in the constellation of the children's group, seeing it as his attempt to assert himself in relation to Kelly, who is slightly older. Ann talks about how Daniel only bites in situations where there is a conflict between him and Kelly, mostly when they fight about toys. He never bites the younger boy. In other words, Ann believes the problem stems from the change in the social dynamics of the children's community. The majority of the professionals nonetheless see the biting as a sign that Daniel lacks attention from his mother, i.e. the problem related to a particular situation in the nursery is understood as being related to Daniel and a lack of motherly care and attention in the family context. This individualized understanding of a social problem can be seen as a reason why the intervention is directed at Daniel and not the whole group of children and their various possibilities for influencing the situation, they are part of. Consequently, a social conflict in the family nursery is addressed as an apparent deficit in the mother-child relationship. Consequently, individualization and mother blaming, to use Burman's (2018) term becomes the interpretive repertoire for understanding the problem.

Detaching Support from the Context of the Problem

Initially, Ann is a little hesitant about doing massages but since she believes that Daniel likes them, she begins to do them daily, as agreed at the meeting. However, as we shall see, she encounters various dilemmas when carrying them out. In the following episode, which takes place in the morning, Kelly and Daniel have just had a spat about some toys and Daniel bites Kelly, causing Ann to think that now is a good time for the day's massage:

> Ann asks Daniel (22 months) if they should find the quilt. He nods, points at Ann and pulls on his shirt. He wants Ann to help him take it off. She laughs and pats his head. She picks up the quilt and a small basket with various soft brushes. Ann helps Daniel with his clothes while talking to him in a calm and caring manner: 'My, you are such a sweet boy'. Kelly watches Ann's every move. When she sees that Ann has brought the quilt and the basket Kelly walks towards Daniel. Ann tells her: 'This is just for Daniel, you know that'. Ann sits down on the floor and puts the quilt in front of Daniel, who sits down and grabs his toes with both hands. He smiles. Kelly tries to sit on top of Daniel. Ann gently pushes her away. Kelly continues. Daniel finally leans forward with his mouth open as though he is about to bite her. Ann grabs him by the forehead and pulls him towards her belly, stating emphatically: 'No biting!' She tells Kelly that she should stop teasing and encourages her to go into the other room and find a book. Kelly, who starts to cry, keeps trying to sit on the quilt. Now Liam, the younger boy, also wants to sit on the quilt. All three children are fighting about who gets to sit on the quilt. Daniel says: 'No, no!' to the other children while Ann is busy brushing his legs with a baby brush at the same time as she tries to keep the other two children away. Daniel does not appear to pay much attention to being brushed but constantly keeps an eye on the other children. After many requests from Ann, Kelly finally gives up, abandons the quilt and leaves the room. Daniel gets up and runs after her.

Daniel seems happy about getting the massage, is eager to get started and is aware of what is to happen as soon as Ann mentions the word quilt. When Daniel sees the basket with the brushes he begins to take off his clothes to help get ready. He is also fully aware that he is the only one who is supposed to sit on the quilt. The other children, also interested in the activity, try to sit on the quilt next to Daniel. He protests and pushes them away. Daniel is keen to sit on the quilt and keep the other children away, but his interest in the quilt seems to relate to the other children's interest in it. When Kelly eventually gives up and leaves the room, Daniel loses interest in the quilt. Notably, her exit provides an opportunity for Daniel to have the adult contact with Ann that the massage is supposed to provide but he runs after Kelly.

Analysed from Daniel's position in the social practice, the relationship between him and Ann alone does not appear to concern him the most. He is occupied with getting attention from Ann but simultaneously pays a great deal of attention to the other children and responds to them when they approach the quilt. Daniel is attempting to integrate what Ann is making an effort to separate. He is prevented from doing so because the massage is for just one child and one adult. Hence Ann considers Kelly's actions and interest disruptive, thwarting her from carrying out the massage as intended. Schwartz (2014), in an analysis of children's daily lives at a residential institution, points out that when a child and a professional educator are involved in a caring situation, it often attracts the attention of other children. Schwartz states 'the children's openness to engagement of other children challenges the caregivers' notions that children need individual time with an adult' (2014, p. 183, Author's translation). The point is that situations where adults give care and attention to a single child means, from the perspective of children, that it may very well include more children.

Paradoxically, the professionals view the massage as a means to get Daniel to stop biting. But in the specific situation, the setup and one-adult-to-one-child approach leads to a new conflict in which Daniel again tries to bite. The point is that Daniel bites in the context of the children's group as part of him responding to what is going on between him and Kelly and their mutual exploration of what they can do together, indicating that the issue must be resolved in this context and not isolated from it.

In the subsequent section, I present one more of the five children. His name is Anthony and the situation discussed involves a morning where I was together with him in his family nursery. In the situation, Anthony – like Daniel – explores how to become part of a community with older children. The point I wish to make with the example provided is that Anthony's caregiver understands his way of approaching the other children as precisely an attempt to orientate himself in what is going on and how to take part in it. Anthony was twelve months old when I started my observations and twenty-four months when the study ended. Anthony has been enrolled in family nursery since he was five months old. He is taken care of by Kate together with two older children, Hannah and Andy, both of whom are twenty months old. Anthony lives with both of his parents, who are in their mid-twenties and have a history of drug abuse. His mother is a student, and his father is a truck driver who works night shifts. Anthony's father has a chronic illness that regularly puts him in hospital, leaving his wife with sole responsibility for Anthony. Anthony spends every other weekend in respite care in a family that also occasionally picks him up from family nursery and supports the parents in their care tasks. Moreover, Anthony and his mother are part of the same group for marginalized parents as Daniel and his mother.

Care as Support to Agentic Participation – Anthony

The caregiver, Kate, sits on the floor with the children one morning. Hannah and Andy play together, and Anthony goes back and forth between Kate and a box of LEGOS:

> Anthony (13 months) gives some LEGO blocks to Kate, squeaking and smiling before going back to the box to pick out new ones. Hannah and Andy play with a large plastic garage with a slide that they glide cars down while making sounds like a motor. Anthony stops and looks at them. He lets go off the LEGO blocks he has in his hands, sits down and begins to pull on one side of the slide while imitating the older children's sounds. The slide falls off. Hannah and Andy protest loudly and try to pull the garage away from Anthony, who looks a little surprised by their reaction. Kate says: 'Anthony just wants to join in'. Addressing Anthony, she says, 'Well, now I think we should find some cars for you'. Kate hands a small car to Anthony, who knocks them onto the floor and begins making the sounds of motor while looking at Hannah and Andy. A little later he goes over to them again. Kate joins in and sits down next to them. Anthony begins to drive his car on the roof of the garage (mostly he hits the car against the roof). Kate keeps the garage in place so the slide does not fall off again.

In this example, Anthony orientates himself in the play situation by observing the two older children for a little while before imitating their actions to transition into the play. His initial endeavour to become part of the play is not successful since his motor skills are not yet as refined and controlled as the older children's.

Consequently, he unintendedly pulls the slide loose, disturbing the children's play. Kate helps Anthony by translating his intentions to the other children ('Anthony just want to join in'), and she helps him by adjusting the conditions (holding the garage in place) to allow Anthony to contribute to the play without disrupting it. Kate translates Anthony's intentions so he can take part of the play, seeing the conflict as a situation that commonly occurs when a toddler wants to participate but cannot do so in the same way as the older children. Kate's support provides the opportunity for Anthony to experience that his attempts to be part of the activity are successful. At first glance Anthony's actions solely appear to be disruptive. However, I argue that the situation provides an opportunity for the older children to learn how to maintain a play and include others in a shared activity without interrupting it even though conditions for the play have changed.

Above, I highlight how Ann prepares well in advance, which is what Kate also does, an approach that allows them to spend more time with the children. They are able to follow the children's interactions and efforts, providing opportunities for them to intervene, adjust and help the children socially in real time. The toy garage example shows the beneficial opportunities that arise for both children and adults when the children's intentions and efforts are observed and explored over time. The meaning-making framework the caregivers draw on to interpret the children's actions and intentions is crucial in terms of the possibilities that are created that let the children transition into and contribute to various situations and activities.

In the next section, I present the third child, Oscar, who is fifteen months old and just recently enrolled in a public nursery.

Becoming Part of the Nursery Group – Oscar

I started my observations of Oscar when he was fifteen months, concluding them when he was twenty-seven months. Oscar, who had recently started attending a public nursery, is the youngest child among twelve children in the nursery group. Oscar lives with his mother (eighteen years old), who the authorities consider very young to have responsibility for a child. Sixteen when she got pregnant, she has no family network and no contact with Oscar's father. Already during pregnancy these circumstances led to inclusion in early preventive interventions involving regular supervision by a social worker and a health visitor to help to care for the newborn. Physically, Oscar is small for his age, which is why the health visitor and social worker who regularly monitor Oscar's weight think that his mother lets him drink too much milk from a bottle, preventing him from eating enough solids. The health visitor advises the nursery caregivers to give Oscar additional meals to get him to eat more during the day. The following observation takes place before Oscar's morning nap at the nursery. I am sitting at a table with Oscar, who is in a highchair, and two older children are playing on the floor while the rest of the children are in the coatroom getting ready to go to the playground.

> Oscar and I are sitting at the table, Oscar has a bib on. Behind us, two children are playing with toy blocks on the floor. Oscar turns his face towards the children to look at them and points with one finger. He struggles to turn his upper body. One of the children points at him, saying loudly: 'Oscar, Oscar!' Holding a block in her hand, the other child stops what she is doing. She walks over to Oscar and hands him the block. He grabs it and puts it up to his mouth. The children laugh and go back to playing with their blocks. A caregiver enters the room and puts down a plate of porridge. She sits down beside Oscar, takes the block he is holding and puts it away before trying to entice him with the porridge. Oscar rejects the spoon whenever the caregiver offers him porridge, turning his face and upper body towards the girls. The caregiver says to Oscar: 'Oh, you want to look at Fiona and Anna! That's okay, you can do that.' She moves Oscar and his chair to the other side of the table so he can watch the children's activities. Oscar looks from the children to the caregiver, eagerly pointing and making happy sounds. She smiles at him and tries to give him some food. He still seems uninterested in the porridge. After a while, she lifts Oscar out of the chair and carries him to the napping area. He starts to cry and wrenches his body in her arms.

This glimpse of Oscar's daily life shows how he turns his attention towards the two children. The caregiver articulates her perception of Oscar's intentions ('Oh, you want to look at Fiona and Anna!'). In an interview, she talked in detail about how her experience with children had made her aware of how much, from a very young age, they were interested in one another. Based on this experience, it seemed easy for her to understand what Oscar was engaged in in the specific situation, even though she did not back up his engagement. What can be learned from Oscar's participation in the situation? Why does Oscar not want to eat? Is it because he is full from the milk his mother apparently gives him? Or is it because other things are more important to him? My aim is not to address these questions specifically, but rather to illustrate the need for analysing children's situated contributions in relation to the social situations they are part of. An analysis of Oscar's activities shows that he does not pay much attention to the food being offered. At first glance, based on insights from studies on children's engagements and abilities concerning group activity, the attention Oscar pays to the other children's activities may not have been conspicuous (Selby & Bradley, 2003). Another factor that should be taken into consideration is the fact that, until recently, Oscar's mother had been on maternity leave since his birth. In this regard, being part of a nursery group with many other children and three caregivers is a new aspect of his daily life. He has not yet participated in many activities with the other children, since he sleeps twice a day. When he is awake, he spends most of his time sitting at the table to eat, while looking intensively at the other children. Until now, the other children have not taken much notice of him. A turning point occurs for Oscar when the two girls in the above excerpt call out his name and include him in their activity by handing him one of their blocks; for the first time, he is part of a shared activity with his peers. Based on Oscar's way of acting (turning, looking, pointing, wrenching), and especially due to insights based on long-term participant observations, I recognize that this situation and the emerging opportunity to participate in the girls' activity is significant for Oscar. It is the first time he appeared to be excited about being in the nursery. Meanwhile, because his lack of interest in food has been designated as the reason to intervene, Oscar's curiosity and attempts to become part of the other children's activities are not prioritized. When the problem is analysed in relation to his family's care and nutrition patterns, Oscar's interest in the other children in the nursery is neglected even though the caregiver is aware of that interest. The point I wish to make is that caregivers create and support developmental opportunities for young children like Oscar in accordance with their interpretation of the problem and the support needed. When children's needs are defined abstractly, isolated from concrete situations, the children's intentional actions and attempts to contribute to the social relations and activities they are part of easily become neglected. The example shows how institutional demands become the primary guideline for the caregiver in the complex social practice of the nursery, where different and contradictory demands are at stake. For Oscar, this way of interpreting his needs in the situation means that his transitioning process from being at home with his mother to becoming a nursery child becomes difficult since he does not get many opportunities to interact with the other children when he spends most of his waking hours sitting at the table, being served food or sleeping. In this way, Oscar does not get many opportunities to orientate himself in the – to him – unknown nursery context by interacting with the other children.

In the next section I introduce the fourth child, Emily, who was nearly three years old (thirty-three months) when I started observing her and nearly four when the study ended. Throughout the observation period Emily transitioned from a public nursery to a day care centre located in the same ECEC centre. Emily lives in two households, one with her mother and one with her father, her time divided equally between the two. Emily's parents are in a custody battle and are unable to collaborate. The caregivers are concerned about Emily's well-being since she is involved in countless conflicts with the other children, and the caregivers think that the parents' battles are possibly the reason for the problems Emily faces at the day care centre. Moreover, Emily does not perform well on the language test. The caregivers believe that Emily is left too much on her own when at home and that she is not included in conversations. As a result, Emily has been given additional support in the day care centre in the form of extra adult resources for language assistance and to help develop her social skills. These extra resources are mostly allocated to a small group, where Emily and one or two other children participate in an activity that a caregiver organizes.

Orientation as Pivotal in Internal Transitions – Emily

Emily spends weekdays at the nursery from 7:30 am to 4:30 pm. She is enrolled in a group with twelve other children (12–34 months), two caregivers and one assistant. Compared to the family nursery, the public nursery has a more systematic focus on the learning curriculum. Consequently, learning objectives are addressed in planned activities, just as they are documented by the staff. The schedule differs compared to the family nursery, where the day's activities are not contingent upon learning objectives and activities. Rather, as illustrated, the weather or group dynamics, for example, guides what the caregiver does. In the public nursery, each day follows a planned schedule. Once all the children in the group have arrived (7–9 am), a typical day begins by sitting in a circle on the floor to sing a couple of songs. Afterward the children sit at two or three small tables to eat a light snack. By 9:30 all three staff members are ideally present, and a planned activity takes place. These activities involve planned, adult-initiated activities such as: excursions, painting, music, dialogical reading, numeracy or geometry activities. Around 10:30 the staff tidy up, get the children ready for lunch, and later have them nap from noon to 2 pm. At this point, some of the staff finish their shifts. Around 2 pm the children get a light snack and play until their parents pick them up between 3 and 5 pm.

The following section contains a description of how two planned activities were organized. One of the activities is the regular morning circle time and the other is a planned learning activity corresponding to one of the topics in the learning curriculum (nature and natural phenomenon). Note that planned learning activities take place in the morning when all the staff is ideally present, allowing them to highly prioritized with enough staff to support them.

> After their morning snack, 10 children, aged 10 months to two years, are gathered and sitting on a big mattress in a circle before starting the daily planned activities. One of the caregivers begins the circle time in the usual way by saying: 'Now, let's see who's here today first'. Each child is then asked the name of the person sitting next to them. If they have difficulties saying the name, the caregivers help. The children smile when their name is said and appear to concentrate carefully on looking around at all the faces. Circle time concludes with singing a few songs. When the singing is over, the caregiver gets out colourful blocks shaped in circles, triangles and squares. The activity is designed to enhance children's early recognition of various colours and shapes. The caregiver lays blocks on the floor and asks a child, Peter (10 months), if he knows the colour of a circle-shaped block. Another child, Simon (22 months), takes some square blocks and tries to pile them up. Emily (33 months) watches him for a little while and then accidently topples his pile when she reaches for a block, causing him to point at her and scream. The caregiver takes the blocks away from the two children and tries eagerly to get them and the rest of the children to focus on the colour of the blocks – for example by asking what colour the sun is, varying her voice and trying to achieve eye contact with the children. A boy, David (10 months), is eagerly sucking on a triangle while observing the activities going on around him. Emily tries to take the triangle out of his mouth.

The staff planned both activities, which appear to have entirely different objectives. The usual morning greeting during circle time appeals to the children, who sit quietly on the mattress. The next activity, however, does not seem to sustain their attention. Why is this the case? A more careful look at the first activity reveals that it is familiar to the oldest children, who have been attending the nursery for a long time. Part of the aim of the activity is for the children to see which potential playmates are at the nursery that day. For the most recently enrolled children, this activity allows them to become familiar with the faces and names of the other children and the staff. This daily activity provides the opportunity for the children to sit quietly and observe their co-participants, who move around constantly at other times. As a result, the situation constitutes an opportunity for orientation as part of, and as a premise for becoming an active part of what is going on in the nursery (Højholt, 2012; Juhl, 2019). Orientation processes take place when children observe peers and caregivers as part of exploring what is at stake in a given situation and how to participate and contribute to what is going on. As Schraube and Osterkamp (2013) state, agency is a striving to gain control over the conditions, and this is a process of orientation (and I would add embodied orientation) as an existential way of being in the world. These orientation processes involve children observing each other. The observations recorded of the children and other activities in the nursery clearly show that they keenly observe each other and appear to be constantly occupied with exploring how they can participate in shared activities, e.g. getting a hold of the same toy another child wants and exploring what and how they can play together. Seen in this light the repeated morning activity with names supports the children in their mutual engagements.

The second activity involves the staff trying to engage the children in focusing on colours and shapes. The children, however, are engaged in exploring the social aspects of the activity, for example by negotiating the right to the blocks. The staff make an effort to distract the children from the social aspects, e.g. the conflicts that arise, and try to keep the children focused on the planned activity. In a subsequent interview, the staff explain that they are very well aware that the children are engaged in the social aspects of the situation and that the situation entails the potential for working with other learning areas as well, for instance social skills. The staff, however, are supposed to evaluate the learning outcome and to document what they do to create optimal learning opportunities for the children in relation to six areas of learning. The staff explain that the requirements for documenting the children's recognition of various colours and shapes, in correspondence with the learning area, are too difficult if mixed with other emerging aspects, for instance, the children's social conflicts. As a result, they try to concentrate only on the colour and shape-related activities. However, as the example illustrates, attempts to detach the social aspects from the activity diminish the children's interest, apparently preventing them from paying attention to the colours and shapes of the blocks. Moreover, the staff do not focus on nor support the children's way of approaching one another.

The point that I wish to make is not that the children, per definition, are uninterested in shapes, colours or other adult-initiated activities, but if they are to be of relevance to the children, they must be anchored in and support the children's endeavours to explore how to participate in the social situation, just as the circle time activity with their names does. As explained earlier, the societal and political changes that have taken place in appraising learning inform discussions on quality in the social practice of ECEC (Juhl, 2018). Activities that enhance the early recognition of colours and shapes represent high quality in a political perspective, for instance, since they help improve later school performance. However, the actions and engagements of children in the concrete situation demonstrate that exploring shapes and colours and their meaning is an ubiquitous part of children's exploration of the complexity of the social practices that they participate in, i.e. what other children are doing and how to take part in it. This circle time situation becomes a resource for the children's processes of internal transitioning between this structured activity and other child-initiated activities and the various interests and demands that children coordinate and continuously relate to and deal with together in a social world.

Early Learning as Related to Transitions Situated in Everyday Living

The subsequent empirical example stems from a different situation almost a year later. Emily is now enrolled in the day care centre for children age thirty-four months to five year:

> It is 8:00 am and children are arriving. Emily (3.5 years) sits at a table doing a puzzle after emptying all the pieces out on the table. She is focused on trying to make the pieces fit together. Another girl, Melanie (3 years old), who just recently started attending the daycare centre, looks at Emily, climbs up on a chair and sits at the table. After Melanie takes some of the puzzle pieces, Emily shouts: 'No!' and points at her while trying to take a piece out of Melanie's hand. Emily lays her upper body on top of the puzzle pieces to protect them from Melanie's grasp. The caregiver, who is sitting nearby on a chair with another girl on her lap, asks Emily if she minds if Melanie helps her with the puzzle. Emily looks from the caregiver to Melanie, glances down at all the puzzle pieces and nods. The caregiver helps the girls cooperate, which requires ongoing input. After a while Melanie puts a puzzle piece up to her mouth and pretends it is a cup, simultaneously tilting her head back while making drinking sounds. Emily stops doing the puzzle and looks at Melanie closely, following her every move with her eyes. Then she takes another piece and imitates Melanie, who smiles at Emily. Melanie takes another puzzle piece and pours an imaginary drink into Emily's cup while saying coffee. Emily drinks again and holds the cup towards Melanie, saying cocoa, after which Melanie replies 'Yes'. The caregiver occasionally steps in to support their play.

Through their joint activities the girls explore possibilities, limitations and contradictions in relation to engaging in shared activities. Protecting the puzzle pieces by lying on top of them, for instance, makes it impossible for Emily to do the puzzle. Sharing the puzzle helps the children gain important experience with being a participant in the complexity of social practice (Dreier, 2008); for example, how to make cooperation work, include other participant contributions and make transitions between various relations and activities. Imagining that the puzzle pieces were cups and saucers comprises as-if aspects, allowing the children to experiment with how to transform a given activity (Winther-Lindqvist, 2017). Melanie initiates the tea party and Emily picks up on it, leading both girls to experience how they contribute to developing the shared activity (Hedegaard, 2014). Taking part in changing social practices requires children to orientate, re-orientate and adjust their way of acting, and develop their intentions and engagements in relation to the changing activities and situations they are part of. Such complex microgenetic events comprise the developmental conditions for children, which is why they possess important potential for children to develop agency and becoming able to transform the social practice, hence also their own and others' conditions.

Together with the girls the staff explore the possibilities for action that the situation makes available. In the case of the example, the caregiver suggests working on the puzzle together, instead of fighting over the right to the pieces, helping the girls to expand and develop their play. Providing support is only possible when the girls' own engagements are explored concurrently. For instance, by noticing how the girls use the puzzle pieces as imaginary cups and saucers, the caregiver supports their change in activity. Mostly, Emily is supported by the caregivers in a smaller group of children comprising Emily and a few other girls with whom Emily often plays. In group sessions, the staff organize activities considered suitable for supporting Emily in developing social and academic skills, for instance waiting for her turn and interpreting the other children's intentions, and for stimulating her language skills. For instance, the staff tell me that Emily must learn to connect her own actions of being too decisive and dominating and the other children's refusal or exclusion of her. In small groups the staff try to support Emily in adjusting her way of interacting with and approaching the other children. Even though the group sessions seem helpful for Emily in the sense that she experiences being included in activities together with other children, she still continually experiences being excluded during activities in the children's communities. Often in relation to transitions from one activity to the next in which dynamics between the children change. Whenever she is part of activities with other children, she most often takes part from a peripheral position from which she constantly is at risk of being excluded. This is particularly the case in the situation where she is playing together with her best friend Melanie.

Even though both children enjoy the play and each other's company, Melanie has several friends in the day care centre and often other children approach her with invitations to engage in play with them when she and Emily are playing. When Melanie accepts their invitations, Emily is left alone with no one to play with. Sometimes she makes an effort to become included in the new play, but these situations often end in exclusion and conflict. In this way, Emily often experiences everyday life in day care as endless endeavours and negotiations to be included, and whenever she is included, to then maintain this position. She makes multiple initiatives and offers contributions to develop the play in ways the other children find productive and interesting. In this way, Emily appears to be capable of interpreting the other children's intentions and of adjusting her way of acting in highly complex ways, across various situations. However, these competences and contributions to the children's community are overseen by the staff. They continue to connect the conflicts and exclusion Emily faces as being related to her inability to understand other children's expressions, a lack of empathy and her being too assertive. This understanding of Emily's situation and the difficulties she experiences as individual deficits impacts what becomes the obvious intervention: small groups with activities that gives Emily the opportunity to practice, e.g. waiting her turn and listening to the other children. Paradoxically, these small groups sessions are mostly rather unproblematic for Emily. In other words, they do not cause exclusion and conflicts. I believe that this relates to the fact that a caregiver is present to constantly helping and support the group – for instance in interpreting the other children's intentions and in expressing their own intentions and contributions in ways that the other children can understand and accept. Importantly, other children do not constantly interfere in Emily and Melanie's activities when the group is small. Due to the staff's understanding that Emily faces exclusion and conflicts due to her individual (in)abilities, little attention is allocated to the children's complex communities during the day when children are constantly transitioning between activities and social relations, even though these are clearly the types of situations where Emily faces the greatest amount of defeat. My observations indicate that these are also the situations where she is deeply engaged, as evidenced by the multiple efforts she puts into making the situations work by trying over and over again to make her contributions accepted by the other children. She invents new ideas and introduces new dynamics into the play to develop it in interesting ways. Emily constantly tries to actively change and develop the activities she participates in. Even though she is constantly at risk of being excluded and losing her playmate, she continues to try. Her friend Melanie, who does not experience exclusion as frequently, has plenty of other possibilities to become part of new relationships and activities since she has numerous friends at day care. In this way, my analysis shows – similar to Recchia and Dvorakova (2012) – that the somewhat same situation in ECEC entails various subjective meanings for different children and that children make use of each other in the processes of belonging in the children's communities, especially during transitions.

When no adult-initiated activities take place and the children play on their own Emily is highly interested in becoming part of joint activities, but she also experiences conflicts and exclusion in these situations. The staff has an important role to play in the way they understand the problems children face and their subsequent way of supporting and intervening. Howers (2011) shows that adults play a crucial role in supporting young children in terms of mediation for the children to become active members of the children's community and to transition between different relationships. The understanding of Emily's problems as related to her individually, and not as a social problem related to children's community, prevents the staff from focusing their attention and support on her attempts to become part of the children's community. Emily's internal transition processes are related to the multitude of struggles she faces, with transitioning often leading to exclusion.

In the next section I introduce Toby as the last of the five children presented in this book. Toby, who is also in a day care, also struggles with moving between various activities and situations. He is not, however, enrolled in any preventive interventions in the day care centre, nor does he spend a large quantity of time with the staff during the day. In this way, Toby's everyday life in ECEC differs compared to Emily's, which includes an abundance of attention from the day care centre staff. What I wish to emphasize is that despite the differences in adult contact, and the fact that Emily is involved in interventions aimed at improving her social and academic skills (which supposedly increase her chance of succeeding in becoming a part of the children's communities), Toby and Emily struggle with similar problems and get involved in similar conflicts related to being excluded or on the slope of exclusion (Kousholt, 2012).

The Periphery of the Day Care Centre – Toby

Toby was almost four years old when I began observing him and nearly five when the observations ended. He is enrolled in the public day care centre and he is in a group comprising twenty-four children, two of whom are children who Toby is specifically interested in playing with. Their names are Magnus and Victor. This observation is based on watching Toby's tireless attempts to become part of their activities and the amount of time he spends observing what these two children are doing. Moreover, he states that being together with your friends is what is important about day care and that being there is boring when you cannot be with your friends. Toby lives with his mother in a nearby apartment. One of the two children from the day care centre lives in the same complex and they sometimes meet up at the local playground.

Toby's father was incarcerated the first couple of years of Toby's life and due to this, the father only recently began to take part in the parental responsibility. Toby spends one weekend every month at his father's. The mother and father have numerous conflicts about Toby – especially about how to create a healthy everyday routine. The father has previously been violent towards the mother, who claims that she is afraid of him. They do not receive any professional help to sort out this problem. Toby's mother, a 23-year-old nurse assistant student, grew up in foster care and has no family network. She has a history of mental illness, and already during pregnancy she asked for support from the local authorities. She has been assigned respite care with a family who Toby visits every other weekend. Every other Thursday, both the mother and Toby spend the afternoon and evening with the family offering respite care. Both the mother and Toby emphasize that this family is an important part of their everyday lives, the mother highlighting that the parents providing respite care give her advice about specific difficulties and conflicts. They also offer encouragement in terms of her parental tasks. Toby is not enrolled in any early interventions at the day care centre. The staff think that he is doing fine but that he can be too rough with the other children.

As outlined earlier in the chapter, one difference between day care centres and nurseries is that day care centres have more adults but also many more children. Toby's day care centre has about eighty children divided into small groups of about twenty children, each group assigned three caregivers. Another difference is the physical environment. The day care centre has various rooms the children can move about in. A third difference is the understanding of what the staff's core task is, where learning objectives in the curriculum plays a much larger role in the day care centre's practice compared to in nurseries, especially in family nurseries. The last-mentioned difference can serve as a stepping stone for understanding why the day care centre staff often focus their professional attention on planned activities with a specific objective compared to nursery caregivers, who also spends a large amount of time supporting children in exploring how to play together. This relates to a fourth difference, which is that children in the day care centre are older, are expected to engage in more self-organized activities and that they are able to move between activities without adult support. For Toby, these situations often lead to conflicts. The day care centre's daily routine is structured, with the morning set aside for planned educational activities. After lunch, the afternoon is most often reserved for the children to organize activities and communities themselves.

Toby's Continuous Efforts to Make Friends and Maintain Friendships

At a meeting between the professionals involved in Toby's case (health visitor, caregivers, social worker and providers of respite care) the caregivers emphasize how well things are going for Toby at the day care centre. They do not experience him being involved in very many conflicts or other problems. Toby, however, does not seem to share their opinion. He tells me that he does not like to go to the centre because it is boring, that there is never anyone to play with. He elaborates by saying: 'my friends are busy'. He says he prefers to spend time on the playground or in the centre's cushion room because the staff are never there. In other words, Toby prefers to spend time in the periphery of the day care centre and stays out of the caregivers' sight. When I have spent time with Toby at the centre, he has been particularly concerned about how to get to play with the two children he defines as his friends. The two children often play together, making it difficult for Toby to become part of their community. Sometimes he succeeds but usually has a peripheral position and is often excluded.

Before presenting excerpts from his everyday life at the day care centre I will go one step back to the first few times I met Toby to describe how he reacted quite differently to having me observe him in his everyday life contexts. Toby's various reactions, I argue, best illustrate how to understand the problems he faces. Before I observed Toby at the day care centre, his mother had given me permission to visit her and Toby in their home one afternoon after day care. During the visit Toby refused to talk to me or even to look at me, ignoring me completely. After a few similar visits, I was close to giving up but a conversation with his mother made me realize that whenever I visited the family, Toby' had to stay in the apartment instead of going out on the playground to meet his friend from day care. Hence, I represented an obstacle to his intentions and efforts to become part of the children's community in the local complex as a means to become part of their community in the day care as well. He worked exceptionally hard at this endeavour during the day and obviously wanted to continue pursuing it when at home but my visits prevented him from doing so.

I decided to give it a final try and agreed with Toby's mother and the various professionals involved in his case that I would finally visit Toby in day care. Based on our visits in his home I was prepared for Toby to run away when he saw me, but to my surprise, he reacted quite differently. He ran happily towards me and took my hand. This welcome took me by surprise until I discovered that me visiting him attracted the other children's attention. They would typically follow us around try to get me involved in their activities. Toby walked proudly around with me, holding my hand tight and showing me how high he could climb the trees, for instance. We were followed by several children who would also show me how fast they could run and how high they could climb. At the day care I became an opportunity for Toby since my very presence attracted the other children and presented new opportunities for him in relation to becoming part of the children's communities. At home I represented the opposite meaning, which is presumably why he protested against my visits so he could continue to go to the playground. I talked to Toby's mother, and we later agreed that when I was observing Toby at home, he should do the things he would normally do when I was not present. After that Toby was allowed to go to the playground, also on days where I was present. After this change, Toby appeared to accept and even appreciate my visits. The experiences I had with Toby in the different contexts of his everyday life learned me about the struggles he faced in the day care and how he tried to pursue his intentions and engagements across his different contexts. The insight I gained in his conduct of everyday life helped me understand the conditions he encountered in the day care. One day at day care the following episode occurred:

> Some of Toby's peers are driving a train of cargo bikes with three empty seats. 'I want on,' says Toby. 'No!' shouts the child in charge of the play. As a group of girls sitting on the train passes, they shout: 'Hi, hello Toby' in a teasing manner while laughing. A member of staff sitting close by watches what happens but does not intervene. Toby looks at the children for a little while. Then he sees a bike and runs to it. When the train passes, he tries to cut it off. At one point the train stops to get new passengers. Toby watches as other children are allowed to get on the train. He picks up a thick branch and puts it in front of a wheel on the train.

This example provides a glimpse of what Toby's everyday life is like in day care. The other children often reject him but being rejected or excluded is a fairly common occurrence that almost all the children experience from time to time. For Toby, however, the majority of his experiences with other children involve rejection and exclusion.

Later that day, the staff explain that the children exclude Toby because he teases them and plays too roughly. They say that he must learn that his teasing causes the other children to reject him. Analysed from Toby's position, the teasing clearly occurs because he is being snubbed. When the problem is understood as detached from the concrete situation in which it unfolds, it becomes attached to Toby as his individual problem of being too rough. The staff do not believe they are capable of addressing the problem since they associate Toby's roughness with his father's history of violence and having a bad temper, as they put it. When detached from the situation, the teasing and roughness are understood as being a result of Toby's family background and not related to his lack of participation and marginalized position in the children's communities. The staff do not appear to believe that they can make a difference since they consider the issue to involve innate qualities in Toby's personality.

Play Activities within and beyond the Adults' View

Toby leaves me with the impression that he has given up on receiving help from the adults to become part of the children's communities as I never see him ask for assistance. The other children, in comparison, often ask for help or turn to the staff for help and consolation. Toby has instead developed strategies to avoid the adults' attention. Often the activities Tony prefers are not permitted at day care, such as climbing on the roof of the playhouse, climbing the tall trees at the back of the playground or fighting. This could be the reason why Toby spends most of his time out of view of the staff. He has developed successful ways to pursue these kinds of activities without being caught.

Whenever the staff plans and organizes joint activities, Toby participates quietly, listens carefully to instructions and follows them. On these occasions he spends a large amount of time watching what is going on around him. I often see him carefully observing how the other children have fun with each other and how he listens to their conversations. Toby does not attract much attention from either the staff or the other children. Often, I observe Toby using his knowledge about the other children's interests and engagements as an access point to become part of the community with his peers. He attained this knowledge based on the many hours he has spent watching them during the day.

In a study of children's well-being in a day care centre, Koch (2012) points out that ECEC professionals have various expectations concerning how children use their bodies in a variety of day care situations. For example, the staff emphasize the importance of the ability of children to attune their bodily activities in accordance to assorted locations and situations. When outdoors, children are expected to be physically active and not just stand still or sit still. When indoors, in contrast, they are expected to move around quietly (2012). Applying Koch's notion of attunement, Toby manages to reconcile his way of moving around and adjusting his bodily activities so that he does not attract any attention from day care staff. On the one hand, this strategy seems to protect Toby from being scolded but, on the other, this attunement and ability to not attract attention also means that the staff have few opportunities to understand Toby's engagements and the difficulties he experiences in day care. When Toby plays too roughly, he does so in secluded areas not often frequented by the staff, e.g. the cushion room or at the back of the playground. These sheltered places provide other kinds of opportunities for activities and new dynamics in the children's community (Sandseter & Kennair, 2011). Toby's activities that occur in open view of the staff are often not especially successful in helping him to become part of other children's play.

Toby's withdrawal to out-of-the-way areas at the day care mean that staff only become aware of his whereabouts when there is a conflict, arriving on the scene after other children have asked them to come. They discover a child crying and the other children pointing out Toby as the guilty party. Consequently, the staff rarely get an opportunity to see the conflicts evolve or to explore Toby's perspective on the conflicts he faces.

The play that Toby is involved in most often contains wild activities, e.g. competing to see who dares to do the most dangerous and forbidden activities or competing to see who can be the strongest and the roughest towards another. In these situations, I see Toby briefly take on a central position in the game because he is often the one who dares to try most of the activities. Since the play frequently ends up being too wild for the other children, they often leave and Toby ends up on his own again. Toby's rowdy approach can serve as an admission ticket to be part of the children's community but activities can also easily get out of control, leading to exclusion and conflict. The following episode illustrates the kind of situation Toby often finds himself in:

> One day Toby wants to show me the forest, which is a small green area in the back of the playground hidden behind big trees. The staff are in the middle of the playground, where the sandbox, swings and playhouse are located. Toby and I walk to the forest. A group of younger children stand by the fence, including a child named Victor. Toby runs to the top of a small hill, lays down and starts rolling towards the fence. On his way down the hill, his legs hit several of the younger children. They laugh. Toby walks up the hill again. Victor also rolls down. Now, some of the younger children also want to try. Toby pushes them so they fall over, one boy so hard in the chest that he falls backward down the hill. The boy cries. Toby looks quickly over his shoulder towards the middle of the playground where the staff are. The smaller children and Victor run off. Toby is left alone with me but follows the other children. He sits down on the edge of the sandbox and observes the younger children telling the staff about what just happened.

The staff have difficulty gaining insight into how situations escalate and turn into conflicts, putting them one step behind in terms of understanding the context of the conflicts. This also hinders them from becoming aware of what Toby struggles with again and again, not to mention his efforts to be included.

Transitioning from a Structured Activity to the Children's Communities

The curriculum at Toby's day care centre is covered in scheduled sessions during the week. There is an enhanced focus on creating a learning environment during the day that stimulates the children's skills in terms of waiting their turn, concentrating, listening to each other and receiving instructions from staff. Planned activities organized by the staff take place in small groups, with children often separated from their friends or those they might want to play with, which sometimes interferes with the children's efforts and intentions. When Toby, for instance, has worked hard to become part of an activity with his peers, the staff often remove him to take part in a group session or they remove the children he is playing with for an activity session. This procedure frequently makes it even more difficult for Toby to pick up where he left off when the group activity ends. The two children he likes to play with most, Magnus and Victor, are in the same group for group sessions, but Toby is in another group. The groups are divided by date of birth, which means mutual interests and relationships are not taken into consideration. Toby, who already works harder than his peers to be a part of the children's communities, becomes even more marginalized, losing ground in terms of maintaining his position in play with his peers.

One day the children sit around a table to get their faces painted by turn. In front of them on the table each child has a laminated drawing of what they are supposed to have painted on their faces. Planned and conducted by the staff, the activity is compulsory and all the children must participate. There is a list of children assigned to be painted on this particular day and another list of who will get a turn a different day so the children can participate without too much waiting time. However, the wait still seems long, the children squirm, fall off their chairs and lie down on the table. Toby sits quietly looking around the other children:

> Toby watches the other children but does not say anything. No one turns to him. He lights up when he sees me, moves a little on his chair and makes room for me on the corner. Magnus, who is not on today's list, enters from another room and watches. Magnus says that clowns are fun. Toby points to a little girl who is painted like a clown: 'There's one, Magnus'. Magnus looks at the girl and smiles at Toby. Magnus leaves the room. Toby watches him go. After 15 more minutes it is Toby's turn to be painted. When finished, he runs into the room, sits down on a couch and looks at Magnus, who is now playing with Victor. They are playing with LEGO on the floor. I sit next to Toby and follow his gaze. He observes what Magnus and Victor are doing. Although Toby also likes to play with LEGO, he tells me firmly: 'But I can't do that now!' without taking his eyes off the two children. Victor suddenly gets up: 'Come on, Magnus, let's fetch our lunches'. Magnus gets up and walks out with Victor, passing the couch but not paying any attention to Toby and me. A little while after they return with their lunch boxes. Toby says to me that he wants to go outside to the playground. He picks up his jacket. A caregiver who is still painting faces asks Toby who is going with him as he passes by. Toby does not answer, and the caregiver does not ask again. Toby passes the room where Victor and Magnus are eating. He is looking at them, then he turns and walks to the door leading outside to the playground. I ask him if he is not going to find someone to go with. He says: 'Nobody can be bothered. I already asked them'.

Toby expends a great deal of effort observing Magnus and Victor without interacting with them. He nevertheless seems absolutely convinced that he is not welcome to be part of what they are doing, nor does he try to persuade them to come outside with him, even though he did not actually ask them. In the situation, I wondered about how Toby came to the conclusion that this would not be a possibility since I have oftentimes observed him playing with these two children. After consulting my observation notes, it becomes clear to me that the majority of examples are when Toby is playing with either Magnus or Victor, but not both. When all three children play together Toby usually ends up being excluded.

For Toby it seems particularly difficult to transition from the face painting, an activity Victor and Magnus would not take part in until the next day. This leaves Toby in a situation where the structure and organization of the pedagogical activity did not allow him to be with the two children, who had time to start playing together without Toby. Situations like this make it even more difficult for him to transition from a structured activity into the children's self-organized activities, in this case playing with LEGOs.

My observations confirm that especially the transitioning processes from an activity orchestrated by the adults to one that is child-led in the children's communities seems difficult to Toby. Keeping in mind studies showing how children use each other in processes of orientation in new situations, Toby's peripheral position in the children's community can shed light on why transitions are notably difficult for him since he does not have many children to orient himself in relation to (Højholt, 2012; Kousholt, 2012; Stanek & Røn Larsen, 2015).

Summary

This chapter highlights how the children in different nursery contexts and in day care centres spend a large quantity of time observing and relating to what their peers are doing as part of orientating themselves in how to become part of the various activities and situations. Moreover, the children, using various strategies – including the use of materiality in their attempts to orientate in what is going on and in involving others in their own activities. This was the case with Daniel who continuously fetched his boots as a persistent attempt to get his caregiver persuaded into going out in the rain. Moreover, the children seem to use each other and the activities of each other as resources when identifying how they can become part of the children's communities in a way that allows them to contribute to the ongoing activities. Pursuing their interests, the children struggle and fight with each other, as they try to relate to each other, negotiate and coordinate interests.

Thus, when children organize communities it involves a continuous effort, the exploration of possibilities and multiple adjustments, negotiations, orientations and re-orientations. My analysis indicates that children in family nurseries receive a great deal of support to manage the aforementioned processes in relation to their social life with the other children. At the same time, the analysis shows that when problems are approached in isolation from the children's community, as in Daniel's case, where biting Kelly is seen as an individual problem related to Daniel's family context, massage as an individual method becomes the answer. The focus shifts from dealing with a social conflict to individualizing the problem. To provide relevant help and support for Daniel, it must connect to the context of the conflicts and thus to his and Kelly's mutual engagements and subsequent conflicts.

An important key point in the chapter is that children's embodied actions and orientation processes are stepping stones for a continuously exploration of what is at stake for young children when in ECEC contexts. In that way, I argue that when children as for instance, Oscar recently enrolled in nursery cries and refuses to eat his embodied actions including his emotional expressions should be taken seriously as a sign of his situated emotional evaluation of how he feels in relation to the concrete situation he is part of. As Osterkamp-Holzkamp (1991) stated, 'emotions function as subjective evaluations of environmental possibilities for acting' (p. 103) and as an emotional reaction, in terms of 'a more or less diffuse feeling of "ease" or "unease" evoked by the complex situation' (1991, p. 105). In this way, the children's embodied actions should be used as an opportunity to explore how the child experiences a given situation, what is at stake, what is happening around the child and how this situation relates to other situations in the complex composition of a child's everyday life – as in the case of Oscar his rejection of the food and his crying is interpreted by the caregiver as a sign of him being tired and he is carried to the napping area. However, when observing him across contexts it comes clear that the concrete situation is the first time, he interacts with the other children whom he has been eagerly observing and directed at. By adopting an understanding of young children as agentic beings, Oscars crying can be considered an occasion to exploring what he is communicating with his crying, smiling, pointing, wrenching and turning.

For the youngest children in nursery contexts, an adult is normally close by to help the children when interacting and in solving conflicts. The slightly older children in day care centres are much more left to solve conflicts on their own. In day care centres children in marginalized positions experience multiple situations with exclusion, which can affect how they understand themselves in relation to other children. As Stetsenko (2019) writes 'how society provides conditions for or, alternatively, deprives individuals of access to participating in social practices and their resources necessary for development is therefore of critical significance' (p. 258). The most important help for children, based on the analysis in this chapter, I would argue, comprises a focus on the ordinary conflicts that children face as related to being part of or trying to become part of social activities together with peers. This involves continuous processes of internal transitions between activities, social relationships and situations organized by ECEC professionals. Stetsenko (2017) argues that agency develops through processes of not only participation but also by contributing to the transformation and affirmation of the activities one takes part in. In this approach to agency, development is a transformative process where 'development is about participating yet is also, and even more critically [...] to contributing to transformative communal practices' (p. 34). Similarly, taking transitions as my point of departure is pivotal for understanding children's agentic contributions underlining how even very young children actively try to orient themselves in the situations that they are part of and how children's actions must be understood in the light of how they orientate themselves and contribute to developing their conditions (Lam & Pollard, 2006). I suggest that Early childhood interventions must focus on the social situations in which conflicts and processes of exclusion evolve since children develop their social self-understanding in these situations as part of their everyday living and transitioning, either as someone who can contribute significantly to what is going on or as someone who is ignored and left out, as someone who is socially neglected.

5

Transitioning Between Everyday Life Contexts

This chapter illustrates how the young children act in relation to their daily transitions between institutional contexts as ECEC centres and family life. Whereas the previous chapter addressed the micro-movements between various activities and situations and locations within the same contexts, this chapter focuses on the horizontal transitions between different contexts in daily living. The concept microgenetic transitions highlights the developmental relevance of the numerous transitions that children make throughout their everyday lives within and across different institutions (Hedegaard & Fleer, 2019). For this reason, I specifically discuss how children contribute not only to the processes of shaping their own living conditions, but also to how they contribute to shaping the action possibilities of other co-participants, and how even very young children through their actions engage in embodied conversations with co-participants and through these conversations young children engage in the world and make the world respond to their agentic contributions. The children through their transitioning processes contribute to the ways in which the social practices of ECEC and family are related. In this way, young children's actions in relation to dealing with transitions contribute to shape, affirm and transform the various social practices as well as how these are connected.

In the chapter I will draw on the analysis from the previous chapter as a backdrop for understanding what children are transitioning from, and then, in Chapter 6, I will use these analytical insights gained to understand how children's way of participating in family life is related to not just what happens in the family and what the parents do but also to the social context they transitioned from. Shifts and movements between different contexts and situations take up a large amount of space in my fieldnotes from the study of young children, indicating that such movements and shifts represent a key source for understanding how they handle shifts in context, relationships and how scopes of actions differ, in addition to discerning what conditions parents and children have for moving from one context to another. Three different situations will be described to illustrate these themes. One situation will illustrate the transition from being home to being enrolled in nursery, while two situations involve the children on the way home from their ECEC centre with their parents. My aim is twofold, first I would like to show how even very young children orientate in transitions and how they contribute to shaping the process of transition, also for their parents and, second, to show not only how parents have highly different conditions for dealing with the conflicts and conflicting interests associated with transitioning but also how this creates various possibilities for the children during transitioning processes. The analysis, then, illustrates how the exchange of knowledge between ECEC staff and parents concerns how the children's day in the ECEC context provides a backdrop for the parents' planning and organizing family life the rest of the day as I will discuss in the next chapter.

A key point in this chapter is, based on the analyses in the previous chapter, that daily transitions are social processes in the sense that the children use their peers and various caregivers as resources for orientating in different contexts. For children newly enrolled in nurseries, for instance, peers already familiar with the nursery context become points of orientation in terms of what is at stake and what one can do in the nursery, what activities are going on and what toys to pursue (Røn Larsen & Stanek, 2015). The caregiver and their maintenance of daily routines are also important resources for the children in order to become familiar with the ECEC context. Even though routines and activities are somewhat different compared to the children's family contexts there are also similarities. For instance, when children are placed around a table, and getting their bibs on, the children know that these are signs of an upcoming meal. Also, when they have their diapers changed and get some of their clothes off and are walked to the napping area and are allowed to get their pacifier, they know they are supposed to lie down and sleep. Or, when they together with their peers are being directed to the wardrobe by the caregivers and get their coats and shoes on, they know that they are going out on the playground or for an excursion. When a similar procedure is repeated together with their parents in the afternoon, they know they are leaving the nursery. In this way, spatial shifts, routines in terms of sleeping, eating and change of outfit, use of things (as e.g. toys, pacifier), and activities (singing, getting (un)dressed) are resources in young children's embodied orientation and hence, important resources for their agency.

A second key point is that these orientation processes and young children's actions and efforts to deal with the shifts and transitions do not just impact the children's possibilities for dealing with transition. Rather, they also contribute to create possibilities for how their parents and caregivers can deal with transitions. The children's embodied actions as part of their orientation processes become resources for various adults and peers (and me as a researcher) in order to be able to relate to the children's well-being and intentions (Hedegaard & Fleer, 2019). I will take my point of departure in the public nursery with Oscar, who is in the process of transitioning from being at home with his mother, who is on maternity leave, to starting in a public nursery. I will emphasize how Oscar uses the materiality as resources in the process of becoming familiar with the nursery context.

Transitioning as Part of the Conduct of Everyday Life – New Routines

When Oscar initially starts at the public nursery he will not eat. The caregivers think he is having difficulties adjusting to the nursery's routines. He does not eat anything during the day and will not sleep either, causing the caregivers to try in various ways to urge him to eat and sleep. Oscar cries a great deal and does not seem well. Small for his age, the caregivers think that the lack of eating is an issue. As a result, they decide to focus on getting Oscar to eat as a first key step in getting acquainted with being part of the nursery. Across the empirical data in my study and supported in a study by Andenæs and Sundnes (2019) it is evident that babies' sleeping routines, nutrition preferences and appetite are considered important markers of their well-being. The caregivers ask Oscar's mother what his favourite foods at home are. Although she says that he loves porridge, Oscar refuses to eat it, causing the caregivers to enquire further about how the mother makes it. She explains that she buys a ready-made instant powder, which has a different taste compared to oatmeal made from scratch. One of the caregivers tells me in an interview that she gradually began mixing the instant powder in with plain oatmeal and water. After a few weeks, Oscar has become completely accustomed to eating ordinary homemade oatmeal. Until now he has been used to living his everyday life in a single context (home), eating one kind of food. Once enrolled at the nursery Oscar spends his everyday life across various contexts and is presented with a variety of food and must, for example, get used to a new routine for naps. The caregivers explore Oscar's refusal to eat at the nursery as being related to his transition into a new context, which allows them to provide him with support. Oscar navigates the transition between being at home and being at the nursery by relating to and reacting to the differences he faces. Apparently, Oscar does not recognize what he is served as porridge, but this issue is solved when the caregivers gradually mix the instant oatmeal with the unfamiliar one, which helps expose his palate to a new taste. In this way, the conduct of everyday life for a young toddler like Oscar also involves orientating and dealing with different routines, food and care practices across various institutional contexts. Through his embodied orientation Oscar explores and communicates what appears to be unfamiliar to him between two care practices. The resistance he demonstrates towards the food allows him to contribute to the adjustment of the care practices. This example illustrates how identifying the problem is done jointly with the mother; her knowledge of Oscar's eating habits at home serving as a resource to support him in his transitioning process. Moreover, the example illustrates how Oscar deals with his changing routines by resisting the food.

The transition from an ECEC context to the home context also entails a shift in relations, from ECEC staff to their parents, and hence also a change in the demands, expectations and interests at stake in these different contexts (Kousholt, 2011). Dreier's (1997) research increases understanding about how transitioning between contexts involves changing how one acts, feels and thinks '[a]s subjects move across contexts their modes of participation vary because these diverse contexts embody particular positions, social relations, scopes of possibilities, and personal concerns for them. Hence they must act, think, and feel in flexible ways' (Dreier, 1997, p. 103).

One example of this is when Anthony's mother picks him (and me) up from the family nursery to go to the family home. In each of his everyday contexts, Anthony pursues different engagements. In the family nursery he shows interest in how to become involved in activities with the other children, while at home with his parents Anthony actively tries to take part in the household activities, e.g. doing laundry, cooking or playing on his own while his parents are busy doing other things and chores. Whenever Anthony visits the family that provides respite care he receives undivided attention. The respite parents – similar to the caregiver in the family nursery – take care of multiple practical tasks and chores in advance to be able to be attentive when Anthony is visiting. The fact that Anthony only stays for one or two days on the weekend gives the respite parents the space to prepare for his visit. They have the day off and do not have to rush out the door in the morning to go to work at a specific time. This provides the opportunity for them to make room for Antony's initiatives and engagements to set the agenda. This differs drastically from Anthony's family as his mother must often attend to multiple practical tasks, e.g. laundry and cooking, while simultaneously taking care of Anthony. Moreover, the time available for these different tasks is limited since the family arrives home late in the afternoon. Since Anthony is tired at this hour, dinner must be prepared quickly. Consequently, the complexity of Anthony's everyday life offers a variety of developmental conditions, and Anthony develops his social self-understanding as part of the processes of orientation and acting upon differences and similarities together with co-participants. Anthony engages differently across connections, ruptures, transitions and contradictions in his everyday life, his actions helping to shape the shared conditions in the various situations he is part of. Analysis of the conduct of everyday life in relation to young children like Anthony sheds light on their activities, engagements and attempts to combine, share and integrate their interests with those of other co-participants. The variations and differences young children face when transitioning between their everyday life contexts require a daily, continuous effort to integrate and relate activities, interactions and interests together with a variety of co-participants in terms of peers, siblings, parents and caregivers. An example of this is when Oscar is presented with differences in terms of new or varied routines in the nursery compared to his home context. Such changes, differences and variations comprise the complexities of everyday living and provide young children with opportunities to develop their self-understanding regarding how to understand themselves in relation to the assorted possibilities present in various situations and contexts, also through their exploration of how to contribute to the transformation and development of these situations and contexts.

Compared to older children and adults, young children do not move around between places independently and they do not choose where they are going, how and when. Their parents decide for them and often even carry the children around. However, as stressed, this does not mean that the children are passive. Rather, the children have intentions, commitments and interests that they are pursuing across situations and contexts. Consequently, children are active co-creators of how movements and shifts between places and situations take place. This is supported by Murray and Cortéz-Morales (2019), who argue that even babies cannot be considered immobile even though they do not move between contexts on their own. The children's actions in transition processes set conditions for how parents can move across places with the children and how care can be provided for the children. However, for young children it is an extraordinary condition that they are to a great extend being moved around by adults and placed in a chair, stroller, bed, on the floor, in the car and the like. And every time the children need to orientate anew. Compared to adults, young children do often not decide or know in advance when they are being moved around. This condition is not tantamount to them being passive – on the contrary I argue that this require young children to orientate themselves and actively deal with even more complex and sudden shifts and changes in activities, locations and relationships. The point is that it takes a great deal of efforts for young children to hold on to and pursue their engagements when being moved around by others. Moreover, it requires a lot for young children to actually move by themselves. For several of the children in this book, they just recently learned how to walk, and they easily lose their balance and fall and have to get back on their feet. This happens many times a day. It often also requires a lot of the children to put on or take of clothes, to get up and down from chairs, stairs and the like. Even though, one could argue that older children and adults also sometimes may feel 'moved' around, or that the movements require a lot of efforts, and that they sometimes experience limited possibilities to influence changes and shifts they have more opportunities to have a say and will be able to anticipate these and, hence, have better opportunities for orientating during the transition processes compared to young children and infants. These examples of young children's transitioning processes contribute to define the conceptualization of conduct of everyday life to also account for how the youngest children involve in these daily agentic processes.

Shifts and Transitions – Conflicting Interests

Parents organize different routines in everyday life to make situations work, such as mealtimes, and getting out the door in the morning, all of which are activities that are often routinized in the conduct of everyday life. According to Holzkamp (2013b), time is a limited resource in everyday living, which is why time and activities continuously must be prioritized and coordinated with co-participants. Consequently, some things are foregrounded, while other activities are omitted. Holzkamp states further that routines and repetitions are important aspects of human life because they allow one's time and attention to be focused elsewhere, prevention repeated, everyday activities from devouring resources in terms of planning from scratch. However, the fact that everyday life partly consists of routines and repetitions that provide the space for other activities does not mean that everyday life can be defined as static or pre-arranged. To the contrary, Axel (2011) states that variations and continually making adjustments are necessary aspects of the effort involved in maintaining a daily routine. This means that parents adjust their routines in accordance with concrete and changing situations. Orientating oneself in situations and adjusting strategies and routines are thus central aspects of parents' conduct of everyday life. When parents and children leave their home in the morning, they are moving away from family life as a particular setting with conditions different from the contexts they are moving towards (e.g. ECEC contexts). This involves a change in the interests and considerations that the family members act in relation to – for instance when the parents need to drop off their children at the nursery before making it to the bus or train at a certain time to be on time for work. This means that the conditions in the various contexts the family members are moving towards also shape the conditions for the present transition. In this way, everyday contexts are connected to each other through the family members' conduct of everyday life. For example, Anthony's mother, Sarah, must drop off Anthony early enough for him to have breakfast there, and then she has to catch a bus to get to her internship. These external demands and considerations require the family to operate under a strict timeframe in the morning. For Anthony, this means that his possibilities for contributing to the activities are limited compared to other times of the day and during the weekend. Things are often done *for* the children in the morning. For example, Anthony is not allowed to put on his clothes or to walk by himself, which is not the case in the afternoon when Sarah picks him up in nursery.

Thus, demands from other contexts become conditions for how parents organize movements between places. Dreier writes 'A social context can only be understood through its interrelationships – connections as well as separations – with other contexts in the structure of social practice' (1997, p. 104). For this reason, it is necessary to focus on what children and parents move from and where they are going to in order to understand the ways in which their transitions between these places take place. This is a common issue related to everyday living across contexts. However, there is a difference between how this transitioning process unfolds for young children and for their parents. For example, children are not responsible for making everyday life work and do not, like the parents, pay attention to time or planning and anticipating what is going to happen next. For example, Sarah is busy getting out the door in the morning because she knows she must be on time for the bus. Anthony, who does not know this, is more concerned with the possibilities in the here and now, walking by himself so that he can explore what he finds on the road. Sarah is more focused on achieving what she knows is waiting in other contexts which leads her to most often carries Anthony to the car in the morning while allowing him to walk by himself in the afternoon. As a result, children and adults often have conflicting interests that need to be coordinated and integrated when moving between contexts. The children challenge and negotiate situations and routines to find out what the various situations and routines mean to them and '[children] must find out how to live in relation to arrangements and rhythms. They must consider how arrangements suit them and what they can do to make the arrangements and rhythms suit them better' (Dreier, 2009, p. 178). Thus, a significant difference between the ways that children and adults move between places is that, while adults have some influence and responsibility for what places they want to move between and how, children have no influence or responsibility for where they are going and when. Parents are responsible for the orchestrating of the family's life, where many different and conflicting concerns, tasks and interests must be coordinated and integrated. Children do not have responsibility for these matters but, like their parents, children have interests and commitments across their life contexts to pursue and they explore the possibilities for doing this in various ways during transitioning processes.

What I have so far sought to address, and which I demonstrate with the excerpts in the next sections, is that analysing how transitions take place cannot be done in isolation but must be understood through the interrelatedness of the social practices that children transition between. The transition processes, then, are part of and must be analysed as a component of the conduct of everyday life. Moreover, an active effort is required from both parents and children when moving across these places. Even though the children are sometimes carried or physically moved by adults they contribute to how the movement can unfold by acting in ways that shape the conditions for the adults. I wish to illustrate this point by highlighting how movement between places is often associated with contradictions and conflicting interests between children and adults. These conflicts turn our focus towards what the children are concerned about and what the situation means to them, as well as the opportunities the parents have for supporting their children's shifts.

Previous Situations Create Conditions for the Current Situation

The following excerpt, which is from an afternoon when Sarah picks up Anthony (and me) from the family nursery, presents a portrait of what a transition in daily living between the contexts of a family nursery and a family home is like:

> Anthony (15 months) runs towards the door when his mother enters and he hears her voice saying 'Hi!'. Kate greets her and describes how Anthony's day has been. He has not eaten much and Kate thinks that Anthony is about to catch a cold. He has been a bit needy and more tired than usually. For this reason, Kate allowed Anthony to nap twice during the day. Normally he only sleeps once. Kate explains that he slept for half an hour in the morning in addition to his usual afternoon nap, which was then somewhat shorter than usual. Sarah says that he woke up at 3:30 am so she understands why he has been tired. Kate takes her time when talking about Anthony's day. As they talk, Sarah helps Anthony get his outerwear on. Once dressed, he runs into the living room. Kate goes after him, lifts him up and explains that he is not allowed to wear shoes inside. He laughs. She kisses him on the cheek and puts him down next to Sarah, who takes him by the hand. We walk towards the parking lot.

This exchange of knowledge between Sarah and Kate about Anthony's day takes place daily when Sarah picks up Anthony. Sarah tells me that she uses the information to take stock of how to arrange the rest of the afternoon. Today, after hearing that Anthony has not eaten much and slept less than normal and at other times, Sarah tells me that she is aware that the family needs to eat earlier than usually. Hence, she has to adjust the dinner routine, making it possible to put Anthony to bed a bit earlier in the evening.

The next excerpt is a continuation of the situation described in the last one. Sarah, Anthony and I walk along a path leading from Kate's house to the parking lot:

> Sarah holds Anthony by the hand, but he pulls his hand away and places both arms behind his back. Sarah lets him walk by himself. Along the path there are small white stones that capture Anthony's interest. He pauses, bends down and picks up a handful. Sarah takes him by the hand and pulls him away. He then pulls his hand away and heads for the playground, which has a slide, next to the path. Sarah goes after him, lifts him up and walks towards the car. He starts screaming and squealing. Sarah sighs and says: 'Okay, but only one ride today'. She quickly lifts him up, walks over and puts him on the slide. He laughs and claps. As he slides down, Sarah lifts him up just before his feet hit the ground.

She starts walking towards the car with Anthony on her arm. He protests loudly and throws himself to the side. Sarah quips: 'I said only one ride'. Sarah unlocks the car and puts Anthony in his car seat. She struggles since he is resisting with his whole body while screaming. When the car begins to move he stops crying. When we get to the parking lot situated near their home, Sarah lifts Anthony out of the car and he wiggles vigorously to get down. He wants to walk by himself. Sarah takes some grocery bags out of the trunk. Since we are both carrying bags, our hands are not available. Anthony walks alone making happy sounds. Sarah puts a bag down, unlocks the front door, holds it open and lets Anthony go in by himself. He stops just before the door and then starts to run in a different direction. Sarah sighs and puts everything down to run after Anthony before lifting him up to carry him inside.

For Anthony, changing from the family nursery to riding home means that the structure of the activities and movements changes. The lack of time constraints in the afternoon compared to the morning transitions means that Anthony does not need to hold his mother's hand but is given the opportunity to walk by himself, allowing him to pick up stones and dash to the playground. He can do something on his own. Not everything is planned down to the last detail in the afternoon when Sarah takes over responsibility for Anthony from the nursery caregiver. However, Sarah wants to get to the car quickly to get home faster on this particular day because Anthony is more tired than usual. Anthony, though, manages to get one ride on the slide. He negotiates by protesting and squirming against how the movement between the contexts, according to Sarah, should take place. Anthony is highly engaged in exploring his surroundings, including the slide and the small white stones. These things are part of a well-known routine for Anthony; he often walks in this area with Kate and his peers from the family nursery, in addition to walking on the path daily with his mother. In other words, Anthony knows which possibilities are available for exploring the stones and the playground. He explores the change of meanings that these activities entail in different situations and with various adults.

Anthony orientates in the transitioning process by exploring what he can do in the same place but in various situations and together with different co-participants. Moreover, he experiences a change in expectations and demands from the various institutional contexts he leaves and enters. When on the path with Kate and the other children, he is not allowed to walk alone unless he holds someone's hand. He is not allowed to make a detour to the playground without Kate's permission either. When he walks the same route together with his mother, he is allowed to walk by himself, which means that new opportunities for agentic participation open up when he leaves the family nursery. Through his intentional and embodied actions Anthony orientates himself to these new opportunities by pursuing the same interests in a familiar place but together with various co-participants.

The Subjective Meaning of Conduct of Everyday Life

Up to this point, I have highlighted transitions between two everyday life contexts as associated with different possibilities for action and different interests and demands. At this point I will go into more detail about how the transition affects how Sarah tries to arrange the movement from nursery to home to execute it as quickly and easily as possible. To understand Sarah's eagerness to get home we must turn our focus to the situation in the family, i.e. the context Anthony and Sarah transition to. Anthony's father, Ben, has an illness that occasionally hinders him from taking part in their family life because he cannot tolerate noise and stress, preventing Ben from regularly carrying out practical tasks in the family. Sarah also knows that Anthony is extremely tired today. Sarah's aim to get Anthony home quickly is based on the situation on this particular day and on her assessment of what tasks await at home. The days' situation places extra demands on Sarah because Anthony has not napped properly, but the information from the caregiver allows her to take this into account when planning, e.g. dinner and bedtime. The point is that routines need to be adjusted for them to be meaningful in a complex everyday life in which children's transitions between contexts comprise their developmental conditions. Anthony communicates with his mother through his embodied actions and in this way, he contributes to change the way the transition is taking place and he seems to make the daily transition between his everyday life contexts by exploring and orientating in the differences between contexts and the possibilities for actions and agentic dealing with the various demands he encounters. However, Anthony is not concerned about the many tasks waiting ahead and he does not seem concerned about the potential consequences of his tiredness. In other words, the transitions are part of Anthony's conduct of everyday life in qualitatively different ways compared to Sarah's. For her the transition is an important part of her and Anthony's collaboration about the common conduct of everyday family life they are entering and the integration of their various interests.

The situation awaiting at home is complex; Sarah must juggle various tasks and interests based on all the factors that must be taken into consideration. In addition, due to concerns about Anthony's well-being, various professionals regularly monitor the family and provide Sarah with advice about carrying out childcare routines satisfactorily. She receives instructions about health promotion, child nurturing, daily routines in the family and responding adequately to a child's needs. These instructions represent yet another concern that must be taken into consideration in the complexity of making everyday family life work. Sarah explains how she finds the instructions contradictory because the family situation is not the same every day, which presents a problem as the professionals instruct her to maintain the same routines daily by repeating the same things in the same way every day. Instructions given beforehand about children's needs fail to take a changing and complex everyday life into account. The rather fixed guidelines about structure and routines in the family life they are transitioning into shape how Sarah prioritizes and deals with the transition.

Parental Expectations towards Their Children

Although Anthony and his mother have different interests concerning how the transition should proceed, Sarah later explains to me that she does not expect Anthony to go directly to the car, even though she tries to get him to. Haavind (1987), who studies mother and child interaction in everyday family life, points out that the mothers in her study emphasize the importance of their children developing self-reliance and of the children developing an interest in taking part in and collaborating in terms of daily routines and tasks in the family. The mothers, however, do not expect their children to comply immediately as they believe that showing the children what to do and repeated exposure to the tasks and responsibilities is required over time. By encouraging the children to collaborate and take part in tasks without expecting them to do it will, the mothers believe, eventually lead to the desired result: compliance. Haavind draws attention to how the balance between wishes and demands changes with the age of the children (1987). The mothers assist and collaborate with the children before expecting them to execute tasks independently, for example, bathing and getting dressed when they are small, and hope that the children will be able to do the tasks alone in time (Haavind, 1987). As children grow older, mothers increasingly expect them to be able to and to want to do things by themselves. Haavind (1987) also shows how mothers continuously adjust their expectations and demands on their children, which is why they help them in situations when the child is tired or upset, even though the mothers know that the children usually can carry out the task themselves.

On the way home from ECEC, Sarah prioritizes adjusting and re-adjusting her own interest in coming home quickly to somewhat suit Anthony's interest in exploring his surroundings on the way to the car. Sarah has discovered that it is often best to compromise to avoid unnecessary conflicts by allowing Anthony to do some of the things that he wants to do, for example walk by himself and ride down the slide at least once. Sarah does not yet demand that he collaborate to rush home. Sarah responds to Anthony's protests with indulgence, likely due to what she was told about Anthony's well-being during the day. According to Haavind (1987), these circumstances and Anthony's age are important to being able to understand how Sarah responds to Anthony's actions and initiatives.

In the next section, I present a situation where Toby, who is four years old, is on his way home from the day care centre after his mother picks him and me up. The situation differs from that of Anthony and his mother in two main respects, creating completely different conditions for how Toby and his mother, whose name is Jane, transition together from the day care centre to home. First, the caregiver and Jane do not exchange any information about Toby's day, which means she has no knowledge about what Toby's day was like, which is not the case for Sarah. Jane is unaware of whether there is anything she should pay special attention to. Second, she expects more from Toby compared to what Sarah does from Anthony, likely due to Toby's age. In this way, certain cultural and societal norms for children's development and what is considered appropriate and fair to expect from children at different ages become part of the children's conditions – including the support they get – in the transition processes.

Lack of Insight into the Difficulties Toby Dealt with in Day Care

I spend the day with Toby at his day care centre, which allows me to gain insight into what situations he deals with during the day. Joining him on the way home with his mother provides the opportunity to observe how Toby tries to connect the efforts he makes in order to play with his peers across contexts.

During the day Toby has a tough time becoming part of the other children's communities, causing him to experience exclusion. Chapter 4 describes examples of the difficulties he faces. When his mother arrives to pick him up Toby is in a bad mood. Jane had a busy day at school but managed to hurry home to peel potatoes for dinner before arriving at the day care centre. Tired, she is eager to get home quickly to finish preparing dinner. Jane likes to hurry in and out of the day care as quickly as possible, so she most often does not talk to any of the caregivers. Due to the sheer number of children, a digital system is available to check out the children, making it unnecessary to talk to the staff. Sometimes, however, a caregiver sees her and engages in a conversation. They generally say that Toby has had a great day, leaving her unaware that Toby has difficulties becoming part of the children's communities. On this particular day when Jane finds Toby, he is wandering aimlessly after trying in vain for a long time to play with a group that includes his friend, Magnus, but is excluded:

> The mother finds Toby, says hello and tries to give him a hug but he wriggles out of her arms and runs away. She follows him and eventually catches him in the coat area. She says that he must come now and that she will not wait any longer. She grabs Toby by the hand and enters the coat area. He wants her help with his coat but she gets annoyed, saying that he is old enough to be able to manage these things by himself. When Toby has put on his coat he says: 'I want to play with Magnus!' The mother says: 'No, it's time to go home. You've already played with your friends all day'.

Later, when I talk to Jane, she explains that she got annoyed because she is convinced that Toby is acting unreasonably. She does not know what Toby's bad mood is about. She wants Toby to come immediately when she arrives, and she especially wants him to do as he is told. Jane elaborates, saying that she thinks that Toby needs boundaries. When he cries and asks her for help with his clothes, she sees it as an expression of him being cross and not wanting to bother to do things himself that she otherwise knows he is capable of.

For Toby, the transition between day care centre and home means that there are different understandings of him at play and he is met with different demands. The underlying cause of Jane's annoyance appears to stem from the fact that none of the caregivers help Toby connect his engagements across contexts by telling his mother about the problems he dealt with during the day. Consequently, the mother does not know that Toby's desire to play with a friend must be seen in the light of his efforts and difficulties involved in joining the other children's communities during the day. Another issue is that Jane sees Toby's bad mood as a manifestation of being cross. The situation continues on the way home:

> Toby slows his bike down and hangs his head. His mother calls for him. Now increasingly annoyed, she says: 'Come on now! Now I really want to get home!' Toby walks even slower, and he cries and shouts: 'I want to play with Magnus!'

When we get to the block of flats where they live, the conflict between Jane and Toby escalates because Toby refuses to park his bike in the correct place and he throws it on the ground instead. For Toby, the change in context from day care to the trip home implies a shift in expectations towards him. Later, when I talk to Jane about this conflict, she tells me that she usually does not have the energy to make play dates for Toby with other children in the afternoon because she has to get home and prepare dinner. She believes that Toby has been playing with other kids all day long. From her perspective, arranging additional opportunities for Toby to play with other children as part of their family life is unnecessary. The main issue, however, is that Toby struggles to be included and often has not managed to play with others during the day. Toby is insistent and tries to persuade his mother to arrange a play date with Magnus, which can be seen as his attempts to pursue his engagements from the day care centre in a different context. The way Toby insists is through embodied actions as hanging his head and moving slowly, as well as verbally encouraging the mother to help him with his endeavours. The mother, in contrast, is eager to get Toby to collaborate and do as he is told. Her lack of knowledge about Toby's life at day care seems to have an impact on Jane's priorities, for example that play dates with other children are not prioritized because she believes that Toby's needs in this regard are met at day care. This essentially means that supporting peer relationships does not appear to be part of her understanding of proper care tasks related to family life. This can be seen in the light of the values and discourses mediated to Jane through collaboration with the professionals within the early childhood interventions. The social worker and the health visitor emphasize healthy food, structure and predictability as important aspects of creating a good developmental environment for Toby in the family. In this way, an understanding of parenthood as comprising tasks 'inwards' in the family rather than 'outwards' is mediated by the professionals (Kousholt, 2018).

The situation with Toby and his mother illustrates how many conditions coincide to make the situation problematic for Toby. First, the multiple experiences of exclusion. Second, the lack of collaboration between the caregivers and the mother means that she lacks insight into what Toby experiences during the day when she is not present. Third, the mother's understanding of what Toby needs and what she can expect does not appear to undergo adjustment in accordance with his well-being in the specific situation. Instead, the mother interprets his mood as being related to him being too much like his father. Thus, Toby's mother does not adjust the demands she puts on Toby in this particular situation. She insists that he should do what she knows he can do in other situations. Moreover, another important aspect of understanding the situation is that Toby's mother has primary responsibility for Toby, even though Toby is with his father occasionally. Toby's mother considers it her responsibility to compensate and counteract the assumedly bad influence she imagines that the father has on Toby. As a result, she considers it an important task to be consistent and strict to avoid Toby becoming like his father, as she explains in a later interview.

Summary

The chapter showed how young children act in relation to transitions between their various everyday contexts. I have illustrated how the children, even though they do not organize the actual movement between the contexts, must be understood as anything but passive. The children act in relation to and explore the different possibilities entailed in varying contexts and relations. The differences and similarities across contexts seem to become important for the children's ways of orientating in their everyday life. This was the case with Oscar, who refused to eat what was apparently the same food in the nursery because it differed from what he was familiar with at home. Moreover, young children seem to compare differences across similar situations, for instance, naptime, meals and walking the same route with varying co-participants. These differences create new ways for the children to gain experience in how daily activities, as, for instance, walking, can be conducted, and these differences expand the children's understanding of their action possibilities across contexts, and they develop their self-understanding and personal preferences in relation to the differences they experience. As emphasized it is an extraordinary condition for young children that they are being moved around compared to older children and adults. This prompts them to continuously orientate anew and deal with many and sudden shifts. In this way, I have argued that young children relate agentic to a great deal of complexity in relation to the numerous transitions during their daily living.

Even though routine and familiar situations and activities, the transitions do not simply proceed automatically. Rather, transitioning processes involve great effort for the children and their parents. As shown, Anthony's mother receives information about his care and well-being during the day before they head home, providing her with information so that she knows that Anthony will probably be tired earlier than usual and that she must plan to eat dinner early. It is therefore urgent for her to move quickly between the family nursery and home contexts. Anthony, on the other hand, is eager to explore his surroundings as he seems to use these surroundings (things and places) to orientate in the transition. The situation where parents and children are moving from one context to another is thus characterized by different and often conflicting interests, which must be coordinated and negotiated to create a situation where the parents and children can move in a common direction together.

The possibilities Toby's mother has for taking over responsibility for Toby in the afternoon are different since she does not receive any information from the staff about how the day has progressed. Consequently, she does not know that he has been excluded. She perceives Toby's desire to play with Magnus as unreasonable because he comes straight from day care, where she is convinced that Toby has been playing with other children all day. Toby, when the adults do not communicate with each other on what care is relevant, is prevented from receiving help to pursue what is relevant to him in the next context he will enter into. In this way, it becomes difficult for him to connect his different engagements across his life contexts.

Young children are dependent on the adults around them to arrange opportunities to participate here and now, which is relevant to the composite life that is also lived elsewhere and with other children and adults. One relevant caregiving task seems to be to support young children's complex lives and the children's development of agency. Analyses based on Toby's conduct of everyday life, this type of support could include the opportunity for Toby to play with peers outside the context of the day care centre and, in this way, support his engagements and possibilities for taking part in and influencing children's communities across contexts.

The analysis in the chapter also indicates that the opportunities parents have to care for their children involve more than just tasks or conditions related to family life contexts. Rather, taking relevant care of young children depends on the opportunities available to the parents to gain insight into their children's lives, well-being and experiences in the contexts in which the parents do not participate. Knowledge of children's daily lives across places is the starting point for organizing care in the family. Thus, professionals who are together with children in other contexts, e.g. ECEC, have an important task in the form of helping children and parents to reunite and connect with each other after they have been apart. Professional care tasks can thus be said to reach into other contexts, just as parental care tasks extend beyond the family life. In the next chapter, I will elaborate on this topic when exploring children's family life.

Part Three

6

Young Children's Family Life

This chapter analyses the part of children's everyday life that unfolds in the family context. Apart from one child, none of the children live with both parents. Consequently, the children's family lives comprise at least two home contexts because four of the children have a family that regularly provides respite care for one to two days at a time. As a result, family life is not just confined to one setting and involves various people besides the parents. As explained in Chapter 4, most parents in Denmark take paid parental leave for the first year of their child's life. After that period parenthood generally involves taking care of children in collaboration with professionals in shared care arrangements (Andenæs, 2011; Kousholt, 2011; Singer, 1993; Ulvik, 2007). Family life, hence, is shaped by the complexity related to the family members' lives elsewhere – including the children's everyday life in ECEC contexts. Consequently, family life must be understood as a social practice linked to other social practices connected through societal structures since 'no context can be understood by itself as if it were an isolated island' (Dreier, 2008, p. 26). Daily transitions across contexts, hence, are a common condition for most families in the West (Dencik, 1999; Singer, 1993; Thorne, 2001). This way of arranging children's lives involve that when children and parents reunite in the afternoon they must coordinate and integrate their different lives into a shared life together. Reunifying is commonly conflictual and challenging, as the examples in the previous chapter illustrate, and conditions for family life and family members' interests are formed in interaction with the lives of the children and parents in other contexts. An example of this is the example in the last chapter, where Toby wants to play with his friend. Conditions in the family life, hence, are set elsewhere and have an impact on the different interests and engagements of family members. For this reason, I draw on an understanding of family life as an activity requiring ongoing negotiations and coordination of conflicting concerns related to family member's lives and relations to various institutional contexts (Dreier, 2008;

Kousholt, 2012; Morgan, 2011). Historically, however, the Western modern nuclear family has been regarded quite isolated as 'the basic unit of social organization, fulfilling the social and economic needs of its members and of society' (O'Hagan, 2010, p. 67). This function of the family as a private unit caused the family to turn inwards as an arena for emotional fulfilment during the late eighteenth and nineteenth centuries. Only, from the 1950s, the function of the family changed and was regarded as a unit of socialization of children, turning the family life outwards towards the society (Parsons & Bales, 1956). Since the 1950s the demarcations between family and other institutional contexts have changed accordingly to fluctuating and historically and culturally changing responsibilities ascribed to the parents and has shaped the division of labour between parents and other caregivers (Schmidt, 2017). I will elaborate this in relation to the parental tasks and responsibilities in Chapter 7. Historically family research has placed the responsibility for the well-being of the child on the parents in a rather private and individualized family. Even though this perspective has been criticized, it remains a central interpretive framework in professional practice of early childhood interventions (Kousholt, 2018). As a response to this problem it is pivotal to understand family life as fundamentally social and part of changing societal conditions, and as framed by Højholt, Juhl and Kousholt (2018), this involves 'conceptualizing how family life at one and the same time is quite a personal matter involving great differences in regard to life forms, care practices and perspectives on the development of children *and* a common matter related to the welfare society's general responsibility for children' (p.13, original emphasis).

Since children's lives are organized across various institutional contexts, the daily processes of transitioning between these contexts become crucial developmental conditions for children. Even though it is mainly from the age of one Danish children begin to live their everyday lives across these various institutional contexts, the welfare state, however, is present in the family life even before the children start attending ECEC centres. As part of a health promotion and prevention approach, every new-born child in Denmark is enrolled in the health visitor programme, which includes several routine home visits from the child's birth to age three. The health visitor supervises the developmental well-being and health of the child. If the health visitor has concerns about the behaviour or appearance of the parents or the child, the health visitor is obliged to report the concerns to the social worker employed by the local authorities, who will determine whether or not it is necessary to proceed with an investigation. If so, the parenting abilities of the parents and potential risk factors will be scrutinized. The local authorities in Denmark provide a large number of preventive interventions that can be initiated if a child's well-being is deemed to be at risk. An example of an intervention is additional visits from the health visitor or having the mother take part in a group for vulnerable mothers that receives regular supervision by a social worker and a health visitor, or respite family care can be provided. In the subsequent sections I will zoom in on the conditions in family life and what these mean for the young children's possibilities for developing agency. Part of the conditions shaping the family life for the concrete children in this book are the early childhood interventions initiated.

Family Life as a Shared Care Practice

Kousholt (2012) highlights the cooperative aspect of the family members' shared family life in the concept of common conduct of family everyday life, which is a theoretical development of Holzkamp's (2013b) conduct of everyday life concept. This concept highlights the transition from being separate places to gathering in the family in the afternoon and how these processes are not to be understood as harmonious alignments of the different interests of parents and children, but rather as the ongoing efforts of children and parents to coordinate and negotiate their different interests to arrange and make everyday situations work.

In many aspects, the families in the book live ordinary lives in terms of shared care arrangements, and that everyday family life involves coordinating various and sometimes contradicting interests and concerns. One aspect, however, that separates the families in the book from other families in general is the fact that they are defined as marginalized and that the parents are given detailed instructions and advice on how to organize their family life by various professionals. Being involved in early childhood interventions decisions and prioritizations in everyday family life add yet another level of collaboration and complexity to the task of taking care of children in collaboration with others. I will focus on how parents organize their family life, including how the instructions from early childhood intervention professionals entangle everyday life practices and concerns at stake for the parents, and then, how such instructions become significant for how the parents prioritize in the family. To illustrate the many complexities at stake in their family life, I include a few excerpts from interviews with the various professionals involved in the families, as well as interview excerpts that illustrate parental reflections on enrolment in an early childhood intervention and how this create somewhat extraordinary conditions for the parents to deal with ordinary conflicts related to parenthood in shared care arrangements. But I foreground how children orientate themselves in relation to the diverse ways in which to organize family life and daily routines. I specifically target the ways in which children explore action possibilities in a variety of contexts, how they create coherence and how they contribute to their own transitioning. Consequently, my main focus in the present chapter will centre on what the children do in their various family settings. How do they participate? How does the organization of their family life create possibilities for them to contribute to the activities that occur? And how does their participation change and develop in and across different settings? How do the children contribute to the transformation of conditions? Even though I also spotlight how the parents organize their family life, a crucial point is how the children also contribute to this organization. I wish to emphasize that various and complex conditions are at stake in entangled ways, and that the apparently same situations and conflicts entail quite different meanings for different children (and parents), depending on the configuration of their conduct of everyday life and the various relationships and situations they take part in various contexts.

Early Childhood Interventions as an Extraordinary Aspect of Family Life

In families where the local authorities consider the children's development and well-being to be at risk, early childhood interventions (e.g. family counselling and respite families) are provided.[1] The instructions parents receive from professionals normally touch on, for example, how to attend to their child's health, nutrition, care and development but also how to organize daily routines. I explicitly pinpoint how the instructions interweave with other concerns and prioritizations as part of the parents' efforts to make family life work. I argue that parents subject to early childhood interventions face several extra dimensions in their lives that add to the complexity of parenthood as the interventions involve receiving instructions on how to parent well. A variety of studies examine this issue, some of which show that parents involved in early childhood interventions experience that the generalized knowledge of the professional has a higher status than the parents' everyday life perspectives, and that parents often struggle to follow social worker's instructions (e.g. Dumbrill, 2006; Hennum, 2014). Inspired by some of the issues brought forward in the above-mentioned studies, I unpack two main issues that I already touched briefly upon in the previous chapter. First, that being a parent and organization of family work cannot be understood as delimited to care activities in the home. Second, that care to ensure the well-being of young children or children's needs is not a static phenomenon that can be supported by doing the same thing every day or by stringently following instructions. The chapter's examples illustrate how the multifaceted nature of the instructions about diverse aspects as health promotion, child nurturing and daily routines in the family disregard the complexity of family into consideration. The professionals' instructions, then, become yet another aspect of the opportunities available for doing good parenting (Hennum, 2014). The chapter presents everyday situations that illustrate rather common conditions related to living and organizing family life, but as we shall see, what may appear to be the same situations or routines in the various families develop differently. The beginning of the chapter provides examples of situations where parents and children have different possibilities for dealing with the conflicts and problems that arise. I give examples of how children have the opportunity to orientate themselves and contribute to the common activities that take place in the family. Later in the chapter, I describe situations characterized by the limited opportunities children have for contributing to what is going on. Finally, I will present situations where conflicts lead to clashes and powerlessness. The point I would like to highlight in terms of escalation is that problems in family life unfold in relation to everyday situations, which for all families are generally associated with complexity, changing conditions, fluctuating dynamics and conflicts to be dealt with (Kousholt, 2012). Hence, what is conspicuous about the families is not that they experience challenging situations, conflicts, contradictory conditions and diverging interests that must be prioritized but that the parents and children I present in the book have fewer opportunities to engage in these conflicts that are commonly associated with family life.

In the next section, I will focus on Anthony's family life. To furnish the analysis of the family as a social practice Anthony as well as his parents' actions must be analysed as a part of, I will start by outlining some of the instructions given to the parents. These instructions as well as Anthony's life elsewhere are significant for understanding the parents' prioritizations and organization of the daily routines family life. Later, I show other examples of similar transition situations from afternoons in the families where children and parents have returned home and now have to find their way into family life after spending the day in various separate places. The reason I chose to focus on precisely these situations is that situations like this usually constitute cross-pressure in relation to the gathering and reuniting. It is precisely in these afternoon situations that I observe that family life is the most difficult for the children and the parents.

Anthony's Family Life

Sarah and Ben's son Anthony is now eighteen months old and when he was a new-born, the local health visitor came for a routine visit. In an interview, the health visitor explains that she was somewhat concerned because the parents did not appear to be awfully familiar with how to take care of an infant. For instance, the parents did not dress Anthony properly according to the weather, and they generally seemed unaware of Anthony's needs. Another issue of concern was the parental history of drug abuse and of growing up in foster care. The health visitor was worried about whether the parents' own experiences meant that they lacked basic parenting skills. Due to these concerns a social worker got involved and suggested that Sarah attends a mothers' group for vulnerable mothers as a preventive intervention. The parents reluctantly accepted.

When I interviewed Sarah and Ben, they explained that they both find everyday life difficult, especially because of the chronic disease Ben suffers from which often prevents him from taking part in caring for Anthony or doing domestic chores. Sometimes Ben is admitted to the hospital for weeks, leaving Sarah with primary responsibility for everything in the home while simultaneously trying to keep up with her studies. When Ben is doing well, most of his energy goes into his work to make up for his high level of absenteeism. When Ben is feeling sick, he and Sarah frequently fight about the care tasks and domestic chores.

When I interviewed the social worker she explained how she thinks that Ben and Sarah are disorganized and incapable of giving Anthony a stable, everyday routine: 'We emphasised how Anthony needs stability and predictability […] One issue is his sleeping pattern. We have reason to believe that the parents put Anthony to bed way too late in the evening and that means that he is exceptionally tired the next day in the family nursery'.

Anthony's apparent need for stability is used as an argument for instructing the parents to ensure stability and predictability. By presenting these concerns and giving instructions the social worker introduces how to be a parent is based on a certain understanding of children and their developmental needs. This perspective includes ensuring healthy sleeping patterns and being able to maintain a stable routine for Anthony. In an attempt to establish this stability, the professionals instruct the parents to make sure that Anthony only naps once in the middle of the day and that he is put to bed around 7:30 or 8:00 pm every night.

Instructions and Complexities of Everyday Life as Contradictory

When I interviewed Sarah and Ben about what they thought about being subject to early childhood interventions, Sarah explains:

> It's really difficult because they [the social worker and the health visitor] urged us to have a stable pattern. We had to try to eat at the same time every evening and keep to a bedtime schedule for Anthony. I think they have some kind of standard formula for how everyday life should be conducted and when to do this and that, but you know what, that just doesn't go very well together with our working hours and the whole situation with Ben's disease and Anthony's mood.

Sarah explains how she finds the instructions contradictory because the family's situation is not the same every day, which presents a problem as the professionals instruct them to maintain the same daily routine. Another problem is addressed by Ben who does not feel that he is involved in the interventions, stating: 'It's only about Sarah and Anthony ... I don't have a say'. Sarah agrees with him and expresses her frustration because, from her perspective, the main problems in the family involve making ends meet when it comes to work hours, studying and picking Anthony up at day care, all of which is compounded by the fact that knowing when and what Ben can help with is unpredictable. Ben, on the other hand, finds it difficult to be included in the family when he is doing well and able and willing to contribute to care tasks and household duties. The fact that the intervention is directed at Sarah and Anthony only appears to reinforce the difficulties and dilemmas that challenge Ben and Sarah as collaborators working to share the responsibility for parenthood.

Other instructions provided by the health visitor and the social worker are directed at Sarah and Anthony's emotional contact. Sarah is told, for example to respond immediately when Anthony cries. The professionals explain that Sarah needs to be a secure base for Anthony, which can be achieved by responding appropriately to his every need. The social worker when visiting the family or when observing Sarah and Anthony in the mothers' group registers whether and how Sarah comforts Anthony when he falls, whether Sarah is capable of verbally expressing what she thinks Anthony is trying to tell her when he cries, and if Sarah gives Anthony a large amount of physical contact and caressing. This illustrates how the professionals in their collaboration with the parents take part in sociocultural activities within institutionalized contexts and that they inevitably draw on structures of meaning or discourses (Burman, 1994), which are inherent in language and in social and cultural practices (Hogstad & Jansen, 2020). In this case, it is the idea of attachment theory that is dominant in early childhood intervention practice. As mentioned earlier, Burman (2020) terms this the 'risk-resilience discourse' about child development, where early childhood experiences, particularly those tied to the parent–child relation, are considered a cause of undesirable psychological consequences in adulthood (Gladstone, Parker, & Malhi, 2006). The psychological concepts about parental ability and attachment appear too isolated and abstracted from social conditions and relations to caregivers and peers, hence insufficient in grasping the complexity of a compound everyday life across various context in which young children develop.

The following example derives from my observations in the family. It is afternoon, and the setting is Ben and Sarah's home. The situation is a continuation of the one presented in the previous chapter in which Sarah just picked up Anthony from family nursery and has returned home, where Ben is waiting. Ben, feeling poorly after recently coming home from the hospital, is still tired and easily becomes annoyed when Anthony cries. Ben describes how he withdraws from the family activities when he is feeling sick. Kate, the caregiver, talked to Sarah about how Anthony seemed particularly tired right from the beginning of the day, which is why an exception was made and Anthony was put to bed for an extra nap in the family nursery. Sarah told the caregiver that Anthony was still suffering from a cold and that he had been awake several times during the night. Sarah learned that Anthony had not slept as long as usual during the day, despite the extra nap. During my visit in the family, Sarah tells me that Anthony seems more tired than he usually is at this time. When Anthony comes home from the family nursery in the afternoon, his father usually is home. Everyday Anthony explores Ben's whereabouts and what he can do with Ben. When Anthony tries to get in contact with his father, Ben meets him differently; some days Anthony lifts himself up on the couch and Ben makes fun of him. Other times Ben gets annoyed with Anthony and does not want him around, which is exactly what occurs that afternoon, as the excerpt below shows:

> Ben sits at the coffee table with a laptop. Anthony walks over to him as soon as he gets his coat off. Anthony is trying to push the buttons on the laptop. Ben, seeming slightly annoyed, brushes his hand away. Anthony stands and looks at him for a moment and then tries again. Ben shuts the laptop. At the same time, Sarah begins to fold clothes from a drying rack placed in the living room. Anthony walks over to her and grabs her leg, eagerly pointing at the basket with clothespins on the table. Sarah gives him the basket. He sits down with the basket in his arms and hands me the clothespins one at a time. Sarah says that he likes to put them together so that they make a long chain. I do this with some of them and give them back to Anthony. Sarah hands Anthony more clothespins as she takes the clothes down from the rack. Anthony seems very preoccupied with them. Sarah puts the clothes aside and walks into the kitchen to prepare the dinner. Anthony looks at her, throws the clothespins to the side and runs after his mother.

In Chapter 4 I described how Anthony orientated himself in relation to the other children in the family nursery. At home in the family, he seems to orientate himself by keeping an eye on what his parents are doing, and he tries to become part of their activities. Family life represents a known setting but one that is nonetheless changing and with dynamic routines and interactions. I view Anthony's attempt to touch Ben's laptop as part of this orientation process in relation to how it is possible to engage with Ben on this particular day. Anthony seems aware of the varieties in the kind of interaction he can have with Ben. Anthony orientates in relation to the responses he gets from Ben. Sometimes his hand is brushed away and at other times Ben is supporting Antony when he lifts himself to the couch. Osterkamp-Holzkamp (1979) writes that 'to orientate oneself is a general endeavour in maintaining agency' (p. 310, author's translation). Based on this, I interpret Anthony's orientation as his attempt to assess the context (family life) that he has transitioned into as part of his possibilities for participating. Anthony explores what is going on and how he can become part of what is happening. Anthony's interests and his intentions seem to be developed and linked to this specific context and his familiarity with it, for example in relation to the situation with the laundry, which he seems quite acquainted with, implying an opportunity for him to be involved in a shared activity. The children's transitions seem involve them changing their intentional actions and develop their ways of participating in new ways, depending on the specific context and its possibilities and demands. The children also create demands which their surroundings respond to, often leading to the change or adjustment of the situations they are part of. Ben, for instance, is urged to relate to Anthony and their relationship through Anthony's persistent approaching him every day. The children appear to pursue quite various engagements in their different settings. However, when entering a new context Anthony seems to deal with the transition by orienting himself in the new context (even if it is well-known to him) by using specific toys or other known items, acting in specific ways in specific relationships and activities, for instance by putting clothespins together in a particular way every time Sarah folds the clothes. However, Anthony's intentions are also developed and shaped as part of his conduct of everyday life through his participation in the family nursery and other contexts. For instance, Anthony expands his repertoire of how to approach others and how to make the world respond to his contributions. The embodied orientation is an important part of transitioning processes and young children's way of exploring how to take part in what is going on. These situated explorative processes appear important for the young children's possibilities for becoming familiar with their various, dynamic life contexts, the differences between these but also how the possibilities within the same contexts vary and how these can be expanded.

When Sarah starts to work on the laundry, it captures Anthony's interest and Sarah engages him in the task. Their interests thus appear to be aligned: Sarah gets the laundry done and can move on to the next task, and Anthony can join what is going on. Sarah has a diverse number of tasks and concerns that she must prioritize, coordinate and relate to together with Anthony and Ben. She is busy getting things started quickly and getting the laundry cleared out of the way so the family can eat in the living room, on top of keeping Anthony busy and in a good mood. Anthony seems to be orientating himself in the activities that occur by participating in the shared activities. I will return to Anthony a little later in the chapter to describe how the afternoon develops. But first, let us see how a similar afternoon plays out slightly differently at Daniel's home.

Daniel and Anthony's opportunities to develop agency differ depending on their possibilities for orientating themselves in situations that are chaotic and difficult to navigate in, making them appear problematic for Daniel.

Strategies in the Orientation Processes

Daniel (sixteen months), lives with his mother, Ashley, twenty, and his older brother, Matt, who is four years old. Matt is enrolled in a day care centre, while Daniel is enrolled in family nursery. The next excerpt is from an afternoon at Daniel's home. Before this situation, I spent the entire day in the family nursery together with Daniel and his mother just recently picked Daniel and me up at the nursery. It is about 5:30 pm, and the transition between family nursery and home has taken much longer than usual due to many conflicts between Matt and his mother. Daniel has been sitting in the child bike seat on his mother's bicycle, observing Matt and his mother carefully. As Daniel is lifted from the bicycle at home he looks at Matt, who pushes his bike to the side and throws himself into a puddle to roll around in. Ashley, meanwhile, is busy locking the bikes. Daniel also lays down in the puddle. Ashley sighs and looks at them for a second before she starts to pull the boys away from the water. After a long time, she manages to get the two now wet and dirty children into the apartment.

> Inside the hallway, Ashley helped Daniel get his outerwear off and takes his bike helmet off as he sits on the floor in the hallway. Matt runs to the kitchen, where the mother has gone out with a bag of items. Daniel pulls the straps to put on his bicycle helmet. I'm sitting next to him. From the kitchen we listen to Ashley and Matt's voices quarrelling because Matt found some chocolate in a cupboard that he wants. The mother says no to Matt and puts the chocolate back in the cupboard: 'It's not for now!' Matt begins to cry. 'But I bought some new instant drink powder for us,' she tells him, 'with strawberry flavour!' Daniel seems to be listening. He looks at me and gets up and runs out to the kitchen as fast as he can, just about stumbling in the hallway.

Daniel spends much time observing Matt, and he tries to do the same things as Matt. Daniel's highchair plays a vital role in his efforts to keep up and orientate himself, as this excerpt from my fieldnotes indicates:

> Daniel comes into the kitchen and looks at Matt, who is sitting on the counter. His mother stands next to him. Daniel grabs his highchair and hangs on one side of it, almost making it fall over. Ashley, who is making the strawberry drink for Matt, quickly steps to the highchair and grabs Daniel by the arm to pull him up into the chair. She returns to the counter and finishes the drink. 'Do you want some too?', she asks Daniel. Daniel grabs the arm of the chair with both hands and lifts himself up and lets himself fall down as he laughs delightedly, saying 'A, a, a', which is what he says when he means yes. The chair tilts slightly off from the floor as Daniel lets himself fall into it. Ashley stands sideways to see what

she's doing at the counter while simultaneously keeping an eye on Daniel in the chair. 'Yes, yes! You'll get some too,' she says to Daniel.

In this situation Daniel stands on the floor and cannot see from down below what Matt is doing on the counter. He seemingly shows that he wants to get up in his chair by hanging on its side, a strategy that works since Ashley immediately needs to respond to prevent the chair from toppling. Other times, when Daniel wants to get out of and down from the chair again, he stands up, which also instantly causes Ashley to lift him down so he does not fall out of the chair and hurt himself.

Daniel's interest in the chair may be related to the fact that it allows him to observe, follow and orientate himself in relation to the (many) things going on at the counter, where Matt can climb up on his own. Possibilities to observe and follow activities seem pivotal as part of embodied orientation processes as well as exploration of what one can do in particular situations and what other co-participants are doing. Listening, looking, moving as ways of connecting their own actions to the actions of others thereby seems pivotal to young children's possibilities for taking active part in occurring activities and for them to engage in communication and interactions with others. At the same time, it is an opportunity to be involved in what the mother and Matt are doing. Matt, on the one hand, seems to be a resource for Daniel in his efforts to orientate himself in family life and the activities that occur. On the other hand, Matt is constantly taking initiatives that require Ashley to respond straightaway, which means Matt also contributes to creating chaotic, hectic situations that make it more difficult for Daniel to orientate himself in them and to be part of them, just as it becomes harder for Ashley to get ahead of the situation. This is an example of how children and parents by their actions contribute to co-create each other's conditions. I observe Daniel's micro-movements up and down his highchair many times during the afternoons I visit the family. Daniel puts immense effort into trying to orientate himself in what is at stake in the interaction between Matt and Ashley, but I do not frequently see Daniel succeeding in being involved in shared activities. I will return to Daniel's family again a little later in the chapter, but first I will look at how Anthony's afternoon is developing.

Concern Becomes Part of Everyday Conditions

Anthony has, as we saw earlier, helped his mother with the laundry and the clothespins, and now he follows her out into the kitchen, where she is about to start cooking. Ben sits in the living room with the laptop and Anthony is tired.

Usually, Sarah explains, Anthony likes to play with some plastic blocks on the kitchen floor while Sarah is cooking. But when Anthony is tired, like today, he does not want to do anything. Occasionally he sits in the living room watching television with Ben.

> 5:20 pm: Anthony starts to whine and rubs his eyes. Sarah puts him on her arm, but he protests by squirming and screaming. He throws himself back and Sarah puts him down. She fetches a small pack of raisins, which seems to calm him down. His crying subsides. Sarah starts peeling potatoes. A few minutes later, Anthony starts to cry again and throws the rest of the raisins on the floor. Sarah makes several attempts to get Anthony to calm down. For example, she tries to draw his attention towards the television, and she fetches water and toys, but nothing seems to work. Sarah looks bewildered and asks Ben if he can start to peel the potatoes, so she can take care of Anthony. Ben nods but is immersed in the laptop.

In this situation, Sarah tries in several ways to comfort Anthony but is simultaneously keen to get dinner ready. Anthony seems to be both tired and hungry at the same time. By delaying the cooking to comfort Anthony, meeting Anthony's urgent need for food so that he can be put to bed becomes difficult. This illustrates how caring for Anthony is a complex, contradictory process that requires constant prioritization of concerns and needs. The situation constitutes a conflict between prioritizing comforting Anthony or preparing dinner. Whenever Sarah turns her attention to the cooking, Anthony cries, and when she comforts him, the dinner is delayed. My fieldnotes show that Sarah considers her options. Sarah looks at the clock [nearly 5:30 pm]. 'You can't be allowed to sleep now. It's too late for a nap', she says to Anthony while carrying him around trying to console him. The guidelines and directions from the professionals about responding immediately to Anthony's needs, having regular sleep routines and nurturing him fail to take into account the contradictory concerns and Anthony's changing and simultaneous needs.

Later that night Sarah explains to me how, in the situation in question, she is well aware that Anthony is crying because he is tired and that what he needs most of all is sleep. Yet, Sarah does not consider putting him to bed an option, stating:

> Some nights are just really difficult when Anthony is tired and cries. Then it's not as easy as they [the professionals] make it sound to just keep doing the same thing over and over! […] Even when Anthony isn't tired, then we come home late in the afternoon and then it gets late until dinner is ready … too late according to them. If Ben hasn't had the energy to peel potatoes or … yeah, you

know, just prepare the dinner or something ... then it's quite difficult to eat as early as they claim is best for Anthony ... but, you know, I try because I'm afraid what will happen if we don't follow their instructions.

This example emphasizes two issues. First, Anthony's needs and well-being cannot be understood merely in relation to what is going on in the family and what the parents do. In the above situation, Anthony's need for an afternoon nap when he is together with his parents is different than usual because of a shorter nap during the day. The specific care tasks, Anthony's needs and the related dilemmas experienced by the parents are connected to what happened earlier in the day and in other contexts of Anthony's life. This suggests that parental care connects to and builds on the care that others provide at other times and in other places. The parents hold responsibility for what Andenæs (2011) terms 'a chain of care' which various caregivers contribute to. The parents, however, only comprises one part of this chain. Second, I want to point out how this shared care arrangement is a common condition for parenthood that becomes particularly difficult for Anthony's parents because of the social worker's narrow focus on parental care instead of focusing on the parents' care contribution as one part of multiple caregivers' care contributions. This focus does not take into consideration how the dilemmas and Anthony's concrete needs evolve situated in relation to his participation in and across different life contexts. What happens in other contexts influences the problems, needs and concerns that emerge at home and, consequently, becomes the parents' responsibility. Kousholt's (2012) study of family life shows that parents continuously arrange and rearrange routines according to changing and complex everyday life in order to make it work. Exploring such action possibilities in everyday life together with the parents – including parental perspectives on everyday struggles – does not appear to be part of the professional interventions aimed at marginalized parents. The family nursery caregiver has the opportunity to adjust the routines around, for example, the noon nap, to make things work and to meet Anthony's needs if she believes he is more tired than normal. The parents do not feel that they have the same opportunity as the caregiver to adjust and break the routines by, for example allowing Anthony to take a short nap before eating dinner. Doing so would be contrary to the advice and guidelines the professionals gave them. Thus, advice based on standards of care and the sleep patterns of toddles becomes part of the parental conditions for arranging care and family life in the situation. Along with advice about sleep, the family has also been told that listening to Anthony's signals, understanding his needs and responding to them is important. Guidelines for creating good regular routines around sleep and diet thus become parallel to other guidelines, such as not letting Anthony cry, which conflicts with other demands in the family's already complex everyday life, where Ben's illness means that the balance between tasks and resources in the family fluctuates.

The task of taking care of young children is thus a contradictory process that requires prioritization of different considerations and needs. The parental care, regular routines and sleep guidelines do not take into account these contradictory conditions. Anthony's mood and well-being are not static phenomenon, which means that supporting his well-being must rely on doing more than just the same thing every day or following a guide. What worked yesterday is not necessarily what will work in the situation today. As a result, the parents must constantly evaluate the variations in Anthony's intentional and embodied actions as a way to assess his well-being. Paradoxically, it becomes difficult for Sarah to take Anthony's embodied orientation as a starting point for a shared exploration together with him of how his well-being can be ensured when the standardized directions about young children's needs are foregrounded. The parents adjust their actions, priorities and routines to take care of Anthony as well as possible and to maintain the routines of family life. One strategy in this regard is to give Anthony a baby bottle filled with water, which helps him to calm down a bit so that cooking can resume. This solution is a compromise that both sooths Anthony and does not go against the guidelines from Sarah's mothers' group about not giving milk in a bottle after the child is one year of age. The parents' statements illustrate that instructions given beforehand about Anthony's needs fail to take a changing and complex everyday life into account. Moreover, the professionals emphasize young children's biological needs as the focus for parental care. Agency, hence, is not a topic.

Hennum argues similarly that instructions given by professionals can lead to a 'hierarchy of knowledge privileging professional knowledge above parental ethno-theories and everyday life struggles' (2014, p. 451). In the situation, Sarah's concern for the family translates into trying to live up to the official guidelines, which has an impact on the solutions she can resort to in the situation. For example, Sarah does not even consider following what her own assessment of what would work best in the situation for Anthony and the whole family. Sarah says that she knows that Anthony needs a nap the most to ease the situation, but she is worried about what the professionals will say if she does not follow their advice down to the smallest detail. Thus, these circumstances indicate that Sarah does in fact have the ability to monitor and sense Anthony's mood and well-being, which the professionals believe is lacking.

In her study of family life, Kousholt (2011) points out that parents make everyday life work by trying different solutions and changing and re-arranging various ways of organizing daily routines if things do not work out. Anthony's respite parents, Paul and Ann, provide an example of trying out what works when they describe how they approached Anthony learning to fall asleep with them 'Yeah … we tried really hard and did what worked with our own children, and if what we tried didn't work, well then we tried something else'. The point is that trying out assorted options requires flexibility and various opportunities to act. Paul and Ann, who have three children, have been a foster family for many years. They have different conditions than Anthony's parents because they have extensive experience with trying new approaches and with what already works. Another significant condition is that no one is concerned about how Paul and Ann organize their family life or care for Anthony. On the contrary, they were selected and employed by the local authorities to supplement and compensate for what Anthony's parents are considered unable to give him. The system trusts the respite family's judgement, assessments and decisions as caregivers, which creates opportunities for action in relation to adjusting to routines and trying them out.

The Hour before Dinner, Priorities and Strategies

I have so far pointed out how being enrolled in early childhood interventions interacts with and becomes part of children's as well as parents' conditions in family life, just as I have shown that conditions in the family are formed not only in the family but also in relation to the child's life elsewhere and based on other people's care contributions. In the following, I will present one last example from the afternoon at Anthony's home. The aim is to show how Anthony contributes to Sarah's change in priorities concerning the tasks at hand. My fieldnotes describe how Sarah tries to get on with preparing the dinner during that same afternoon:

> Anthony sits with a baby bottle in his highchair, and when the bottle is empty, he begins to cry again. Sarah sighs, calls to Ben and asks him again to peel the potatoes. Sarah asks Anthony if he wants to come with her and wash clothes. He stops crying as soon as he is being lifted down from the highchair. He follows Sarah to the bathroom and helps her put clothes in the washing machine. He is allowed to press the button. He stomps a little on the floor with his foot and

> laughs delightedly at Sarah and me. Sarah takes him by the hand and walks back into the kitchen again. Sarah sets him up in the highchair with a new bottle. Ben has gone into the living room again. Sarah finishes the dinner.

By relating to Antony's embodied orientation through her own embodied orientation Sarah interprets that he is feeling uneasy in the situation. Osterkamp-Holzkamp (1979) writes that 'one must take a negative emotional state as an expression of some unsatisfactory objective living conditions. Emotions have, so to speak, the function of constituting a subjective orientation to improve the relations of the outside world' (p. 276, author's translation). Anthony's resistance and embodied orientation are his way of exploring the concrete situation and expressing a negative emotional state, and he does so in a way that causes Sarah to temporarily change her priorities and postpone the cooking. In this way, Anthony makes Sarah respond to him in a way that allows for him to get in a position to contribute to transform the situation. Sarah's response helps him to change the conditions so that it is possible for him to become an active part of a shared activity. As soon as Sarah lifts Anthony out of his highchair his emotional state changes. The tiredness seems to be of less importance to Anthony when he is involved in what is going on and the change in Anthony's emotional state allows Sarah to return to cooking.

Sarah's many transitions between activities are propelled by Anthony's bodily actions and emotional expressions. This means that Sarah needs to react and change her focus and her priorities in coordination with Anthony. As shown in Chapter 4, the caregiver in the family nursery prepares the practical tasks and logistics before the children arrive in the morning; that is, she has the opportunity to prepare food and other things that she will need during the day in advance. In the family, the parents do not have the same opportunity to take of practical tasks ahead of time because they get home at the same time as their children, which forces them to take care of their children and the practical tasks at the same time. Kousholt (2011) mentions that prioritizing between different tasks is an integral part of parenting. This prioritization becomes part of the children's conditions in the family because it requires them to be able to do some things themselves or to entertain themselves for a period (Haavind, 1987).

Anthony is often with his respite family on weekends and during the holidays, when there are fewer time constraints, which is in stark contrast to weekdays in Anthony's own family, where not only time but hands and other resources are scarce. Like ECEC childminders, the respite parents have time to prepare for Anthony's visits, for example by completing practical tasks such as cleaning, purchasing groceries and cooking in advance, which allows them to give Anthony all the attention he needs during his visit. In the respite family, there are always two adults around all the time, which means Anthony is not required to entertain himself while they are busy. In the subsequent sections, I will show how the contexts of the two families are part of a complex life, where Anthony is given the opportunity to pursue engagements in diverse ways.

Space and Possibilities Are Combined

A few months later in the spring on the way home from the family nursery with Anthony's family in the afternoon, Sarah talks to Anthony about what they should do once we are home. She suggests that he can play outside on the ground-floor apartment patio.

> 5:00 pm. As we enter the apartment, Anthony walks purposefully through the living room and heads for the patio door. He barely notices Ben when he greets him. Sarah follows Anthony and opens the door for him. Anthony walks out onto the patio and heads for a red plastic tractor, which he climbs onto. He sits on it for a little while and then tries to get it running by moving forward in the seat. He cannot reach the pedals with his feet. He slides down and pushes the tractor and then sits back up and leans forward. Then he slides down again and goes into his room. He picks up books and teddy bears, which he throws into the tractor's trailer. Anthony walks back and forth between his room and the patio many times. The door is open, and he walks inside with boots and outerwear on and fetches many items to carry out onto the patio to throw in the plastic trailer. Anthony pulls the trailer around the garden and goes inside again to pick up new things. He is completely engulfed by this play for almost an hour.

Anthony seems to enjoy being able to move between the patio and his room. The play takes place both inside and outside, and he is allowed to decide for himself when he wants to go in or out. He is given the opportunity to try out various solutions and to experiment. He is also allowed to pick things up from his room and take them outside and vice versa. His parents do not require Anthony to take his boots on and off every time he moves between being inside and out. The family nursery and the respite family have several restrictions on how Anthony can move between places – for instance from outside and inside, which things he is allowed to bring back and forth and to what extent he plays alone.

For example, when Anthony plays outside in the family nursery and is wearing outerwear and boots, he is not allowed to go inside with his boots on. He must also wash his hands when he has finished playing outside. Thus, there are several routines to go through in the transition between distinct kinds of activities and spaces in the family nursery and with the respite family compared to Anthony's home context. Due to all the routines and the goal of being with Anthony at all times, the nursery caregiver, as well as Paul and Ann must engage in extra work when they let Anthony change from inside or out, which is why Anthony must play either inside or out in these settings. The toys in family nursery are not allowed to be taken outside, just as buckets and items from the sandbox are not permitted in the living room. All of this, however, is allowed at home with his family. When with the respite family, Paul and Ann stay outside with Anthony while he plays, which the caregiver also does at the family nursery. At home, Anthony is often allowed to be out in the garden by himself, which means that there are no adults who become impatient and eager to go back inside, delimiting the time Anthony can play outside. Because Anthony's parents are usually busy with other chores while Anthony is outside he can often play outside as long as he wants to.

This is also the case today as Anthony freely goes back and forth to his heart's desire between his room and the patio. Anthony is highly engaged in his play, where bringing items back and forth from inside to out and vice versa seems to be a high priority. Anthony is pursuing his interests across spaces inside and outside, embracing the opportunity to connect things and spaces that are separated in other contexts. The point of highlighting this situation is that at home Anthony is given the opportunity to pursue his engagements in a different way compared to when he is with the respite family or at the family nursery, where they generally constantly hold his hand, metaphorically speaking. There is always an adult close by ready to help and arrange activities for him. This was the case with Kate at the nursery and, in a moment, I will provide examples of how the respite parents behave similarly when Anthony is with them. In the situation above and in many other situations at home, his parents do not arrange situations for him in the same way. They let him try to accomplish things on his own, for example when he climbs up on a chair to fetch something, opens a package of cheese or struggles to put his outerwear on alone. As mentioned above, these differences can partly be seen in the context of the different conditions in the family compared to the other contexts in Anthony's everyday life with fewer/more hands and more/less time. Another reason for the difference is linked to his parents' understanding that it is important for Anthony to be allowed to do things himself and to get the opportunity to influence the situation. I will elaborate the perspectives of the parents in the next chapter.

While observing Anthony I saw that he seemed to enjoy being involved in common activities with his parents but also doing things himself. This does not mean that his well-being can be understood as equal to self-determination or being solely left to himself. My point is that the importance of having possibilities for participating and contributing to create and to change the situations one is taking part of must be assessed in relation to the compound life situation. This must include the possibilities for adult support when needed, and, in relation to how these possibilities are in other everyday life contexts, i.e. the entirety of Anthony's developmental conditions. In the following, I will illustrate this with an example from a day spent with Anthony and the respite family.

Protection and Variations between Family Contexts

The example I will present is from a Saturday afternoon. Anthony has been with the respite family since the day before when Paul and Ann picked him up at the family nursery to bring him to their home, about a 45-minute drive away by car. Anthony is supposed to stay until Sunday, when his parents are invited to an early dinner before they take him home again. In this regard, the respite family is similar to the role that grandparents typically would have but neither Sarah nor Ben's parents can take care of Anthony.

The following situation unfolds in the afternoon with the respite family. Paul is outside with Anthony, while Ann is inside preparing his afternoon snack:

> Anthony (18 months) walks around the courtyard with Paul, who holds both of Anthony's hands. Paul bends over him to continually hold both of his hands so that Anthony does not fall. Once in a while, Anthony stops to bend over and pick up pebbles.

This situation illustrates how Anthony is met as someone who is in need of protection, which is striking since Anthony is quite capable of and used to doing multiple things on his own. For instance, he walks and runs around without holding anyone's hand whenever he is with his parents. Anthony, in other words, is not in danger of falling when he walks or runs. And even if he does, he usually quickly gets back up on his feet. He does not often cry when things do not work out for him. Instead, he tries over and over again. My impression of Anthony is that he is somewhat indomitable and optimistic. The respite parents emphasize in a later interview, however, the importance of Anthony feeling comfortable and safe whenever he is with them. They explain how they are eager to eliminate obstacles for him, for example catching him whenever he is about to fall or handing him the things he reaches for. They are eager to prevent situations that could potentially make him cry or get angry, which is why they to a considerable extent avoid conflicts and try to adjust to his needs and initiatives. Whenever Anthony comes to visit, Paul and Ann are with him all the time. They explain to me that they consider it their duty to compensate for what they imagine as the tough life situation Anthony was born into. This is the reason that they emphasize that, in their eyes, Anthony needs all the protection and support he can get from other adults as a means to support him and relieve his parents of some of the responsibility they bear. In this way, Paul and Ann try to counteract the imagined difficulties Anthony might face when at home with his birth family.

Paul and Ann's strategy means that Anthony gets plenty of attention from them, which he seems to enjoy. He includes them, for instance in his activities by handing both of them small stones or other items when outside in the garden or courtyard. He carefully includes both of them when they are both present. When playing or walking, Paul and Ann do not require Anthony to walk in a particular direction or urge him to hurry. Rather, they let him lead the way and they follow his every movement, supporting his engagements. At the same time, the respite parents organize the same routines every time Anthony visits. Anthony, on the other hand, does not seem to spend much effort to orientate himself in relation to the situation in the respite family or to the transitions between situations and activities. The situations seem calm and rather predictable to him, following familiar routines and daily rhythms. At home with his family, in contrast, Anthony needs to orientate himself and reconcile with a complex family life, including a web of various interests, tasks and changing conditions, e.g. in relation to Ben's well-being. Anthony needs to integrate his own interests with what else is going on, which varies from day to day. Even though Paul and Ann have their routines they adjust each activity according to Anthony and his need for food and sleep. These two different family contexts thus open up quite diverse ways for him to participate. From a conduct of everyday life perspective, Anthony's birth family context provides the opportunity for him to orientate and act in complex situations with multiple activities going on, as well as he learns how to orientate regarding the various interests and demands, and at a pace much faster than compared to the respite family context. In this way, Anthony gains experience from distinct kinds of family life with changing conditions and he gets experiences with engaging in various kinds of interactions and encounters with adults. With his birth family, he can try out things on his own in ways that the respite family does not allow, for instance in the following situation, which occurred on another afternoon a few months later:

> Anthony (20 months) walks toward the coffee table, where Ann has placed fruit and coffee. Anthony notices the grapes in a dish on the table. He takes one. Paul and Ann both rush over and Ann takes the grape away from Anthony. They discuss whether the grape should be cut in half to prevent Anthony from suffocating if he swallows it wrong. Paul certainly thinks the grape should be halved, stating: 'I'm so scared he might suffocate'. Ann halves the grape with a knife and puts one half directly into Anthony's mouth. She continues feeding him with other pieces, one at a time. Anthony also gets water from a cup, which Ann holds for him while he drinks. He leans his head back against Ann's shoulder and looks relaxed.

Paul and Ann often talk to each other about what Anthony can handle and what is too dangerous to let him do. Anthony is being protected, which largely involves Paul and Ann doing things for him instead of allowing him to do things by himself – even though he actually is capable of eating and walking by himself in other contexts. The adult support, on the one hand, opens up opportunities for Anthony, providing him with a variety of new experiences compared to the experiences he gets in his family. On the other hand, too much adult support may prevent Anthony from gaining experience with other aspects of life with the respite family. In his birth family Anthony has various opportunities to try something and (occasionally) succeed. With the respite family, he more often experiences being protected and is treated like he is vulnerable and unable to achieve things alone. Sandseter and Kennair (2011), both of whom are Norwegian psychologists, argue that '[i]n modern Western society there is a growing focus on the safety of children in all areas [which] is problematic because while on the one hand children should avoid injuries, on the other hand they might need challenges and different stimulation to develop normally, both physically and mentally' (p. 258). In accordance with Sandseter and Kennair, a key point is that, if Anthony only had the opportunity to develop within the protected respite family environment, he might lack some of the developmental opportunities he is exposed to in his birth family. Dreier (2009a) argues that 'human beings learn by having chances to compare similarities and differences' (p. 179). In terms of Dreier, the differences between the various family contexts that Anthony transitions between provide him with varying opportunities to participate in relation to adults and in family life. These differences comprise various possibilities for gaining experiences while being supported and met in a variety of ways. In this way, the differences he transitions between provide important conditions for Anthony's development of self-understanding. Thus, Anthony's complex care arrangements complement one another in a way that allows Anthony to explore how to pursue his interests in multiple contexts and to engage in different interactions. He develops his self-understanding as part of this conduct of everyday life. The examples from Anthony's everyday life illustrate that what creates conditions for young children's well-being is not associated with only one form of care or one form of developmental support but rather is generated by different adults with varying ways of understanding Anthony and his need for care and hence distinctive care contributions.

Changed Routines and Changed Family Dynamics and Care Relations

A few months later, Sarah explains that several changes have occurred in the family. The afternoons have become much easier now that Anthony is older and able to stay awake longer in the evening. Due to this developmental change, the family life has become less stressful since the parents have more time for routine activities like preparing dinner. Another change is that Ben has been feeling better over the past months. In addition, Sarah has started a new internship with a new schedule and location that prevent her from getting back in time to pick Anthony up from day care in the afternoon. A change for one family member results in the need for the whole family to rearrange its daily routines, leaving Ben to pick up Anthony every afternoon. Ben has changed his schedule so that he now sleeps for a short while after his night shift before picking up Anthony. The family conduct of life is organized in a new way, which has also changed the dynamics between the family members:

> 5:30 pm. Sarah is in the kitchen preparing dinner, while Anthony (25 months), Ben and I are in the living room, where Anthony is playing with Ben's keys. Ben sits with his laptop. Anthony pulls his father's sleeve and says 'Cheese!' Ben replies: 'You want cheese? Well then, let's see if there's any in the fridge'. Anthony runs fast headed for the fridge. Ben gets up, heads for the fridge as well, opens it and gives a snack cheese to Anthony, who immediately begins to pull off the wrapper. Struggling to get it open, he is just about to topple when he pulls hard on the plastic. Ben stands next to him, looking at Anthony, who now is seated on the floor working on the wrapper. After a little while, he succeeds and pulls out the cheese. He puts half into his mouth. After eating it all, he points to the refrigerator again. Ben laughs and tells me that Anthony knows there are stickers in the cheese box since he and Anthony repeat this routine every day. He takes a

sticker out of the box and hands it to Anthony. Anthony gets on his feet and pulls Ben by the hand, and they walk to Anthony's room and Anthony use his whole body and his arms to close the door so that they can put a sticker on the inside of the door. There are already many other similar stickers on the door.

The changed routines in the conduct of family life affect not only the practical tasks but also the interactions between the family members. The new routines (putting stickers from the cheese box on the door) have become a shared activity between Ben and Anthony which opens up new possibilities for both of them to develop their relationship and their common conduct of family life. In this way, Anthony's intentional actions and initiatives to engage Ben in shared activities contributes not only to him getting new experiences together with his father but also for Ben to develop his self-understanding as a father in new ways through the shared activity with Anthony. The new routine involves that Ben takes care of Anthony while Sarah takes care of the cooking. In a subsequent interview, the parents explain to me how this creates fewer conflicts and a better atmosphere, especially because Ben says that he feels like he makes a difference in the family and that he and Sarah are equal partners in making things work in the daily life. Ben reflects on how he has become better at taking care of Anthony and understanding what he wants because he has spent more time with him. Ben explains how he knows how to interpret Anthony's intentions and what he is communicating through his embodied actions and with the few words he articulates. Ben is pleased that Anthony seeks him out directly, as in the example above. In the past, Anthony has mostly preferred Sarah, who also enjoys the fact that she and Ben share their family responsibilities to a greater extent. She describes how things are 'really nice' between her and Ben and in the family as a whole.

After the new routine has worked well for some months, however, problems begin to arise. On several occasions Ben has overslept in the afternoon, failing to wake up in time to pick up Anthony before the family nursery's closing time. This created conflicts with both the municipal social worker and Kate the caregiver. These incidents also create problems between Sarah and Ben because Sarah feels like she cannot focus on her internship if she is unable to count on Ben to take care of things. The pressure grows when the social worker tells Sarah that things must change, causing Sarah to feel that she is being made solely responsible for the problems, even though they derive from Ben's failure to pick up Anthony. Kate has watched Anthony several times after closing time, but is unwilling to continue doing this. The social worker also underlines that the situation causes concern about whether or not Sarah and Ben can provide sufficient care for Anthony, including maintaining daily routines. The situation is unsustainable, and Sarah is considering her options. She tries a variety of solutions, including calling Ben every afternoon to be sure he is awake in time to pick up Anthony, but that does not always work.

When Ben is subsequently admitted to the hospital, Sarah is forced to find a more stable solution. Paul and Ann from the respite family work on weekdays, making it impossible for them to provide sufficient support. Sarah considers whether she needs to quit her internship to pick Anthony up herself. In a last effort, Sarah tries to get two neighbourhood schoolgirls to help her out but being able to afford the expense represents a dilemma, especially if Ben risks losing his job every time he is hospitalized. Sarah nonetheless decides that this is the best solution. In the West, parents with young children commonly involve grandparents, other relatives and people in their social network, in addition to ECEC childcare, in their lives (Thorne, 2001). This approach helps make it possible to make ends meet when both parents work or study. The social worker, nonetheless, problematizes that Anthony will be picked up by too many different people, which is not usually considered a problematic solution for families with children in ordinary circumstances. One reason for this could be that to children enrolled in early childhood interventions, mothers are considered the most important persons (Romagnoli & Wall, 2012; Woodhead, 1999). Due to the interpretive framework of attachment theory, dominating among the early childhood intervention staff the emotional contact between primarily the mother and her young child is emphasized as a relationship that should unfold without to many disturbances. Because of a dominant picture of young children as vulnerable, being at risk of lopsided development, the solutions available to parents in general do not seem to be available to Ben and Sarah. Paradoxically, they are left with fewer options and less flexibility to make their family life work. Being involved in an early childhood intervention increases pressure on parents, making it even more difficult to stay on the labour market and complete an education or internship.

Situations Become Critical and Conflicts Escalate

Now I will leave Anthony for a little while returning to Daniel's family life. The situation I will explore in this section is a continuation of the late afternoon described earlier in the chapter. In situations involving multiple tasks, for example cooking late in the afternoon, Ashley must both focus on getting dinner ready while simultaneously taking care of two young children. The following excerpt from my fieldnotes illustrates how Ashley copes while trying to cook and respond to her son Matt's activities. This situation comprises the context for Daniel's attempts to orientate himself in order to be able to take part in what is going on:

> Matt sits on the counter, grabs a large knife and swings it toward Daniel, who is standing right below him, watching. Ashley rushes to Matt to take the knife away from him. This leads to a conflict between Ashley and Matt. Daniel observes them from the floor. Ashley lifts Matt away from the counter to put him down on the floor. He is crying. Ashley and I start preparing dinner. Shortly after, Ashley suddenly says that she wants to bake a cake with Matt. The counter is full of dirty plates, bowls and groceries. Ashley stacks some of the dirty plates and consoles Matt. He stops crying and she lifts him back up on the counter He says he wants to make the batter for the cake, which Ashley lets him do. Daniel starts to whimper a little and pulls at Ashley's blouse. 'Dang you, please don't do that!' she says, sounding annoyed. Daniel walks to the highchair and hangs on to the side of it. Ashley sees this, quickly steps close to him and grabs his t-shirt to prevent him from falling down. 'Do you want some raisins?' she asks him. Daniel says 'A'. His mother lifts him up into his highchair and pulls the chair over to the counter so that he is able to see what she and Matt are doing. She puts some raisins in Daniel's hand and returns to making the cake and Matt, who has just poured flour all over the counter. Ashley sighs.

As I scan observation notes from my visits with Daniel's family, I see that the situations are often hectic and somewhat chaotic, as the above excerpt illustrates. Although many things are happening all at once, a pattern begins to appear: proactive, Matt constantly starts new activities and takes numerous initiatives. Most of them require an immediate reaction from Ashley, for instance when he gets hold of a knife. Daniel then often does something related to what Matt is doing. For example, he tries to do the same as Matt, or he observes what Matt and his mother are doing as part of his attempts to orientate himself. Ashley then responds to what Daniel is doing, for example when he climbs onto his highchair, hanging on one side of it until it nearly tips. Ashley mainly only responds to Daniel to prevent him from hurting himself. Then, when Ashley turns her attention towards Daniel, Matt does something new, and the pattern repeats. The various situations appear to lack direction and often get stuck, in the sense that Ashely seldom succeeds in getting all the food ready for dinner and she does not have time to wash the dishes. The situations and the boys' initiatives constantly keep her on her toes without a chance to get the situation under control or to get one step ahead. The mayhem at home differs greatly from what Daniel experiences in family nursery, where the smallest detail is planned and checked by the childminder, as illustrated in Chapter 4. Daniel appears to have difficulty orientating in the chaotic situations at home, making it a challenge for him to figure out how to become part of the activities. Since Ashely is almost always one step behind she is stuck preventing things from happening and only responding to the boys. She does not have a chance to be proactive, take control and help Daniel (or Matt) to find a way for all of them to productively be part of the activities and move forward. Ashley nevertheless does occasionally take the initiative, for instance, with the cake, an activity that seemed only to add to the chaos, conflicts and confusion. Moreover, making the cake delayed dinner even further by adding additional complexity to the situation. The empirical examples from everyday situations in Daniel's family, hence, help expand understanding how young children's agency develops as social processes of embodied orientation situated in the conduct of everyday life. Moreover, agency can be more or less supported by the adults present in and responsible for the everyday living of the children. The examples from Daniel's everyday family life offer the opportunity to theoretically understand the social and situated processes of young children's agency as interrelated with their possibilities for embodied orientation. This involves the arrangement of situations in which the young children have the possibilities for orientating in what is going as this orientation is part of their possibilities for agentic, transformative actions.

I see Daniel's attempts to get up and down from his highchair as a clue about how he perceives the situation. Almost everything happening between Matt and Ashley takes place on the counter. Daniel is not tall enough to see what they are doing when he is standing on the floor, which is why his constant attempts to get up in his highchair are so he can see what is going on. In other words, he pursues a position from which he can watch his mother and Matt and that he can also use to orientate himself in the situation. He loses interest in the chair whenever Matt is on the floor. The situations in the context of Daniel's family life illustrate that his personal development is linked to how the situations develop, but they do not seem to unfold in ways that open up new possibilities for the family members to participate in ways that contribute to them proactively transforming and develop the situation. The situations instead escalate and limit the scopes of actions for everyone involved. When the situations are chaotic and family members continuously initiate new activities and actions that push the others to react, it prevents them from having the space to become proactive instead of reactive making it difficult for the children to orientate themselves and explore what is going on and how they can be part of it. The situations in Daniel's family life often seem to go in circles, until the mother gives up, for instance her plans for activities and daily chores. The impossibilities characterizing the situations in their family life complicate or even hinder the progression of the situations, constraining the options available for the family members to pursue their interests by coordinating and collaborating with the other family members. These situations with limited scopes of actions also shape the conditions for Daniel's personal development. Since he cannot participate in ways that allow him to be part of the activities, but only to follow along, this also limits his possibilities for personal development and hence affects his self-understanding as a person who can proactively take part in shaping his own conditions and the activities he takes part in. In this way, Daniel's experiences with who he is and what he can accomplish as part of his family relations differ from the experiences he gets in the family nursery, where he is capable of influencing the situations and pursuing his engagements to a more considerable degree. A key point is that the situations in the family nursery, to a much larger extent compared to the family context, allow Daniel to orientate in what is going on. A related point is that despite the difficult situations in the family life Daniel does not resign or give up. Instead, he continues his efforts to become aware of what is going on. His attempts to get up and down from his chair, which at first glimpse may seem trivial and pointless, I interpret as part of his agentic actions. His moving up and down the chair adds to complexity in the situation, and hereby he also contributes to create conditions for his mother and for Matt.

To illustrate the level of complexity that Daniel is orientating himself in I provide yet another excerpt from the same evening of observations in Daniel's family. In the middle of making the cake, Matt also wants to be involved in preparing the dinner at the same time, which Ashley allows him to:

> Matt wants to taste one of the sausages for the sauce. Ashely picks one out of the pot with her fingers and hands it to him. Daniel, who is sitting in his highchair, looks at Matt, reaches out and points while saying: 'A'. Ashley hands him a sausage as well. Daniel starts peeling off the sausage skin. He looks at his hands, soon covered in small pieces of sausage. He looks very intent, puts his fingers in his mouth and takes them out again before looking at them. Matt wants to taste the cake batter, which his mother allows him to do. Ashley states: 'That's the last time now, Matt'. Matt says: 'Yes, yes'. He continues to eat the batter. Daniel stands up on the seat of his highchair. He is just about to fall out, but Ashley grabs him by his arm and lifts him down on the floor. Meanwhile, Matt has accidently

dropped the bowl filled with batter. Ashley yells at him. Daniel looks at them, then returns to the highchair and hangs on the side of it.

Ashley allows Matt to join all the activities she engages in, and she helps Daniel to get up and down from the highchair many times while trying to cook and bake a cake.

In a later interview, Ashley tells me that it is important to her that she and the boys enjoy themselves and that the children's initiatives are not constrained. Ashley also explains that, in her opinion, a good life for children is when the children are happy and is allowed to do what they want to. I often see Ashley say yes, allowing almost everything in the situations with the children. She also involves them and initiates baking a cake to create a cosy situation in the afternoon. In this way, Ashley works hard to create what she perceives as a nice family life for the children. For Daniel, the above situation urges him to try to position himself so that he can keep up with what Ashley and Matt are doing, but so much is going on all the time that he is not given the opportunity to orientate in a way that permits him to become part of what is going on. However, he does not give up. Instead, he again tries to get Ashley to lift him up and down from his highchair, which in turn allows Matt to start new things that Ashley needs to respond to. In other words, the situation seems difficult and chaotic for everyone since they seem to progress aimlessly, leaving each family member confused and overly alert. The situation in Daniel's family illustrates how young children depend on adults to organize situations in ways that allow them to orientate and thereby for them to explore how to take part in co-creating and transforming the situations and activities as part of their developmental conditions. What I wish to point out is that it is not enough for Daniel to be able to observe Matt and Ashley's doings in order to orientate. Rather, in order to contribute to shape and transform his conditions in the situation Daniel needs to be an active participant in what is going on. Embodied orientation, then, is first and foremost a social process since it is through relating his own embodied orientation and his actions to the embodied orientation and actions of others that Daniel gets in a position from where he can explore what is going on and what this means to him. He also, through the shared activities, learns how to make his surroundings respond to him and in this way he contributes to the development of the very same situations and premises that also comprise his own developmental conditions.

The guidelines, Ashley receives from the early childhood intervention staff, are similar to those Anthony's parents receive in the sense that these guidelines are rather abstract, not taking their point of departure in the concrete configurations of everyday lives, and the concrete problems and conflicts Ashley, Matt and Daniel experience. Also, the early childhood intervention professionals stress the importance of creating calm, and cosy atmosphere in the family and they stress the importance of avoiding conflicts. According to Ashley, she is aware of the difficult situation, but to her the guidelines seem irrelevant, and even impossible to follow, which is why she disregards them. For instance, when, the early childhood intervention professionals stress the importance of Ashley creating fixed structures and being firm towards the children while at the same time ensuring a cosy atmosphere in the family and the importance of avoiding conflicts.

Escalation of Conflicts

In the following excerpt, the food is ready and the family gets ready to eat:

> Ashley sets plates on the table and then places the pan with meat sauce on the table. Daniel wants to get up in his highchair. I lift him up. He is constantly trying to stand up to be able to grab the pot of meat sauce. Matt claims that he does not want any food. He would rather have cake. He has to eat his food first, Ashley says. He reluctantly sits on his chair. He starts beating his fork on the empty plate. Daniel looks at him laughing, grabs his fork and hits the table with it. The mother says angrily and loudly that they must stop. They continue. Ashley takes away their forks and moves Matt's plate away. Matt starts crying: 'No! Mom!' He gets up and runs to the hallway, where he starts throwing things around. Daniel turns his head and looks out into the hallway for Matt. He pulls off his bib and wants to get down.

The conflict escalates, and neither Ashley nor the children get any food or cake. Ashley, who has given up on getting Daniel to eat anything, puts him to bed and gives him a large bottle of milk, which he holds by himself. His baby bed is in the same room as Matt's, so Ashley explains to me how it is important that Daniel is asleep before she puts Matt to bed. Otherwise, Matt will keep Daniel awake. She needs to wait until Daniel is asleep so she tries to calm Matt down in the meantime. The room where Daniel's bed is has a large TV screen hanging on the wall. Ashley turns the TV on and finds a cartoon for Daniel to watch while drinking his milk. It is late, and he soon falls asleep. Ashley's attempts to calm Matt down are unsuccessful. Instead, a new conflict starts between Matt and Ashley because Matt shouts and insists on eating cake before going to bed. Ashley gives up and lets Matt eat a large piece of cake.

This example of how an afternoon and evening take place in Daniel's family is characteristic in the sense that situations frequently end in chaos, with Ashley giving up on her plans and routines. Often the children do not get the meal she prepared but milk, cake or candy. In the mornings both children are very tired and hard to get out of bed. Since Ashley does not work or go to school, the family often sleeps in and the children do not get to day care until late in the morning. Everyday situations like the one described above form part of Daniel's developmental conditions. Højholt and Kousholt (2018) write that development is characterized by the fact that children gain experience in how to get through conflicts, move on together and thus develop new action possibilities. However, Daniel is gaining an extensive amount of experience in how conflicts cause activities to grind to a halt, leading to the abandonment of meal and bedtime rituals. Additionally, development is characterized by the possibilities for developing agency through embodied orientation and contributions to the transformation and affirmation of the social practices young children take part in.

Similar situations in the late afternoon with tired and hungry children that also cause difficulties in Anthony's family are exacerbated in Daniel's family as Ashley is alone all the time, just as there is not only one child but two with various needs, making the somewhat same situation more complex. This is a key point since the same situations and social problems (including what in other strands of research would be defined as risk factors) entail quite different situated meanings in different family contexts. Moreover, the children – even though they cannot be seen as responsible for the situations – are co-creators of the situations. In this way, the most demanding situations that lead to continuous conflicts are more than just a matter of parental intentions and understandings about what creates a good life for their children. Numerous conditions, relationships and interactions are complexly interrelated, comprising possibilities and impossibilities in everyday family life in unpredictable and changing ways. Ashley does not have a network to support and assist her in everyday situations, nor one she can discuss priorities and solutions with. She is left to organize everyday situations alone. Even though she gets counselling from the health visitor and the social worker, none of them are present when the everyday situations around mealtimes and transitions to and from home in the morning and afternoon lead to conflicts. Ashley becomes more and more exhausted as time goes by. The family nursery caregiver and the social worker are concerned since the children are often absent from day care, their home is untidy and Ashley seems depressed. Sensing the pressure in the home situation, the professionals notice that Daniel does not follow the weight chart for children, causing them to suspect that Ashley still gives Daniel milk in a baby bottle, even though she has promised to quit. The professionals do not think Ashley is cooperating. They express their growing concern, especially because the family nursery caregiver says that she thinks that Daniel seems overly tired, which makes her wonder if he gets to bed too late at night. Overall, the professionals are concerned about the lack of structure and the well-being of the children.

For this reason, a few months later Daniel is assigned a respite family, with whom he stays every other weekend, whenever Matt is staying with his dad. Although the respite family helps by giving Ashley a break, it does not provide any help or alleviate problematic issues in the family's everyday situations described here. The professionals all think that the problems in Daniel's family are caused by Ashley's lack of cooperation and her poor lifestyle with no job; she sleeps in and gets the children to bed too late. This understanding of the problem hinders any focus on the options Ashley has for dealing with ordinary conflicts, prioritizing and coping with the dilemmas associated with being a parent and making everyday family life work. These ordinary situations related to family life entail a personal and situated meaning for Daniel that depend on his personal configuration of his compound everyday life and the variety of situations he is part and, hence, the various developmental opportunities he faces.

Structure and Lack of Action Possibilities

Now, as the final example in this chapter, I will present an example from Toby's family life. The professionals are, unlike in Daniel's case, not particularly concerned about Toby since Jane is considered to be good at organizing everyday life, and she has regular routines. The reason why a respite family has been assigned is that Jane has no family network and she is suffering from mental illness, which means her mental state varies and sometimes she does not feel able to provide for Toby's needs.

The example that I will present takes place one afternoon when I went home with Toby and his mother from the day care centre. While Anthony's, and especially Daniel's, family life is characterized by many things going on at once, with terribly hectic afternoons, Toby's family life is different. Jane strictly structures every activity and routine, which means she is always in control of things and ahead of the game – never trailing behind like Ashley. This difference, however, must be understood as more than just a difference between Ashley and

Jane and the skills they possess. For instance Ashley has two young boys while Jane only has one. Their ideals and definitions of what makes a good family life and how to be a good parent differ, even though their interpretations at times overlap. Factors such as the children's ages, the personal configuration of the children's life situations and what the parents consider important also impact how their ideals diverge from one another.

The example reflects the pattern of most other days when I have been at the family home: Jane picks up Toby from the day care centre and they bicycle home together, Toby riding his own bike. Jane has normally already shopped and prepared part of the dinner in advance, for example chopping vegetables to make sure she can stay in control of things when they are at home together and to ensure that dinner is served by 6:00 pm. Jane explains that she grew up in a home without routines and with no adults taking responsibility for the family. These experiences shaped how she perceives her responsibility as a parent. She prefers fixed routines in the family's everyday life. Every afternoon Jane serves Toby a light snack when they get home, usually yogurt or fruit. He then plays in his room while Jane finishes making dinner. When they have eaten dinner, Jane gives Toby a bath and they watch TV together before she puts him to bed.

Conflicts chiefly occur between Toby and his mother when she insists that things should be done in a certain way or that Toby does things himself. When Toby refuses to do what Jane says, she perceives him as being cross or stubborn, which often makes her even more insistent; she never gives in. Toby rarely experiences an opportunity to successfully negotiate a way for him to contribute to changing things. Jane is persistent and consistently sticks to her plans, while Toby gives in, apparently giving up on trying to change things. He seems resigned, responding chiefly to adjust to his mother's demands and refraining from negotiating the conditions his mother sets.

Toby only lives with his father, whose name is Joe, part of the time, ranging from every other weekend to sometimes once every other month, depending on the father's situation. Joe, who is involved in criminal activities that sometimes send him to prison, is unemployed. Consequently, Jane is the parent who is considered to have the main responsibility for Toby. Whenever the father is out of prison and asserts his right to have Toby stay with him, Jane cannot refuse even though she is uncertain that Joe takes proper care of Toby. The professionals do not seem to worry too much about Toby staying with his father since he spends most of his time with Jane. The underlying reason for conflicts between Toby's parents is that the father only occasionally participates in the parental tasks. Consequently, Jane is left with all the responsibility without the possibility of respite. Further, as the sole provider, Jane is caught in an economically and socially vulnerable position. At the same time, she is obliged to hand over Toby when Joe asserts his right to have his son stay with him. A related problem is that the father seems to fly under the municipality's radar, as Jane describes it. For example, Jane received support during her pregnancy to stop abusing alcohol but the father, who also abuses alcohol, did not. This means that in addition to her own difficulties and having sole responsibility for her son, Jane must work together with an alcoholic father. In this context, Jane, who sees Joe as unstable, is left to handle conflicts with him on her own, which may involve violent episodes and threatening behaviour. Researchers examining this issue point out that only the mother's care contribution is in focus when concerns raised about children come to the attention of local authorities (Burman, 2020). For example, Haavind (2006) points out that the contributions of fathers to their children's lives are often considered positive, regardless of the level of quality, whereas the quality of the mother's contribution is seen as crucial.

Jane does not share the professional's unconcerned approach; she is worried about what Toby learns when he is with his father. She underlines that she finds it necessary to compensate for what happens whenever Toby is with his father. As a result, many conflicts arise between her and Toby because Jane has the primary responsibility for raising Toby but still has to share custody with his father, leaving her without any influence or insight into what happens to Toby when he is in the family context of his father. Jane makes an extra effort with their family life when she has Toby, which she believes involves being extra vigilant and consistent about dealing with conflicts by not giving in to him. Jane worries that Joe does not set any boundaries, raising Toby to be 'tough, disobedient and violent' like his father. As Jane sees it, Toby comes across as tough and rude every time he has spent time with the father. She believes this is a sign that Toby might become like his father and that Toby's actions and expressions are something she needs to correct. For Toby this means that his mother does not use his embodied actions and emotional state as a stepping stone to figure out what he is engaged in here and now and how to best adjust conditions to support him.

When visiting the family, I usually find that Toby largely complies with what Jane wants him to do. One afternoon, I sit next to Toby on the floor of his room shortly after we have returned from the day care centre while Jane is preparing his afternoon snack. Toby is just about to show me a car:

> We have been looking at the car for a while, when Jane calls to Toby (4 years old) from the kitchen. His yogurt is ready. He immediately begins to collect the car and all its accessories before placing it in the shelf. He walks to the living room

and sits down at the dining room table, where Jane has put his yogurt. She wants to know if he has tidied up his toys. He nods and lets himself slide gently into the chair, sitting completely still with his head bent over the yogurt, eating. I sit next to him on a chair. Jane stands in the kitchen, from where she can watch him. 'Sit up straight in the chair and do not slouch,' she admonishes Toby. He tries to straight while also bending his head forward to prevent the yogurt from making a mess.

This example from my fieldnotes shows how Toby tries to follow Jane's directions and Toby only occasionally tries to resist. One example of this was in the previous chapter in which I presented an excerpt of Toby resisting when they were on their way home from the day care centre.

In general, when the members of a family gather in the afternoon after having spent their day in separate places they need to integrate and coordinate their various interests in a common life (Kousholt, 2012). For Toby, the transition to home seems to imply that he must orientate himself to the demands that he meets and for him to try to align his interests with Janes. His own engagements slip into the background, his efforts chiefly shaped by what he must do to help maintain the routines in the home. This was incredibly different for Anthony, who we saw actively negotiating with his parents about the family's routines and priorities. Toby appears rather resigned, making him reactive rather than proactive.

Transitions between Various Contexts, Conditions and Demands

Toby also has a respite family that provides him with the opportunity to gain experience with participating and being met in different ways when he visits compared to at home with his mother. In the respite family Toby is just one child among four to seven other children, as the family has some of its own children, foster children and other children in respite care. Thus Toby is under much less scrutiny; when the respite family eats, no one watches how Toby sits or whether he slouches. Everyone talks animatedly and there is a lot going on at once, which is in stark contrast to dinner with his mother, who focuses all her attention on Toby during meals. I rarely observe, however Toby saying anything at the table when he is in respite care. He watches all the activities going on, the other children, who are a bit older than him, talking loudly and interrupting each other. One of the foster children in particular, a slightly older child, is called Jonathan and often allows Toby to come into his room, where they play together. Jonathan primarily decides the progression of the play but Toby does not appear to be in danger of being excluded from the play, in contrast to at day care. Together with Jonathan, I see Toby eagerly engage in negotiations for the first time, for example, to get the toys he wants most. At the same time, Toby is amazed that Jonathan is allowed to make all the mess he wants to and that he even sometimes destroys a toy:

> Toby is driving around a car with a horse trailer in a circle on the floor. 'Look! I can open the roof and then you can sleep under it,' he says enthusiastically while he shows me how it works. I sit down on the floor and admire the car together with him. Jonathan is busy loading lots of animals into cages and putting them on one of his trucks. Toby looks at him and says: 'I want the truck ... the blue one'. Jonathan replies: 'No, it's too expensive'. Toby says: 'Well, I have hundreds of thousands of millions!' Jonathan answers: 'Okay, you can get that one,' pointing at a yellow truck. 'Ok,' Toby's face lights up. He inspects the vehicle. 'Look, you can take the man out,' he says eagerly. 'You can also open a drawer,' adds Jonathan, taking the truck. He uses a small screwdriver to try to open a drawer at the bottom of the truck. It breaks. 'Can you fix it?' Toby asks a little anxiously. 'I don't know,' Jonathan responds, shrugging his shoulders, and continues to play.

In this situation, Toby is completely engulfed by the play, in a way that I otherwise have not observed, and he takes numerous initiatives to contribute to the play. Although Jonathan clearly is the one in charge, deciding who should have what vehicles, and Jonathan has most of the vehicles himself, Toby negotiates with him, and most importantly, Toby often succeeds in getting what he wants and is able to contribute to the play. He is not constantly in danger of exclusion, as in day care centre, or being watched and corrected like he is most of the time at home. Thus, the respite family offers an important context for Toby to acquire a range of new experiences with participating in peer communities with other social dynamics compared to the experiences he gains in day care. Hence, this family context is important to Toby developing his self-understanding in other ways than in his other family contexts and at day care. He gains experiences with being an active part of transforming and developing the shared activities he is part of.

Summary

The examples in the chapter have shown how early childhood interventions rely on a rather narrow, static understanding of parenthood as related to care contributions within the family home context and a focus on young children's biological needs and ensuring appropriate emotional contact between the mother and the child, even though the field of family research has developed diverse understandings of parenthood as practical and processual in recent years (Lind, Westerling, Sparrman & Dannesboe, 2016; Marschall, 2013; Morgan, 2011). In general, parenthood in Scandinavia involves tasks in relation to supporting children's lives engagements across various contexts (Kousholt, 2012). In this way, it seems paradoxical how the early childhood intervention professionals emphasize only parental tasks concerning tasks related to the child's emotional and biological needs. The young children's interests and intentions in relation to a social life across contexts and their development of agency do not seem to be recognized as important dimensions of young children's development and well-being.

Early childhood intervention professionals emphasize the importance of regularity, stability and parents (mothers) fulfilling their children's needs in specific ways – for instance by ensuring a calm and harmonious atmosphere with no or only few conflicts and ensuring a lot of emotional contact between the child and the mother. This implies an understanding of children as a more or less passive individual dependent on the parents (mother). The point is not to say that young children do not have needs, but that these needs are not universal, static or predictably independent of the concrete situation. On the contrary, children's needs are dynamic and situated in time and place. For parents, the intricacies of everyday life mean that they organize caring for their children in a complex collaboration that involves coordinating with multiple actors who contribute differently to the childcare. The contributions of these actors also become a premise for family life and for the children's needs. Children's well-being is not just shaped by their parents but is co-created by various actors, such as childminders, teachers and other professionals. Conflicts and varying routines cannot be seen merely as a result of parents being disorganized or being unable to interpret and fulfil their children's needs. Instead, these conflicts are inevitably connected to the process of doing parenthood situated in a cultural and historical context drawing on certain ideals concerning doing good parenthood (Lind et al., 2016). Care practices, hence, must be considered as interwoven in the complexities of everyday life and the care practices must also accommodate for the young children's development of agency.

The everyday life situations of Daniel and Toby are examples of how the conditions in family life are shaped partially by the parents' various understandings of what their children need. These understandings develop based on the children's compound everyday life involving multiple caregiver contributions to the children's care and development and also to the parents' discursive and cultural interpretations of how to be a good parent or how to create a good family life for children.

To navigate the contradictory and conflictual process of doing parenthood, parents can benefit from receiving not only support in exploring children's varying needs but also assistance with the challenges changing situations in family life offer. The instructions professionals give to parents often fail to sufficiently consider the degree of complexity and conflicting conditions that exist in everyday life. The instructions and advice offer a fixed, standardized understanding of good parenting and how to execute it. In Anthony's case, the instructions appear to exacerbate the challenges the family faces when trying to make everyday life work.

In the chapter I aimed to show how everyday life in the family becomes important as one out of several contexts in the children's lives. I also described how what happens in these other contexts also establish the terms for family life. Moreover, the chapter has also pointed out that when action possibilities develop, i.e. in situations where there are opportunities to adjust and act in flexible ways, there is the possibility for conflicts to be overcome. We see this, for example, with Anthony during periods when his parents are able to collaborate, share tasks and incorporate Anthony in what they are doing. Situations in which the conflicts escalate, in contrast, lead to a sense of mutual abandonment and powerlessness, both for the children and for the adults. This can become problematic for both the children and the parents because they experience defeat rather than a feeling of success. The analyses illustrate how situations in which it is difficult for children to orientate themselves in family life are associated with various problems that often hinder the children from becoming part of the shared activities with their parents and/or sibling. Most of Daniel's experiences occur in chaotic situations filled with conflict, leading Ashley to at times give up. Young children's agency, then, unfolds as social processes that can be supported by adults' organization of situations that the children can orientate themselves in. However, the fixed guidelines, provided by the early childhood staff, do not seem to support the parents in the problems and conflicts they encounter in daily life.

The empirical material from the various family lives of the children described in this book and also over time in each individual families shows that problematic conditions cause clashes and reinforce conflicts. For example, if one parent is constantly or for a long time responsible for all tasks and simultaneously isolated, with no possibility to act flexibly, incorporate additional resources or draw on networks the situation frequently worsens. The data shows that the problems are largely practical, involving making ends meet in everyday life. Adhering to rigid standards for what a good routine is can lead to a reinforcement of the problems, causing the parents to feel they lack any options to act or that no possible solutions exist. The professionals often cite lack of structure as a problem for the children. In Anthony's family, this understanding of the problems means that the parents do not feel that they can support and adjust to Anthony's changing needs because they believe that the basic advice they received on the circadian rhythm and bedtimes is written in stone. The parents are then tremendously hampered in terms of make an ongoing, concrete assessments of their child's well-being to meet the child's needs. This lack of ability or belief that they can adapt certain rhythms and routines aggravates the conditions in their family life. My point, however, is not that one should entirely refrain from structuring children's lives, but the structure must not be understood as a static phenomenon but as dynamic that requires a continuous effort involving assessment, changes and adjustments to create and maintain a well-functioning structure in an ever-changing everyday life work.

Thus, the problem for Anthony and his parents, for instance, does not seem to be a lack of routine and structure or of being unable to read Anthony's embodied actions, but that the intervention's guidelines for care limit the latitude parents feel they have to act flexibly based on specific everyday situations and to take the children's embodied orientation into consideration as a stepping stone for exploring children's perspectives in terms of how they experience the situation.

7

Parents' Self-understanding and Agency

In this chapter, I turn my attention towards the parents' perspectives on responsibilities and on parents' organization of everyday family life. Parents largely provide the infrastructure of children's daily lives in terms of creating routines and establishing other care contributions in a 'chain of care' (Andenæs, 2011; Marschall, 2013). These issues are important to the topic of the book since, as I have focused on in the previous chapters, agency is not limited to the individual child. Rather, agency emphasizes how children contribute to shaping their life conditions and transition processes in a social life across contexts and through interactive processes with peers as well as adults. Hence, the agency of young children is partly framed (but not determined) by the conditions parents and other caregivers create but is also shaped by the agency of the parents, i.e. the possibilities parents have for influencing and transforming the life conditions. Moreover, how parents interpret what constitutes a good parent and family shapes how they organize everyday life, and how and why they prioritize as they do. Consequently, the chapter addresses the topic of parenthood as one of the conditions that frame young children's agency in three steps.

First, I outline how cultural, social, historical and political aspects shape the contexts for contemporary family life and the definition of parental responsibilities, and I also describe how these are mediated through the collaboration between parents and professionals (Westerling & Juhl, 2021). Second, I discuss a current tendency to instrumentalize parents and how this especially becomes a difficult premise for the organization of everyday family life for parents in difficult life conditions. Consequently, in the third step, I address what I have termed parents experiencing parenthood on the edge (Juhl, 2016), which refers to parenthood being scrutinized and called into question.

I use the category 'parents', which nonetheless mainly covers single mothers. I do not discuss the issue of gender directly but, as already discussed previously in Chapter 2, I consider the societal and cultural meanings ascribed to mothers and to their apparent significance for young children as co-constituting what mothers perceive as pivotal parental tasks. A key point in the chapter, thus, is that parents' self-understanding and the way they understand their parental tasks develop through social meaning-making processes situated in collaboration processes with professionals, as well as develop through the parents' current as well as previous life situations, including the imagined and envisioned future life for their children. Collaboration between parents and professionals is situated in and mediated by institutional (and thus political) agendas, discourses and understandings of family life, parenthood and children's needs. When professionals, in their collaboration with parents, take part in sociocultural activities within institutionalized contexts, they inevitably draw on structures of meaning or discourses, which are inherent in social and cultural practices (Hedegaard, 2008a). The meaning-making processes of parents in relation to being enrolled in early intervention programmes mean that being identified as inadequate and under surveillance become important to their way of understanding themselves as parents and to the scope for action that they deem possible. Especially for parents who are in a vulnerable position and do not, for example, have experience with being part of a family themselves or only primarily have had bad experiences with family life in their own lives, the daily meetings with various professionals in ECEC contexts and being part of an early childhood intervention have a huge influence on how parents perceive their responsibilities, tasks and understanding of what defines a good parent. Children's transition processes, on the one hand, can be viewed as a specific manifestation of how the conduct of everyday life plays out for children within and between institutional contexts such as the family and ECEC. On the other hand, children's transition processes also become part of the conditions that shape parents' understanding of their tasks in relation to this, as well as how their own care contribution relates to other caregivers' contributions, responsibilities and tasks in a chain of care that the parents are mainly responsible for (Andenæs, 2011). Within the framework of the welfare state, parents are designated with the responsibility for ensuring the well-being of their child (Mierendorff & Grunau, 2021). Whenever a child causes concern among the ECEC professionals, the attention is turned towards the family context to understand the cause of the problems – even if these difficulties occur in the ECEC context. Burman (2008) uses the terms 'parent blaming' to describe this tendency to turn the focus towards the parents. Due to the social and culturally embedded meaning ascribed to the responsibility and accountability of the family – chiefly the mother – I will include a short overview of the tasks and responsibilities put on parents and the significance ascribed to the family context.

The Parental Task of Taking Care of Young Children – a Crossroad between Family and ECEC

In Scandinavia parenthood is characterized by extensive collaboration with various caregivers. Nonetheless, the literature about family life and parenthood only sparsely addresses the topic of parenthood as embedded in children's daily transitions, though e.g. Kousholt (2012), Andenæs and Haavind (2018) and Hedegaard and Fleer (2019) are exceptions. These research contributions approach parenthood and, relatedly, parental self-understanding as social phenomena that develop, change and are shaped by relationships and collaborations with others. They also include the specific cultural and societal context in which the parenthood unfolds and, more specifically, through the collaboration with the other care givers in the care chain. Parents negotiate, take up and transform cultural and societal norms and parenting values through this nexus of social relations and institutional practices.

As explained in previous chapters, parental tasks are related to a nexus of political, institutional and personal engagements in ongoing encounters with various professionals in the task of taking care of their children in shared care arrangements (Andenæs & Haavind, 2018). As a consequence, I take my point of departure based on the premise that parenthood, inevitably, is social and implies interacting with multiple others (Andenæs, 2011; Juhl, 2016; Kousholt, 2012; Lind et al., 2016; Morgan, 2011). However, how collaboration and the distribution of tasks are configured has been changing historically in the West in recent years (Westerling & Juhl, 2021). According to Grunau and Mierendorff (forthcoming), this change can be understood as a transformation of the state from being distributive towards being a social investment state – especially in Western Europe. This transition involves a change in parental responsibility in terms of ensuring that childcare must emphasize education and early academic learning as a central tool for addressing social inequality. The stress put on early learning represents the culmination of a broader historical development in European ECEC policies, with an increased focus on learning as a means to enhance children's life chances and later academic performance (Bach, 2017; Juhl, 2018; Schmidt, 2017). Scholars (e.g. Bleses, Jensen, Høje & Dale, 2018;

Bleses et al., 2018; Heckman, 2006) argue that preventive measures in ECEC in terms of supporting children's early skill formation and a strengthening of young children's learning environments are the new silver bullet in fighting inequality. International studies similarly indicate that active parental involvement in learning activities as early as infancy positively affects children's cognitive development and that parent-led learning activities in the home setting prepare children for further education later in life (Love et al., 2002; Lugo-Gill & Tamis-LeMonda, 2008). This comprises what some scholars term 'the home learning environment' (Kelly, Sacker, Del Bono, Fransesconi & Marmot, 2011; Melhuish et al., 2001, 2008).

By focusing on the importance of early learning as an investment in early childhood that will apparently yield a positive outcome later, parents are to an increasing extent considered to be both the problem (for instance, due to social background) and the saviour in terms of ensuring their children's well-being and future life chances (for instance, by establishing a home learning environment). In this way, the transformation has accelerated towards the social investment state, which involves preventive measures and policies – not only in Western Europe but in the West in general.[1] When education and early learning in children's lives politically is considered the best solution for preventing poverty and alleviating social inequality later in life, and parental activities at home are emphasized as important, the societal discourse seems to be that the task of parenthood subsequently becomes too risky to leave to random parents (Grunau, in press; Lee, 2014). Parenthood, then, has at the same pace become increasingly professionalized and the growing number of preventive programmes aimed at monitoring young children's well-being and increasing parental knowledge and skills can be seen in this light. For parents in general, this tendency appears to problematize modern parents as insecure and self-doubting as they confront vast demands and pressures related to raising their children (Sieben & Yıldırır, 2020). In Denmark, the tendency towards guiding parents manifests itself in ECEC centres introducing learning programmes and instructions for parents designed to support learning activities in the family. These programmes may include instructing parents to do certain activities with their children, such as singing or reading stories to cultivate language development. In the 2018 reform of the Day Care Act in Denmark, the establishing and supporting the learning environment of young children across ECEC and families has become a mandatory topic in the collaboration between parents and ECEC professionals (Westerling & Juhl, 2021). Placing responsibility for stimulating children's early learning on the parents has no historic precedence in Denmark, where early learning has been the domain of ECEC. Politically, the apparent benefits of early learning in children's lives are underlined and parent-led learning activities are inevitably defined as crucial since a child's first twelve months are most often spent at home when parental leave is taken. In this way, parents and the educational activities they do at home are considered a key factor in supporting young children's learning. However, this ambition does not take into consideration how much the conditions that parents live under vary in daily life and, consequently, that all parents do not have the same opportunities for conducting learning activities in a family life already being under pressure.

A recurring feature in all of the interviews I conducted was, however, that parents felt that doing well in school and getting an education later in life were an important key to achieving what they called a normal life. When asked about what they consider a good family life for their children, parents highlighted getting an education and having a job so that they could provide for themselves and their children, in addition to being a role model. This is significant since political discourse on the importance of learning activities in the family context mediated through collaboration with ECEC professionals increases the pressure put on the parents and what family life should contain.

'I Want Her to Do Better than Me'

Caregivers in the nursery that Emily (twenty-nine months) goes to told her mother, Monica, that Emily had not performed well in a mandatory age-appropriate language test, so they suggested that she join a small group of children that focuses specifically on developing language skills, especially building vocabulary. Monica agreed, underlining that she feels supporting Emily is a crucial part of her responsibility as a parent. Monica explained that she has developed a close relationship with the caregivers and that she tries hard to do whatever they suggest as 'they know what's for the best'. Monica's own life history involved bullying, being excluded and failing academically, her lack of education heightening her belief in the strong importance of doing good from an early age. In Monica's view this is the single most important factor in terms of Emily's chances in the future. The caregivers also told Monica how to do activities that involve Emily at home, e.g. reading aloud, conversing with her more and naming things to help Emily learn new words daily. Monica explained that her daughter is often tired when they get home and unable to concentrate when Monica wants them to read books. This created numerous conflicts between Monica and Emily, causing Monica to get frustrated because she is afraid that Emily will fall behind if she lacks the right skills and that Monica is to blame if she does. Monica said that the conflicts arising from educational activities added to the struggles that inherently arise during obligatory tasks such as brushing teeth, eating, sleeping routines and Emily being obstinate whenever Monica says 'no' to Emily. Monica explained how the suggested learning activities turned into a difficult extra task that increased the complexity of their lives, increasing the amounts of struggles in making their everyday family life work. The institutional demands entangle themselves in other concerns and demands at stake in family life, adding to the complex constellation of contradictory tasks related to taking care of young children. Moreover, Monica told me that she felt like a failure since her child had fallen behind on the test, putting pressure on her to make up for this and to ensure that Emily would be able to perform later on in school and get an education so she would not end up on unemployment benefits like her mother. The future life Monica envisions for Emily shape the here and now of her care practices. Societal, cultural and historically situated values about what constitutes a good life for children and what is important in terms of developmental support also shape the developmental trajectories envisioned. Political discourse and societal values about the importance of enhancing young children's early academic learning are especially mediated through the daily interactions and collaboration between parents and professionals in ECEC (Hedegaard, 2008a). Hedegaard's concept of institutional demands offers an opportunity to understand how societal values and discourses about child development become part of the conditions in everyday life that the five children in this book and their parents encounter when taking part in institutional contexts and through collaboration with various professionals. I argue that societal values are important to include in the analysis of the nexus of social practices since it helps expand understanding of the situations in which child developmental processes are situated. These demands and understandings are developed culturally and become part of the conditions in the everyday lives of children and parents because they are embedded in encounters in daily living situated in various institutional contexts and the collaboration with early childhood intervention professionals. Meanwhile, my point is not that values and the demands determine parents and children, or professionals for that matter. On the contrary, institutional demands are not fixed but rather constantly 'coauthored' and 'transformed' by the individuals, as Stetsenko stresses (2019, p. 257). How people, adults and children alike, relate to and deal with their conditions (including institutional demands and societal values), not to mention how they contribute to changing them is a process that involves developing agency – for instance when parents take up the advices they receive from professionals and adjust the advices to fit the everyday life situations as illustrated in Chapter 6. However, values shape the parents' priorities and how they organize everyday living – hence also the developmental conditions for children. When early learning is defined and directed by ECEC as an institutional agenda, it can cause collaboration between parents and professionals to become antagonistic since the parents have no sense of ownership and are cast as not-knowers who must contribute to the learning agenda in specific ways that do not depart from the concrete conditions of everyday life situations (Westerling & Juhl, 2021). Another problem is that all parents – independently of their specific life situation – are considered to have responsibility for engaging in learning activities, leaving individual parents with inequal conditions for dealing with the task. In this way an institutional task defined by the social welfare state is distributed and assigned to individual families to deal with. This entails the risk that the same inequalities that the system is seeking to prevent may become amplified since parents may not possess what living up to the task requires. Moreover, the demands put on the parents to do learning activities add to the level of complexity in the family life, entangling multiple concerns and conditions in unpredictable ways. To explore how interventions of this nature influence family life, sometimes for the worse, situated knowledge about how the parents perceive this is needed. The parents in my study, however, do not experience that their perspectives are taken into consideration.

When Parenthood Is Scrutinized and Questioned – Parental Self-understanding

According to the parents, the problem of not being listened to is pervasive in the collaboration with early childhood intervention professionals. In the interviews I conducted with the parents two mothers explained that they felt that especially during meetings with multiple professionals their perspective on the problems and solutions were not included:

> Ashley: 'at the meetings … with the municipality, I just felt like they come up with some suggestions that I literally just have to comply with. And as soon as I come up with some proposals myself, and when it concerns situations I am actually more familiar with than they are, they don't even want to listen to me'.

Monica: 'All my explanations ... they don't bother to listen; they just point their fingers at me and then I totally withdraw, because they have their own opinion of what is best, and then it doesn't matter what I say!'

These two mothers indicate that their perspectives on the problems they deal with and how to possibly solve these are not deemed important. They find that the professionals come up with (unsuitable) solutions that the parents must adhere to because the professionals have their own opinion of what is best. During the interviews, the parents clearly felt tremendously frustrated by the collaboration with the social workers, health visitors and other professionals who only know the family peripherally. These professionals often give parents general instructions from national health guidelines about nutrition, sleep and how to establish an emotional attachment to the child. For this reason, I argue that the other side of this way of understanding young children's needs creates a parallel understanding of the good parent as a parent capable of providing a secure base for the child, and, relatedly, as stated by Grienenberger, Denham and Reynolds (2015) provide a 'reflective and mindful parenting' (p. 446) in terms of being reflective, attentive and capable of mentalization ad containments of the child (p. 447). In this way, the agency expected from parents is 'self-agency' in terms of impulse control and affect regulation (p. 447).

'The Most Important Thing for Him Is to Grow up in an Ordinary Family, I Think'

All of the parents who were interviewed stressed the importance of creating what they term an ordinary family life for their children. The parents are referring to what Burman (2008) calls the 'textbook model of family', which is a nuclear family consisting of a heterosexual couple with their genetic children as the picture of normality (see also Burman 2008; Kousholt, 2011, Woodhead, 1999, 2005). Nonetheless, four of the families included in this book consist of a single mother living alone with her child/children; only one family was the nuclear family they all wished for. Listening to these mothers, their strong desire to create a nuclear family can be understood based on the backdrop that almost all of them did not grow up in an ordinary family of their own as children. On the contrary, they either grew up in foster care or with parents who abused drugs and alcohol. Their experiences came from what they called a broken and unstable family, where their own parents often had various partners, often leading to multiple break ups, moves and changing schools. The parents accentuated that they wanted to make sure that their own children did not experience too much commotion, that creating normality and stability was a high priority, i.e. establishing a life like the ones their peers lived. One key priority stressed by all of the parents in order to ensure stability is having a job, and all of the parents except one are studying or working. Even though the parents say that maintaining a work-life balance is difficult, they make clear that the pride they feel about living a liveable life (Phoenix, 2017) ameliorates the adversities. O'Hagan (2010) asserted that mothers generally find that achieving a work-life balance is tricky. However, as explained in Chapter 6, parents without a family network to count on when their children are sick or when their working hours do not align with ECEC opening hours, this general problem becomes a significant extra burden.

Another key aspect that the parents give prominence to regarding what they deem important for a good life is their children's enrolment in ECEC, just as they reaffirm that the caregivers help them better handle daily logistics and preserve a better work-life balance. They are aware that the ECEC context provides other developmental opportunities and life experiences compared to family life, e.g. learning to be with others, trusting adults beyond the parents, playing with other children and developing friendships. In other words, the children learn to become social beings and to deal with conflicts. This aligns with Kousholt (2012), whose research indicated that parents view ECEC as an important developmental context in which children can do other things and gain other experiences compared to in the family. In this way, the parents' ideas of what comprises a good life for children involve aspects of the family context, including the physical settings of the home, the relationships between parents and children, and everyday living outside the family.

When discussing what a good life for children is, the parents' concerns involve not just the here and now but the future they envision for their children. These conceptions of what a good life is partly derive from expectations based on the parents' own experiences, from the parents' wishes for a better future for their children and from the values and demands communicated through collaboration with professionals. Anthony's parents, for example, describe how important it is to them that Anthony learns how to become strong, tough and independent, because the parents' life trajectory has shown them that these traits are necessary to cope with resistance and adversity in life. At the same time, they hope that Anthony will have the opportunity to have a better life than they did. Toby's mother, Jane, similarly dwells on wanting Toby to do well, but her focus is not to make Toby tough but rather that he learns to behave properly, is obedient and does well in school. For example, she insists on teaching him the alphabet at an early age because the day care centre caregivers told her about the importance of early learning in performing well later on in school. Throughout her school career Jane was frequently absent, causing her to lack behind, which is why she wants Toby to get a good start. Jane tries to give Toby the same opportunities as other children by making sure he 'does not stick out', as she puts it. She reiterates that clean clothes and a nice and tidy appearance make a good impression on others. At the same time, her perspective on a good life is also shaped by what she imagines Toby experiences when he stays with his father. Jane wants to be a counterbalance to what she is worried about Toby might be learning from his father. She fears that the father's – in her view – chaotic way of living, his criminal activities and his history of violence are a bad influence on their son. This is why Jane is extremely consistent and wants Toby to think about the consequences of his actions, even from a very young age. As shown in Chapter 6, this parenting approach often leads to conflicts between Jane and Toby, sometimes hindering the nice, calm atmosphere that Jane also sees as highly important. In this way, the effort and prioritization required to create a good life in the here and now may end up working against one another in the long term.

Ashley, Daniel's mother, believes strongly that her boys should experience a careless and harmonious everyday life:

> a good life is when children have a safe everyday life and that no one pushes them to do something they don't want to do. They should have freedom and be allowed to do lots of things ... it's also important that they experience a harmonious everyday life at home, in nursery and at day care centre, and that they are happy and can play.

Ashley explained that she moved constantly as a child, with frequent conflicts and broken relationships in her family. This is the reason, she explains, that from a young age she had to take responsibility for her younger siblings. As a result, she believes that a top priority is letting children be children and that they know that she is the responsible adult.

Lack of Social and Family Networks – the Significance of Collaboration with Welfare Professionals

This section illustrates how a lack of social and family networks is a common feature of the parents' lives. Consequently, ECEC professionals and other professionals become even more pivotal since they are the main network for parents to rely on to exchange knowledge about their children. This collaboration serves, as already stressed, to communicate societal values and is where institutional demands are mediated and negotiated. The ECEC professionals become key mediators of underlying ideals and practices concerning childcare, child rearing and children's needs, which also gives them the role of defining what a good parent is (Lind et al., 2016). This is the case for parents in general, but for parents who do not have good experiences of their own to draw on in terms of what it means to be a well-functioning parent and who do not have grandparents or other kin who can pass on experiences and support them, the ECEC professionals are often the only reliable adults available who can provide advice and teach about childcare. For the parents of children who have a respite family, the respite parents also become important role models and supervisors. Due to social isolation, the parents, consequently, deeply depend on the collaboration with ECEC professionals and respite parents – not only in terms of contributing to the actual care of the children and to make both ends meet in everyday life, but also as resources for the parents' development of self-understanding. Social workers, therapists, health visitors and other professionals often provide specialized support but do not engage with the family as a part of their everyday lives. The daily collaboration with the ECEC professionals is a different case since it is based on the situated examination of the well-being of the children across their everyday life contexts. The exchanges between Oscar's childminder and his mother about his transition into nursery show that the interchange of ideas and information became an important part of the solution.

The ECEC professionals interviewed underscore that good parenting is characterized by democratic and equal relationships between parents and children, and that parents should involve their children in daily chores and prioritize doing shared and stimulating activities with their children, e.g. talking, reading and singing to them. They are also proponents of issuing demands and instructions for creating and maintaining a fixed structure and daily routine to ensure a harmonious atmosphere with a minimum of conflicts and no scolding. Leaving young children to entertain themselves is not considered a proper approach. Bach (2017) and Andenæs (2011) both state that such institutionalized expectations align with the values and experiences of family life of middle-class parents. The parents in this book do not have an equivalent framework for interpreting their parental tasks and responsibilities. As illustrated, Anthony's parents value him growing up to be capable of taking care of himself and of doing things by himself since the parents' own experiences demonstrate that these abilities play a key role in surviving the challenges of daily life. Their child-rearing strategy often causes concern among the professionals since Anthony's parents do not comfort him when he falls and hurts himself unless he is highly upset. During the observations in the family, the parents always observed Anthony closely but contented themselves to encourage him to get back on his feet on his own. They did not comfort him unless he did not get back on his feet again after a little while. According to the professionals, appropriate childcare is to immediately respond to the children's needs, especially when they cry.

In this way, parents with life experiences that are less fortunate and whose life situations diverge from the norm have to deal with major disparities in their own values and the values and demands they encounter across contexts. Moreover, they have to engage in shared care practices across these dissimilarities since their children transition between these various demands and values. The parents described how they often feel that their way of doing things and their own values are less appreciated by the professionals compared to, for instance, what the respite parents do. In this way, the differences that their children navigate through as part of daily transitioning processes also shape the parents' self-understanding.

A common issue for almost all the parents is inequality – both financial[2] and in terms of access to communities with others, which limits the opportunities available to influence their own life conditions. Inequality is thus linked to fewer opportunities to exchange opinions on parenting with other parents and to see how family life can be organized in multiple ways (Nygren, 1999). Nygren (1999) examined how parents develop agency based on: '1) own experiences as a child, 2) general education and information about children, 3) experiences from social relationships, 4) experiences passed on from their own parents and through social networks, and 5) daily contact with their own and others' children' (p. 57, author's translation). Parents without social and family networks do not in equal measure generally have access to the five items Nygren lists as relevant sources for developing agency as parents.

Moreover, based on the interviews, the parents do not have much experience with what actually works. They, on the other hand, have many experiences with what does not work. The point I am trying to arrive at is that the opportunities the parents have to develop their care practices and parenthood cannot be understood as inherently and naturally unfolding. On the contrary, parental care practices are developed through participation in social life together with others (Nygren, 1999). Inequality arises when parents lack contact with their own family and also lack a social network since they do not have the same opportunities to develop agency or access to forums that allow them to reflect on their parenting practices together with others, to ask others for advice or to discuss solutions and observe alternative ways of organizing everyday life and solving conflicts. As mentioned, several of the families in the study have a respite family that is supposed to compensate for the network that the parents rarely possess themselves. The aim is also for respite families to provide a learning space for parents that provides opportunities for them to see other ways of doing things. The following section describes what the parents experience in the collaboration with the respite family, which also involves conflicts and the parents feeling excluded.

'Now That I Can't Afford to Give Her Those Kinds of Things Myself, It's Good that They Can'

The parents who have respite parents report that they provide an invaluable, dependable and stable network. In particular, the parents emphasize that flexibility is a key issue because problems are often unpredictable, making advanced planning in that regard nearly impossible. The need for help usually arises suddenly, for example when children fall ill and cannot go to day care. The parents, especially single parents, have difficulty covering sick days. Respite parents also work full-time and some have children of their own, which restricts how much and on how short notice they can provide help.

Another important aspect that one of the mothers accentuates is how she learned a great deal when being present in the respite family together with her child. Being part of everyday situations provides her the opportunity to sit back and observe while the respite parents deal with the child, giving her a break while simultaneously allowing her to witness how to handle things differently. The parents nevertheless said that the living conditions in the respite family differs greatly compared to their own, sometimes making them feel they do not measure up. Two adults are present in respite families, which means that one adult does not need to handle all the domestic tasks while simultaneously looking after the child. First and foremost, there are more hands to take care of the tasks, many of which can be done in advance of the child's visit. This positions the child as a guest, allowing the child to be the main focus of attention. In the child's biological home the parent(s) are not home during the day, which prevents them from getting one step ahead, as already discussed in Chapter 6. When the family returns home late in the afternoon after having spent the day in different places and the grocery shopping, preparing dinner, taking care of the child all have to be squeezed into a few short hours before bedtime, which is quite early for the youngest children.

Despite the disparities, the parents nonetheless appreciate the value of the relationship with the respite families. The respite parents are also vital in the sense that they also show interest in the parents and not just the child, remembering to ask about momentous events like job interviews and exams. In addition, they sometimes participate together with the parents in ECEC meetings and social events as, for instance, 'grandparents' day'. Thus, the help and support are directed not only at the child but also the parents. Apart from providing a sorely needed network of other adults, respite families give the children access to other experiences with what family life can be like, an aspect that their parents highlight as important. The respite parents have greater financial and material wherewithal that allows them to take the children to the zoo or on other excursions unaffordable to their parents. Other aspects in the respite family that the parents cannot provide themselves are underlined: access to greater material abundance and contact reminiscent of spending time with grandparents, where peace, quiet and no everyday stress are pervasive. The interview data shows that the parents think that this access is positive, though the parents also have ambivalent feelings because they wish they also had the opportunity to share fun experiences with their child. Parents whose children are in foster families experience a similar longing. The parents, who feeling envious, find it difficult that all the fun activities happen with other adults while they are left with the conflicts and the struggle of stressful everyday situations.

Like the other parents, Monica describes her arrangement with the respite family as indispensable, giving the parents a much-needed break. Monica says that sometimes when she and Emily are at the respite family together, Emily gets a bath after dinner before the family drives them home, letting Monica put Emily directly to bed when they arrive home. All of the parents draw attention to how actions like this are a major help, not least because sharing the experiences and conversing with other adults is rewarding. Feeling cared for gives them more energy to cope with everyday life when alone with their children. Dilemmas are nonetheless associated with working with a respite family. Monica, for example, feels ambivalent about how happy Emily is with what the respite parents do for her and the number of nice experiences she gets that Monica is unable to provide. Consequently, she is worried that Emily might prefer them since the time they spend together is mostly happy, not filled with stressful situations and child rearing. Moreover, the material resources, such as having a garden or a room of her own, are in stark contrast to her own home. During an interview at her apartment Monica elaborates on her ambivalence:

> Monica: She has everything at their place.
> Interviewer: What does she have … ? Is it stuff, or … ?
> Monica: Yes, she has a big garden and a large room with toys and everything. Here, at our place, you can see for yourself, how small it all is. But then, it's not that … it's a *really* good family … but it's just so odd. What happens there and what happens here represents such completely different lives, and it's hard for Emily to transition. And it's also more fun over there, and she is happy about it. And I think that it's also difficult … But, then again, I would never be able to manage without them, because it's great how they help us.

Monica's description indicates that she feels somewhat ambivalent about the collaboration with the respite parents. On the one hand, they help her tremendously, providing a needed network and support in everyday life. Monica cannot imagine how to make everyday life work without them. On the other hand, she feels that what she can offer Emily is worthless in comparison, fewer material things, only one adult and less time and attention, all in a one-room apartment. From Monica's perspective, 'Emily has everything' and 'is allowed to do everything' with the respite family. Monica finds that the transitions are exceedingly difficult to deal with and create conflicts, for instance about the food that Monica serves due to differing rules about what Emily is supposed to eat and taste in the two family contexts. Monica, who does not always agree with the respite family's rules, does not feel that her opinion weighs as heavily as the respite parents':

> Monica: It differs a lot … How they do things there and what I do here.
> Interviewer: Can you to tell me a little more about these differences?
> Monica: Well, the respite parents are a bit more lenient … Emily is generally spoiled more by them, treated like a guest. And here, I don't have the time to play with her all the time. She also has to take care of herself while I cook in the evening and shower in the morning, for example. It's hard for her to get used to that when she comes back from being at their place. She calls for attention all the time and cries if I'm unable to play with her. They also allow her to do more things, for example she is allowed to make a mess with all the toys and they simply just tidy up after her. Here, I want her to do it herself. And there, she's not pushed to eat her vegetables if she doesn't want to, and that's something I'm strict about because I think that's important. And the health visitor really gave me a hard time in the beginning because she did not eat enough of them.

Interviewer: Okay, and what about when you're all there together? Is it you who decides, for example, whether Emily is supposed to eat her vegetables, or how do you do it?

Monica: No, they decide because I find it hard to protest.

Interviewer: Why do you think that's the case?

Monica: I think it's because I feel insecure in a way ... because they are highly educated or something like that, and they are also paid by the local authorities. So ... yes ... they are people who know better ... know a lot about children and such ... They have been hired by the local authorities, and they help me and not the other way around, so yes ... I don't quite know how to say it, or explain it, I mean, but ... I just feel that their opinion is worth more than mine ... Even though she's my child.

Similar to that of other parents, Monica's narrative points out that the relationship between parents and respite parents may be characterized by disagreements about care practices, rules and also the distribution of responsibility. The collaboration appears to raise numerous questions: Whose child is it? In which contexts? And who decides rules? Who knows best? And, how is it possible to create balanced collaboration when one party is paid to help and the other is defined as needing help and advice? Consequently, conflicting interests may arise in relation to the child's upbringing and who defines the right care. As Monica's narrative spotlights she is designated as needing help, while the respite parents provide this help, making them easily appear as the ones who know better. Monica thus develops an understanding of herself as less capable in comparison with the respite parents and convinces herself that what she knows about her own child is of less importance.

Monica describes her relationship with the respite family as ambivalent because she finds herself in a subordinate position. Another problematic dynamic in terms of finding their place in the respite family is often associated with a desire to be part of a family, while the respite family's primary commitment is to the child and to a lesser degree the parents. This example illustrates how children negotiate the differences across social practices as part of their orientation process, which the parents relate to. In this way, the parents' self-understanding and agency develops through their interactions with their children located in and across various social practices. The children respond to the differences they encounter in everyday living, and they develop their engagements in relation to their participation across these different contexts. The variety of experiences, hence, becomes a resource for children to develop their agency and contribute to transform and negotiate the common conduct of family life with their parents.

In addition to the respite family some of the families, as mentioned earlier, are affiliated with a mothers' group for vulnerable and young mothers. The help here is primarily advisory, while maintaining regular contact with the families gives the professionals an opportunity to monitor the children's well-being. In the next section, I wind down the chapter by exploring what this mother's group means to the parents. The point is to show how the mothers perceive the group as an opportunity to interact with other mothers, providing a space to exchange of knowledge about issues that are easily recognizable – for example how to manage preparing dinner alone with a tired toddler or how to support children's daily transitions between ECEC contexts and family contexts. The community between the mothers thus contains some of the opportunities that the respite family does not provide – access to a network of women whose everyday experiences comprise recognizable problematic situations.

Mother's Group: Networking and Exchanging Everyday Life Experiences

Anthony, Daniel and their mothers, Sarah and Ashley join the mothers' group once a week together with five other mothers and their children. This group of mothers are categorized by municipal professionals as marginalized. As a result, the professionals monitor the children closely to ensure age-appropriate development. In Denmark it is a common practice among new parents to enrol in a mothers' group, which is usually run by the mothers independent of the professionals. Normally, the health visitor introduces a group of new women to each other on the first gathering, leaving them to run the group on their own. They often meet in their own homes or for a walk. In this particular mothers' group, they always meet in a municipal building and professionals run the group, which is why they also decide what activities to do. In contrast to ordinary groups, which generally end when parental leave is over after one year, this one continues for three years. If the mothers continue in the group for all three years, their children are given a free spot in the ECEC. The objective is partly to create a learning space where the professionals can provide the mothers with instruction and supervision, and the mothers have a chance to observe how other mothers parent. The group only explicitly includes and educates mothers, not fathers. Specifically, the professionals emphasize that an important learning objective is to instruct mothers to decode their children's signals and for the mothers to learn how to put their own needs aside and focus on the child. Another purpose of the mothers' group is to provide an opportunity for the professionals to keep an eye on the child's well-being and the interaction and emotional bond between children and mothers. In this way, the programme is an important part of the municipality's preventive interventions. The mothers' group mainly focuses on children's weight, nutrition, sleep and the emotional contact between mother and child. The organization of everyday life, conflicts and problems that the mothers face in this regard are not given much attention.

One day while observing in the mother's group, the health visitor looked at Daniel's weight curve. Ashley finds it reassuring that professionals keep an eye on Daniel so that she can be sure he is developing as he should. She nonetheless finds their stressing everything she does wrong annoying, for example Daniel getting too much milk from a bottle for his age, getting too little healthy food on a daily basis and being allowed to eat sugar. Ashley, like many of the other mothers, partially thinks this advice is acceptable because the health visitor is knowledgeable about children but implementing the advice in everyday life is exceedingly challenging. As one of the mothers explains: 'You can easily feel like you are a bad mother'. The health visitor emphasizes that children older than twelve months must not be fed milk in a bottle, according to the guidelines established by the health authorities. Ashley and Sarah, notwithstanding, use a bottle to solve difficult situations, as described in Chapter 6. Sarah partially adheres to their advice by replacing the milk with water to keep Anthony calm while she prepares dinner. Her strategy combines competing concerns: cooking and comforting Anthony. Sarah is pleased that both the professionals and Anthony are satisfied with her solution, which does not go against the instructions provided in the mothers' group. Ashley, on the other hand, refuses to stop feeding Daniel milk from a bottle because it serves as a comfort when he goes to sleep and ensures that he is satiated throughout the night regardless of how much he ate at dinner. Ashley continues to use the bottle, though she tells the health visitor that she is weaning Daniel from it, mainly to avoid listening to accusations:

> Ashley: … it caused consternation when I accidently told them [the staff in the mothers' group] that I still use the bottle every night. It was because Daniel turned 15 months. And they said that we aren't allowed to give our children a bottle after they turn one. And then they want me to take his pacifier away from him too, so he only uses it when he sleeps, but honestly … I really don't think it can hurt … neither the pacifier nor the bottle. And it really helps me a lot to be able to give him both the pacifier and the bottle … but they [the professionals] accuse me of not taking proper care of Daniel. I don't bother to argue or explain because they don't give a damn about my opinion.

In this way, continuing to use the bottle anyway helps Ashley to develop agency as a parent and to deal with the situation. She refuses to follow pieces of advice which she deems meaningless. This is similar to what Dumbrill's (2006) study describes in relation to parents' strategies when enrolled in early childhood interventions; they try to play the game by apparently accepting instructions and then only pretending to cooperate. Corby, Millar & Young (1996) similarly assert that parents often feel misunderstood by social workers. For Ashley, it means that she distances herself from their advice and instructions and declines to confide in the professionals, even though she is aware that the family life situation is becoming too difficult for everyone involved. Ashley explains in an interview that she thinks the professionals are not interested in her perspective on everyday life situations. She feels that she is just supposed to be subordinate and is only approached as part of the problem though is still considered a means for ensuring her children's well-being – not by developing agency as a parent but by solely following instructions. Hennum (2014) similarly maintains that one of the most difficult pitfalls of social work with at-risk families entails an: 'instrumentalization of parents who are to fulfil their children's needs and raise them correctly, as defined by instruction given by professionals' (p. 452).

The health visitor and the social worker attend each meeting in the mothers' group, and once a month a psychologist also comes. The meetings usually start with the mothers, their children and the two professionals sitting together at a table, drinking tea and coffee and eating a light meal. Then, when appropriate, the children are weighed and measured. The professionals follow-up on their advice and give guidance to each mother individually while the rest of the group sit on the floor talking and playing with their children. The professionals make an effort to help the mothers be able to recognize and be aware of their children's needs. One approach is that the health visitor will speak on behalf of the child, saying for example: 'Look at me, mum, I need food' when the child reaches for something on the table. Sarah explains in an interview that this tactic annoys her greatly because she already knows very well what her son wants and that it makes her feeling inferior when they speak to her like she is a child. Despite her exasperation, Sarah emphasizes that she likes going to the mothers' group because it gives her the opportunity to listen to what is said when the others ask questions and get answers. She can listen to the answers without having to articulate her own doubts or problems. Another aspect of the group that Sarah points out as important is the reciprocal exchange of experiences among the mothers on how to solve various problems, the interviews indicating that all of the mothers share this view. The framework of the mothers' group is seldom able to accommodate many of the topics that the mothers think are relevant to discuss; hence they speak about them during the breaks – preferably outside while they smoke and are out of earshot of the professionals inside. When asked about the best thing about the mothers' group, Sarah enthusiastically replies: 'The smoking breaks!'. They provide a space for open conversations and exchanges about recognizable issues that the mothers face. For example, they discuss how to find a boyfriend as a single mother, how they make everyday life situations work and how to handle conflicts with ex-boyfriends, in addition to sharing strategies and experiences from various encounters with the local authorities. The mothers think that health, nutrition, smoking cessation and how to sing to the children take up too much space as they think they are of less importance compared to conflicts with the children's fathers and maintaining a work-life balance. The mothers agree that the irrelevant topics chosen by the professionals are 'just something you have to accept' when in the mothers' group. Thus, the problems and issues that the mothers actually deal with are discussed on breaks because they are not part of the official. In this way, the professionals deem other aspects of parenthood as more relevant than the mothers do but these aspects ignore the daily struggles related to being a single parent, the conflicts with the children, the effects of not having a social network, being ill and other problems that characterize the lives of these mother. The aspects valued and presented by the professionals reflect a family life constituted by other conditions in terms of time and resources. In this way, the values about parenthood communicated to the parents can be difficult for them to relate to, which is why they often explain that they feel like they are bad parents in their collaboration with professionals. With ECEC professionals, however, everyday life situations can more easily be discussed, shown in Chapter 5. However, with the political early learning agenda and the new learning activities stemming from this for parents to do at home, the collaboration increasingly focuses on supporting parents in how to conduct those activities, as was the case for Monica and Emily and for Jane and Toby, rather than on supporting young children's agency.

The mothers' perspectives on the mother's group highlight various dilemmas, for example, that the interventions sometimes fail to include parents' perspectives on the problems they face and the issues they struggle with. Consequently, failing to include the parents' understandings of what problems are relevant for the interventions, the supportive efforts are at risk of being isolated from, or even neglecting, the mothers' everyday lives and problems. The parents' perspectives on what is important about the mothers' group, hence, help to shed light on the problems the mothers experience, i.e. that they lack networks and that they yearn to have someone to discuss difficult and recognizable situations with and to get new ideas from about how to deal with the situations they face.

Parents' Self-understanding

By intervening in the multifaceted everyday life processes, preventive help sometimes adds to the problems and marginalization it is meant to remedy. In other situations, the help makes parents aware of new action possibilities. This is partially the case for Monica, who on her own initiative asked for help due to her own family background when she gave birth to Emily. She grew up in a violent family and she has a bad temper, as she explains. She often experiences a feeling of powerless and anger in situations when her daughter is cross, which is why she asked for help in the hope of learning alternative ways to handle conflicts and frustrations. Monica explains how cooperation with the respite family and the possibility of learning from other adults' ways of dealing with conflicts contribute to developing self-understanding from being a potentially violent parent to one with alternative action possibilities in difficult situations: 'I learned how to handle Emily when she is being cross and screams. I learned what to do and say, and that works very well, I think. I have become more self-confident, and I trust myself to be able to handle situations without becoming violent.' Her self-understanding and changing practice emerge from being part of the respite family practice and experiencing other ways of handling frustrations. At the same time, the collaboration with the respite family leads to new conflicts between the mother and daughter, as already stressed. Monica explains that there is a chasm between the rules in her home and in the respite family's, also in terms of their routines and perspectives on childrearing. The respite family provides support and a reprieve in another home context, exposing Emily to an additional transitioning process that she must orientate herself in relation to. The major differences in routines and resources in the various family contexts add to the intricacy of Emily's complex life. The respite family expands her experiences of what being part of a family can be like that neither Emily nor her mother would have access to otherwise. Nonetheless, the variations between the various family contexts lead to yet other conflicts that Monica must deal with when alone with Emily. The variations that the children experience, hence, on one hand are considered a resource for them but, on the other hand, also add to the complexity of their lives and generate unintended conflicts. Transitioning and orientating themselves in relation to the different contexts set the stage for the children's developmental possibilities in terms of being able to compare different action contexts and possibilities for participation across different family configurations but also involves conflicts and experiences of exclusion. For the parents the transitioning processes of their children also entail opportunities for them to develop their parental self-understanding and conduct of family life.

In general, parents coordinate and negotiate together with other parties in shared care arrangements. The mothers of the children studied in this book, however, do not have access to the same resources as, for instance a family network, which means that on the whole they do not have the same opportunities to negotiate, evaluate and cope with the conflictual issues as a family. Being treated as someone who lacks ordinary skills causes the mothers to perceive the demands from the municipal professionals as non-negotiable as they live with the constant fear of having their children taken away and put in permanent foster care hanging over them. The self-understanding of being someone who is incompetent manifests itself in encounters with the professionals who lead the mothers' group, at meetings with other municipal professionals and when spending time with the respite parents, as was the case for Monica.

Summary

This chapter focused on the parents' perspectives on what is important for their children and on the parents' experiences of their possibilities for making everyday family life work. Hence, I centred on the parents' perspectives on everyday life and the obstacles they deal with in relation to their children's lives across contexts and in relation to shared care arrangements with various professionals. Children's daily transitions between various contexts and the multiple differences that children and parents need to relate to and deal with, in relation to different routines, understandings of childcare and values about being a good parent are the underlying conditions of the social practices that comprise part of the context for parenting. A key point of this chapter was to analyse the parents' perspectives related to the general dilemmas of being a parent and to show how aspects of being a parent are generally associated with conflicts, predicaments and an ongoing effort to juggle and adjust everyday routines. One general issue that I examined in relation to parenting is that parents collaborate with various adults about the care tasks in the chain of care. The parents thus share their tasks involving the child with others, but the overall responsibility for the child's well-being rests on the parents.

The parents call attention to how the problems they experience in everyday life largely derive from having to single-handedly execute all the care tasks in relation to the child. It may appear paradoxical that they feel overwhelmed when they are part of an extended care arrangement, especially in Denmark and other Scandinavian countries, where public services are pervasive. However, I see this linked to the fact that – despite the fact that both ECEC contexts and the respite family carry out tasks in relation to the child – the parents are left to fend for themselves when dealing with the most difficult situations in everyday life. For example, in relation to transitioning from ECEC contexts to the home late in the afternoon when, e.g. the children are tired and the parents need to combine cooking, taking care of their child(ren), eating, putting the child(ren) to bed and doing laundry, all within quite a tight timeline. Seen from the perspective of the parents, the supportive interventions are directed away from these challenging situations. The respite parents, however, are not bogged down by these tasks, which means they have the surplus time, energy and resources to give the children new experiences and perspectives on how to deal with everyday situations and conflicts. The conditions for making everyday situations work in the two highly disparate family contexts mean that one is more likely to succeed than the other, which makes the mothers feel defeated and at times dejected, as shown in the chapter.

The leap between the help provided and the parents' perspectives on the problems they need help with, I argue, is linked to the understandings of problems dominating the municipal intervention system. One issue is that parents' conflicts and problems are addressed as a lack of parenting skills, poor emotional contact between mother and child or the inability to organize routines and a properly structured daily life. As a consequence, this leads to the mothers being given instructions on how to establish emotional contact, sing and read to their young children to stimulate language development, in addition to advice on nutrition, sleep and creating a calm, harmonious atmosphere with no conflicts, all while insisting that the mothers adhere to tight structures and time schedules in their family life. These guidelines stem from cultural understandings of how to properly care for children and reflect what Burman (2008) terms the textbook model of a nuclear (middle class) family, which is seldom corresponds to parents enrolled in early childhood interventions, who often are single mothers with other kinds of life experiences (O'Hagan, 2010). Moreover, the help offered does not take the agency of young children into consideration. Neither does it address how the children could be supported during transitions in everyday living or how parents can deal with the conflicts that occur in relation to these processes. Various political, cultural and historical conditions entangle family life and shape the underlying values and demands on what to do to be a good parent and which tasks to prioritize in an everyday life pressed for time that is filled with multiple tasks, dynamics, changing concerns and demands. In this way, the present chapter elaborated on the previous chapter's key point: conditions for family life and parental care are also set outside the family. One example is that parents are given responsibility for their young children's learning in Denmark, which means the individual parent is assigned (a private) responsibility for (a public) educational task, which earlier was only defined as a task for the welfare state. Assigning the individual parent with this task entails the risk of amplifying the inequality that early learning activities are designed to prevent, as parents have different prerequisites for taking on and succeeding at this task. Moreover, the chapter has shown that societal values and institutional demands for shared care arrangements or early childhood interventions do not address how to support young children's orientation processes as part of developing their agency. This leads to the related point that the perspectives of parents and children must be included to provide relevant support since the parents' perspectives are rooted in the concrete everyday life with their children. They inherently contribute important knowledge about the child's life, which the professionals otherwise do not have access to. For example, when Ashley does not feel that her perspectives are respected or seen as valuable in terms of finding a solution, she stops confiding in the professionals and discussing the problems she experiences. Instead, she pretends to align with their agenda to stop bottle feeding but secretly continues. This type of withdrawal restricts the professionals' ability to help and curtails access to concrete information about the family context and their problems, somewhat defeating the purpose of the intervention.

Part Four

8

Summing-up and Future Perspectives

The aim of this book has been to contribute to developing the theoretical understandings of young children as agentic subjects, and thus to specify the conceptualization of agency to also account for young children. Specifically, I focused on young children's daily transitioning within and across everyday life contexts as a productive empirical site for gaining a deeper understanding of how children – even from an incredibly young age – pursue engagements and develop their intentions together with others and in relation to an everyday life across various contexts. This way of understanding agency allows for a broader understanding of the young child as an active person in the world, instead of focusing on some of the child's isolated psychological functions. Regardless of how detailed various functions are described, the descriptions cannot replace an understanding of the acting child in the world since the child's acting provides an idea of how the child perceives his or her own action possibilities. Descriptions of functions fail to grasp how the child creates meaning in concrete situations, where not only the child acts, but numerous others do as well (Hviid, 2008).

Since the everyday lives of young children in most countries in the West constitute a situation where children live their lives across different societal institutions, e.g. ECEC contexts together with a group of children, the peer communities that young children are part of become important condition for the children's personal development, as well as the care practices caregivers embrace. Observing the same group of children in ECEC contexts and family contexts, therefore, provided the opportunity to learn about how young children develop their engagements and intentions in relation to the complex and various situations and interactions of which they are a part. Moreover, the long-term participatory design I used afforded opportunities to learn about how young children orientate themselves in the situations, activities and contexts they are part of as a pivotal aspect of developing agency. My aim, based on empirical accounts, was to challenge predominant depictions in the literature of young children as vulnerable and passively exposed to their conditions, largely without any acknowledgement given to the children's creativity in terms of their efforts to influence their everyday lives.

The empirical accounts in the book assist in refining the prevailing conceptualization of agency and, consequently, also to further developing theoretical knowledge on how the development of young children is interrelated with the development of the social practices in which the development is situated. I used the everyday lives of five specific children to establish a basis for focusing on the more general aspects of how to understand the agency of young children. My aim was to describe and analyse the dialectical processes through which the youngest group of children contribute to developing and transforming the conditions under which they live and develop. To accomplish this, I explored the agency of young children as social processes of embodied orientation situated in everyday living. A key point is that in situations that the children have difficulty orientating themselves, and hence in how they can take part in the situation, their opportunities for developing agency become limited.

The empirical chapters highlighted important aspects of how the processes of embodied orientation unfold. The present chapter will highlight these aspects as a way to conclude on how the agency of young children comprises processes of (1) being both responsive and proactive, (2) utilizing material, spatial and social surroundings to explore, through embodied orientation, the situations and contexts they take part in, (3) transitioning in daily living and how these processes are important resources for young children's development of intentions and engagements and (4) interrelations with the agency of caregivers. A fundamental issue is that when the action possibilities and agency of parents are restricted, the agency of the children is also hampered. In this way, the agency of young children is framed (but not determined) by the care practices of their caregivers.

Initially, I will start by elaborating how embodied orientation serve as pivotal part of the process through which young children enter a situation and how they explore this situation and the possibilities for participation. This orientation is an important part of the process of developing agency in terms of making influential and transformative contributions to the situations they take part in. The second part of the chapter, then, examines what can be learned from the book's analysis to qualify professional practice with young children. To conclude I discuss how the book contributes to the research fields.

Agency as Processes of Embodied Orientation Situated in the Conduct of Everyday Life

The book illustrates how processes of embodied orientation constitute a link between the child and the situation. Including the body and emotional expressions in studies of young children as acting and purposeful subjects expands the modalities and sources for intersubjective understanding, inviting a discussion of concrete epistemological and methodological consequences in designing studies that examine the agency of children as the embodied and pre-reflective ways of co-creating and changing the world that others can attempt to relate to through their own embodied orientation.

Young child feels and experiences the world subjectively in first-person mode, as does the researcher and caregivers. Emotions emerge and are felt by each individual in concrete situations. Given these emotions, we can learn about the world from our perspective. However, to act in the world, we need to relate to and to cooperate with co-participants and we need to learn about how they perceive the shared situation from their subjective perspectives located in social practice. In this regard, emotions, thoughts and experiences are not considered private phenomenon. Psychological processes are mediated by the world and by other people, and the first-person perspective transcends the dualistic division of world and person, which also implies an epistemological change of research perspective. Taking this type of 'I' and 'we' standpoint, in accordance with the 'epistemic asymmetry' discussed in Chapter 3 as the point of departure for exploring what life situations mean to different subjects, contributes to transcending the development and well-being of young children as determined by external stimuli. Agency develops through (embodied) participation in social practice together with others, which is why agency continually must be explored through processes of intersubjective understanding located in social practice. For this reason, I argue that including embodied orientation means that all participants can be taken more seriously as acting subjects who are exploring (new) possibilities for action.

Inspired by Hedegaard (2019) I consider the process of orientation a link between the intentionally acting child and her or his living conditions in various everyday contexts. I take the standpoint of the subject as a point of departure for exploring young children's personal contributions to the development and transformation of their living conditions. Concerning young children, such contributions and transformative actions are embodied and involve explorative and social processes of orientation. For this reason, I have argued that embodied orientation is pivotal for young children's possibilities for participating in influential and transformative ways, hence making the social world respond to their intentional actions while the children simultaneously relate to and deal with the situations, they are part of. Societal values mediated through the institutional contexts that children live their lives within and across are part of these life conditions. When transitioning between these contexts young children develop and transform their intentions and engagements in relation to the new experiences they gain, activities they take part in, interactions with peers and caregivers and the conditions they encounter. These new intentions and engagements that young children pursue across contexts provide a backdrop for the children's transformative actions across their various everyday life contexts. For this reason, I suggested that young children orientate based on a backdrop comprising the various experiences they acquired in situations and contexts elsewhere. Moreover, I suggested that a juxtaposition of the concepts embodied orientation and conduct of everyday life foregrounds an important aspect of the development of agency in young children, i.e. that the children orientate themselves in relation to the concrete situations and contexts they enter into and that the conduct of everyday life comprises a resource for this orientation. In this way, young children develop their engagements and intentions through their subjective configuration of a conduct of everyday life and based on this, they also contribute to developing and negotiating the demands they meet. Accordingly, the concept of conduct of everyday life helps decentre the analytical attention given to the complexity of children's lives in the attempt to understand how the various experiences children gain from participating in assorted situations and activities shape their way of acting in a specific situation and, moreover, how agency also develops in relation to linking their participation in various situations and contexts in meaningful ways by contributing to shaping and transforming these. This means that the situations and activities often take other directions than the ones caregivers wish to go or can even imagine or predict. However, my ambition has not been to depict the young child as either 'a privileged author nor as a self-initiating agent' (Waldenfels, 2008). Inspired by scholars such as Køster and Winther-Lindqvist (2018) I instead wished to emphasize how children are creative, proactive as well as responsive beings. I will elaborate this in the next section.

Agency as Responsiveness and Transformative Actions

This book, which dissects how young children, both as historical and responsive beings, as emphasized by Waldenfels in Køster and Winther-Lindqvist (2018), orientate and respond to activities initiated by others, and thus always start from elsewhere. I perceive the processes of embodied orientation as a part of the responsiveness and exploratory actions through which children respond and relate to the historically developed situations they are part of. Simultaneously, this responsiveness is exactly what guides young children when they, through their intentional, embodied actions, contribute to the development and transformation of their surroundings by proactively interacting with these surroundings (Stetsenko, 2017).

I focused on children's micro-movements in everyday living to spotlight the multiple transitions children make during their everyday lives within as well as between institutional contexts. This focus helped highlight and identify the processes through which children contribute to creating, reproducing and transforming conditions in everyday life. For instance, I elaborated on how children are already intentional agentic beings when entering historically and socially developed nexuses of social practices. Children simultaneously orientate in these practices and new situations, putting them in a position to contribute to interpreting and creating them, as well as to transform the values, routines and demands they encounter within various institutional contexts. An example of this was Daniel, who on his way to nursery played in the rain with his mother. At the nursery, by picking up his boots again and again he succeeds in making his childminder respond to his initiative and support his efforts to go out in the rain. Daniel utilizes his experience from a situation in another context to alter his childminder's plans.

I aimed to illustrate how even very young children are anything but immobile and how they are active parts in transitions in daily living, contributing to shaping not only their own but also the lives of their parents, peers and caregivers. The purpose was to transcend how children do more than just respond to and act in relation to already established social practices, embracing the agentic contributions of young children to the development of social practice. However, I did not wish to depict young children as eminently rational, independent agents. This type of depiction would overlook the responsibility adults have for children's everyday lives and would disregard the fact that young children generally have fewer life experiences compared to adults and, hence, are cared for by adults. I stress the importance on being aware of the unequal power relationship between adults and children. Children dependent on the care and protection that parents and other caregivers are responsible for providing. My aim has been to show how young children still have the opportunities to influence their life conditions and the routines of everyday life, though fewer than the adults who surround them. In this respect children are dependent on how the adults orchestrate the everyday life conditions that they have overall responsibility for. This interpretation identifies how the agency of young children is framed but certainly not determined.

It is precisely through their transitions in a complex everyday life and the various experiences derived from transitioning between different contexts that children gain opportunities and experiences that develop their engagements and pursuit of them by entering, for instance, the nursery with experiences from being outside in the rain like Daniel who responds to the day care practice in a way that also is proactive and transformative of the daily schedule. Also, participation in various contexts provides children with alternative understandings of how, for instance eating, sleep and walking routines can be done in various ways. The description I provide of walking with a parent and a caregiver on a daily route illustrates that it entails a variety of diverse opportunities for the child. Spaces, things and social relationships, hence, are part of young children's processes of embodied orientation.

Materiality, Spaces and Social Relationships as Resources for Embodied Orientation

Young children use their experiences with spaces, activities and materiality in their attempts to orientate in what is going on and become familiar with routines in everyday life, just as they use them to involve others in their own activities. This is the case with Daniel, who continuously fetched his boots. While inside at the nursery, he associated his boots with his positive experience of being outdoors in the rain earlier in the morning with his mother, pointing out the window where he could see the rain. He persevered even though his childminder initially rejected or misunderstood his wishes. He repeatedly communicated his intentions to get her to understand that he wished to go from an inside to an outside space.

In other situations, the children use each other and one another's activities as a resource when identifying what is at stake and how they can become part of it, as also emphasized in other research contributions in Chapter 2. One example of this is when Toby watched the other children playing train with cargo bikes and then acted like a passenger who wanted to get on. The children observe how their peers use things in a specific way; in this case cargo bikes were linked together to make a train with one driver and the other children as passengers. Young children coordinate as well as fight with each other in their attempts to relate to each other and to negotiate their engagements. This was also the case when Emily allowed a younger child to influence the play in the nursery for her to be able to have someone to play with. Another example is Daniel constantly wanting to use the same toys as his peers in day care and imitating the actions of another child named Kelly. This is part of Daniel's orientation process for exploring which playthings are relevant to get a hold of to become part of the ever-changing social dynamics in the peer community in the context of the nursery.

The way the children use things and spaces form the possibilities for other participants to make situations work. For example, Anthony walks in various ways along the route with his mother and the family nursery caregiver, orientating himself to explore how the same path and playground offer diverse opportunities for him to influence the walk and explore his options. Anthony's mother relates to his way of using and exploring things on the path as a way to cooperate with him on how to make the transitioning process between the nursery and the car function as smoothly as possible. Another example was Daniel's use of his highchair in his family context, which provided a stepping stone for him to be able to observe what was going on between his mother and brother in the kitchen. However, the example also illustrates his inability to influence what he is taking part in ways that lead to transformation or development of the conditions. Daniel's continuous attempts to climb either into or out of the chair demonstrate how he experiences the situation as chaotic, his attempts to orientate himself adding to the complexity in the situation, making it even more difficult for his mother to handle the situation because she constantly needs to attend to him to prevent him from falling down. Based on my analysis, I suggest that young children try to get the world to respond to their initiatives and intentional actions, and to do so, they need to be able to orientate themselves in relation to what is at stake and what other co-participants intentions are. In this way, agency is not about developing autonomy and becoming an independent agent as some strands of research argue (see Chapter 2). Rather, agency is embedded in social, material and historical practices and the children's possibilities for developing agency are created through processes of embodied orientation in material and social surroundings, just as they are supported through processes of intersubjective understandings and multimodal communication with others.

Transitions between the Everyday Life Contexts – Differences as a Resources and Source of Conflict

My analysis emphasized the differences between the contexts children participate in as resources for them to develop their intentions and for them to gain a variety of experiences in how to understand and participate in, for instance, the same kind of activities and routines in different ways, e.g. walking the same route holds various possibilities for action depending on who one walks with. Children play an active part in creating coherence across their various everyday life contexts, and they seem to use daily transitioning processes for orientating in the various opportunities available and for exploring various ways of influencing what is going on. These processes of embodied orientation, as already emphasized, are social as children use things, co-participants and spaces to explore and orientate themselves. This section, however, focuses on the multiple ways in which caregivers encounter young children in their various contexts. Anthony's parents, for instance, approached him as intentional and agentic, and they let him do plenty on his own. His respite family approached him differently, viewing him as being in need of protection and constant care and his childminder in nursery in a third way. The caregivers differing approaches served as a resource for Anthony, allowing him to learn, e.g. that how you eat and walk can be done in numerous ways. To a large extent his respite family does everything for him, even holding his hand when he walks to prevent him from falling. This is in contrast to the approach his birth family takes, where his parents encourage and allow him to do things on his own. Even though he struggles more with accomplishing his engagements in his birth family, he has the opportunity to transform his conditions and gain experience in having the ability to influence the situations. Moreover, Anthony's actions prompt his parents to act, allowing Anthony to transform the way his parents conduct the everyday family life routines they have otherwise planned. Consequently, Anthony's embodied orientation and intentional actions not only affect him but also shape his parents' scope of action possibilities. For Emily, it was a different case. The differences between her two family contexts lead to conflicts rather than serving as a resource for her development of agency. This is due to the fact that she is allowed to do more things and that her respite family does not require anything of her. When at home with her mother Emily starts to protest against her mother's routines and demands because she has experienced other ways of eating (e.g. not required to eat her vegetables) and other routines (e.g. tidying up her toys before dinner). These differences make Emily question her mother's routines, creating additional conflicts between them. These differences became too difficult in this case and led to conflicts that restricted the possibilities for action of both the child and the mother rather than serving as a resource for development.

As illustrated, important differences exist between ECEC contexts and family contexts. Daniel, for instance, seems to have more opportunities to influence the situations he is part of when in the family nursery, even though the caregiver has created a rather fixed structure and daily routines. These fixed and foreseeable routines specifically appear to provide Daniel with the opportunity to orientate himself in other ways compared to his family context, where life is quite chaotic and hectic. The routines in Daniel's family are carried out in an entirely different way compared to his family nursery. For this reason, Daniel seems unable to use the routines in his various everyday life contexts as a stepping stone for linking the routines in his various everyday life contexts.

As shown throughout the book, the children's daily transitions also are a source of development for the parents since they find that their children act in novel ways or develop new preferences, at times pursuing new interests that the parents are unfamiliar with. In these situations, the parents use the child's way of acting to orientate in what the child does and experiences in other contexts. In some situations, through the transitions, the children introduce their parents to new routines, causing the parents to gain new perspectives on their own child when they experience and observe their child together with their peers or other caregivers. In this manner, the way young children engage in their daily transitions aids in developing the various contexts and situations they are part of, and hence how they develop agency.

Interrelatedness of the Agency of Parents and of Children

The development of personal agency is connected to possessing an increasing influence on specific conditions for parents and for their children. Meanings of contributions are mediated through how other participants connect to them and use them for further collective collaboration and common activity. When parents or other caregivers do not respond to the contributions of their children, the children's possibilities for developing agency are limited. This is why concentrating on the parents' possibilities for acting in agentic ways must be in focus in early childhood intervention practice and other kinds of professional practice targeting young children if the agency of these children is to be supported.

When parents are able to relate to their young children's embodied orientation as a way to understand how they perceive a concrete situation and what their emotional state is, and what they are trying to accomplish, the parents can support the children's engagements or at least relate to them and respond to them – as was the case for Anthony and his mother as they walk to their car. Even though Anthony was not allowed to do everything he wanted or for as long as he wanted to his mother related and responded to his agentic and intentional actions. Consequently, she supported Anthony in his engagements, permitting him to influence the unfolding of the transition while she simultaneously maintained the purpose of heading home early to prepare dinner in a timely manner.

Dinnertime at Daniel's is highly chaotic, making it impossible for Daniel (or any other family member) to orientate, which prevents exploration of how to participate proactively. Hence, Daniel mainly acts in reactive ways in his family context. This example shows how the agency of the parents interrelates with that of their children. Due to confusion, disorder and conflicts at dinnertime, Daniel's mother is often forced to abandon her plans and routines, which is the opposite of Toby's family, where a strict, structured approach is taken. On the one hand this might be easier to orientate in due to the predictability and calm atmosphere but on the other hand, leaves little to no room for negotiation, leaving Toby feeling resigned and constantly trying to react to his mother's demands. The two approaches, strictly versus loosely structured, both leave little room for the children to develop agency.

The manner in which the parents organize everyday family life reflects their agency in terms of them feeling like they have opportunities to deal with and influence their everyday life situations and routines. Early childhood intervention professionals monitor the parents and children studied in this book, causing the parents to feel that their options are limited for creating an everyday life that works. They all feel constricted by the pressure to comply with the directions and advice they receive from the authorities. As illustrated the instructions and guidance the parents receive are misaligned and correspond to a different type of family life and other life conditions. This dynamic means the societal values about family life and care practices are hard to comply with, sometimes leaving the parents feeling dejected instead of encouraged.

Transcending Problems in Professional Practice

This section discusses how the analysis and the theoretical development of agency in relation to young children also serves as a resource for developing professional practice in terms of young children and their parents as the target of early childhood interventions. I will discuss how the theoretical insights can provide analytical tools fruitful for exploring the well-being of young children while also including the perspectives of young children.

As outlined, the agency of young children (or their parents) is not an explicit topic in early childhood interventions. One explanation for this is that the literature does not to a great extent focus on agency in children below the age of five, and even less in children below the age of three and especially this age group is the target of early childhood interventions. Another reason is that the huge political focus on early childhood interventions and the objectives of preventive measures are often initiated before problems even become evident in the children's lives. Consequently, the professionals intervene based on abstract understandings of the family situation in terms of risk factors rather than the concrete problems in everyday life situations of the parents and children. Moreover, due to an increasing demand for professionals to document their work they often target aspects of an intervention that can easily be measured in terms of progression, e.g. weight, nutrition and structure. In other words, the interventions are often not designed to ease general problems and conflicts occurring in relation to the conduct of family life, as for instance in conflictual situations like dinnertime or bedtime. They instead sometimes enhance these conflicts by adding contradictory demands, hence delimiting the parents' development of agency. This is problematic for more than just the parents. As illustrated, if situations become too chaotic young children have difficulties in orientating themselves, leaving little room to respond to and influence what is going on. This is why a focus on supporting the agency of young children must also be considered an issue of high relevance in professional practice aimed at children and families.

As discussed, enhancing young children's future life chances is high on the political agenda in Denmark and the West in general. A problem, I argue, is that measures to ensure future life chances are initiated in ways that might exacerbate the problems and conflicts that children and parents face in their current lives. In this way, the fact that this great political interest coincides with a lack of knowledge about the everyday lives of young children and parents is problematic since interventions are initiated without situated knowledge about what they involve or what significance an intervention may have in different families (Juhl & Westerling, forthcoming). One example of this is the early learning agenda. In the last two decades the attention given in Denmark and the West to collaboration between ECEC professionals and parents – especially parents in difficulties – has increasingly focused on early learning and preventive interventions (Westerling & Juhl, 2021). Focusing on the development of isolated skills in children (e.g. language) and their parents (e.g. emotional contact with the child) due to concerns about the child's welfare and future prospects means that important opportunities for supporting the development of agency as embedded in the social complexity of young children's everyday lives decrease.

Today, daily exchanges between caretakers and parents about what was important to a child while in day care, or what conflicts played out in the family in the morning, or even more general exchanges about how to support the child in transitioning between ECEC and home contexts, i.e. the quite different opportunities and demands children face during the day, easily fall out of focus due to the limited time available. When early learning becomes a focus in this already downsized collaboration between the child's two key developmental contexts, multiple related issues fall by the wayside. This leaves parents with fewer resources in terms of their familial network when already in a situation with fewer options to explore and discuss various alternatives in how to organize everyday family life and ways of handling difficult situations with their children and how to relate to and interpret children's well-being.

The United Nations 17 Sustainable Develop Goals, a call to action for all countries to work in a global partnership, include a specific focus on children's rights, and the ambition is to achieve equality and create sustainable lives for all children.[1] Moreover, there is the shared ambition to enhance democracy by including children to a larger extent in making decisions involving the children's own lives and conditions. This international agenda is a challenge for professionals when the children are too young to articulate their perspectives. However, the conceptual work in this book can serve as a stepping stone to further develop tools for exploring children's perspectives regardless of their age. I will discuss this in the next section.

Including Young Children in Professional Work

The concept of orientation, according to Osterkamp-Holzkamp (1991), is substantial in relation to understanding how people sustain possibilities for action. Inspired by Osterkamp-Holzkamp and Hedegaard's (2019) approach to orientation (2019), I suggested embodied orientation as pivotal in addressing the issue of how to grasp what children's diverse life conditions mean to different children. The analytical tools of embodied orientation juxtaposed with the concept of conduct of everyday life help link the child's subjective emotional experiences to a concrete situation located in a social practice that is linked to other social practices. I focused on how embodied orientation guides young children's actions but also those of the children's caregivers, who use children's embodied ways of acting as a clue to explore what situations mean to children. This is an important contribution that pushes past narrowly approaching young children as having universal needs that caregivers can know in advance, independently of the complexity of the situations and transitions the child has moved within and between. I illustrated how children also take part in their own care practices and guide their caregivers through embodied orientation, communicating and acting. By observing the detailed ways in which children act, develop their actions and orientate themselves, as well as how this develops over time situated in the conduct of everyday life, others can, through their own embodied orientation and insights, explore the child's perspective and develop a shared intersubjective understanding.

The analytical tools of embodied orientation situated within the conduct of everyday life, I assert, help sustain an openness in relation to a situated exploration of a child's well-being. By this, I emphasize that it is not enough to include statistical risk factors as a basis for assessing whether a child's well-being and development is at risk and for, at one point, initiating early childhood interventions (Mashford-Scott, Church &Tayler, 2012; Seland, Sandseter & Bratterud, 2015). Rather, it is pivotal to analyse the situated meanings of life conditions as situated in a specific configuration of the conduct of everyday life. We cannot know in advance a concrete problem or a predefined risk factor means. Consequently, the meaning of what can be considered a general problem in terms of risk factors concerning a child's well-being must be analysed in relation to the specific complexity of the conduct of everyday life. Moreover, this analysis requires an ongoing exploration of the child's perspective across situations and transitioning processes. The embodied orientation expands the modalities for analysing a child's bodily ways of being in the world to explore their actions as reasoned, hence also analysing the child's perspective in non-verbal ways.

Supporting the Agency of Parents in Professional Practice

In the early childhood interventions I touch upon in this book, the concrete everyday family life situations, e.g. dinnertime and bedtime, are not to a great extent taken into consideration as a general problem related to the complex practice of parenthood, or in the context of a family life in which all the family members have been apart during the day and re-join in the late afternoon, merging their various needs, experiences and interests in a common life (Kousholt, 2011). However, my analyses based on the everyday lives of parents and children show that, precisely these situations comprise the most difficult and conflictual situations. An important aspect to include in early childhood interventions, then, is parental development of agency in terms of arranging everyday situations since this is inevitably important to how the parents can support their young children in developing agency.

I maintain that the instructions and advice the professionals provide on organizing family life fail to see parents and children as agentic beings situated in a conduct of everyday life across various demands and conditions. Interventions aimed at enhancing a fixed structure, good emotional atmosphere and emotional contact between mother and child turn the parental tasks inwards, towards family life. Consequently, care tasks that turn the attention outwards are minimized in early childhood intervention practice (Kousholt, 2018). This means that early childhood intervention professionals largely put no emphasis on and do not recognize the fact that the children's social relationships with peers and other engagements unfold elsewhere, which is an important issue for parents. One of the repercussions of this is that the parents do not necessarily consider the complexity of their children's everyday lives as an important issue when supporting their children's development. In this way, the young children are often not supported in finding a sense of coherence in the various contexts in which they take part. That was the case with Toby, who tried to involve his mother in supporting his endeavours in his home context in becoming part of his community of peers in the ECEC centre.

The huge focus on the significance of the family context and the parents for the children's development predominant in early childhood interventions partially explains why the outward focus of parental tasks is neglected. However, as illustrated, conditions in family life are set in more than just the current situation. How everyday family life is organized depends also on the care contributions of other parties, e.g. in the nursery. Anthony's parents, for instance, must take into consideration how Anthony's day in the nursery went: did he nap, or is he tired? What did caregivers in the ECEC context prioritize and decide during the day? What kind of communities and relationships was the child part of in ECEC? What kind of experiences did the child have? And what significance do these experiences and situations have in the child's family life? These are all key questions that must be addressed and considered when trying to understand children's development and well-being, but also the contributions various adults and other children make during daily life and how these comprise a compound life for children and the efforts children make to create coherence between these different experiences and situations. These conditions and experiences across contexts, then, shape the family's afternoon schedule in relation to which priorities and choices the parents make, e.g. will they rush to make dinner before Anthony gets too tired or do they have more time? All these details become significant for how to be a parent, for what Anthony needs. Moreover, the overarching concern for the parents is to balance all of these concerns and conditions with the instructions they received from the early childhood intervention unit. In this way, the contexts for children's daily transitions are dynamic and changeable, and the children act in relation to these changeable conditions. Moreover, their ways of acting also contribute to changing and shaping these conditions, not to mention how the transitions evolve. In this way, the transitions are key to exploring agency in young children and also key to exploring the nexus of political, institutional and personal aspects of daily living for children as well as parents. In continuation of this, parenthood must be considered politically, culturally and historically shaped, but also seen in the light of the hegemonic cultural understandings and values of parenthood that are reflected in the interventions provided for families in marginalized positions. Parenting culture studies, for example, argue that the hegemonic ideals mediated by parenting programmes are part of a wider, comprehensive tendency of intensified parenthood (Lee, 2014; McVaris, 2014). Faircloth contends (2014) that intensified parenthood implies that parents are constantly held accountable for their children's health, well-being and future failure or success. She terms this parental determinism (2014), emphasizing that parents are considered both the source of – and responsible for preventing – risks in their children's lives (Furedi, 2008). I suggest that instead of approaching parents in terms of the risk-resilience discourse (Burman, 2020) they must be approached as agentic and as trying to make their everyday lives work. Hence, supporting the agency of parents in relation to organizing family life as related to children's lives in other social practices needs to be the starting point of exploration in professional interventions. To do so, including the perspectives and situated knowledge of parents about everyday life situations is pivotal and can be done by focusing on the concrete and detailed aspects of everyday life (e.g. using life forms interviews, a research method developed into professional practice by researchers in Norway; see Ulvik & Guldbrandsen, 2015). Relatedly, Hopwood and Mäkitalo (2019) suggest that early childhood intervention practitioners should built partnerships with parents aiming for exploring how parents perceive problems and needs rather than taking a point of departure in a professionally determined agenda (p. 600).

Parenthood on the Crossroads between Family and ECEC

In Scandinavia, where collaborating with various professionals in the ECEC system is an important parental task, professional caregivers become significant for the parents' ways of understanding and interpreting their parental task and responsibility in the chain of care. The daily transitions between ECEC and family entail opportunities for parents to develop their self-understanding in productive ways but also the risk of parents experiencing failure and exclusion. Even though this is particularly relevant in a Scandinavian context, since the majority of children are enrolled in the ECEC system, it is also relevant in an international context as ECEC systems become more common and because of the fact that parents worldwide include other parties outside the birth family to make everyday life work with family and work (Thorne, 2001). The transitions and crossroads between family and other institutional and more informal everyday life contexts contain huge developmental potential since children as well as parents learn and develop by participating in various contexts and by expanding ways to participate in and contribute to developing the situations they take part in. When parents are isolated in the sense of lacking a family network and social networks, they rely heavily on their collaboration with ECEC professionals, who represent an important resource for how to be a caregiver, how to solve conflicts and how to deal with children. Often the parents' network does not contain any examples of how to be a parent or how to organize family life. In this way, transitions in daily life become opportunities for parents to collaborate with other caregivers and to exchange knowledge about their child. These situations and the collaboration provide the conditions for how children transition between their everyday life contexts. As a result, engaging parents in an ongoing dialogue about their children's everyday life is a pivotal task for ECEC professionals also in relation to children in difficult life conditions leading to the development of joint knowledge about the specific child and what needs to be in focus in the various contexts.

The last two issues I touch on are gender inequality and social inequality, both of which are highly relevant to address in the professional practices of early childhood interventions. The mothers in the book emphasized what O'Hagan (2010) terms time pressure and time poverty since they often have the main responsibility for caring for their children and are also the target of early childhood interventions. They also do not have a social network to draw on in everyday life to help them balance domestic chores, childcare and work or education. However, the social position of mothers is also privileged in terms of a hegemonic status in society, despite the inequalities it also creates. Fathers are basically ignored in early childhood interventions, leaving the mothers with all the responsibility. If the parents have disagreements about child custody, domestic violence occurs or other severe conflicts arise, the mothers are left with yet another problem because the children have the right to be in contact with their fathers. This pushes the mothers to communicate and cooperate with the fathers under often highly challenging conditions and without any help from the authorities. This apparent gender inequality affects more than just mothers negatively. In one of the families I observed, the father faced hurdles to become part of the intervention; his participation was rejected even though both he and the mother wanted him to take part. This unfolding of events aligns with the authorities' belief that it is in the best interest of preschool-age children to spend most of their time with their mother to ensure attachment, an idea based on attachment theory that is dominant in early childhood intervention practice. As mentioned earlier, Burman (2020) terms this 'risk-resilience discourse' on child development, where early childhood experiences, particularly those tied to the parent-child relationship, are considered the root of undesirable psychological consequences later in life. Such understandings of young children's psychological needs and parental tasks contribute to maintaining gender inequality and essentially exclude fathers as a resource in their children's lives.

A Final Word – Situating the Knowledge Contribution

In this book I have studied the various ways in which agency develops in the lives of specific children. My examination of the process from both a general and concrete perspective contributes with complex and situated knowledge about the dynamics, feelings, interests, intentions, concerns, well-being, possibilities, difficulties and conflicts each child experiences related to the social practices in which these aspects unfold. However, the social practices share common features in the young children's lives. In this way, what I contribute with is 'knowledge about the everyday realities of living, experiencing, and changing in social practice and about how general aspects are present and matter in varying ways therein' (Dreier, 2019, p. 191). My analysis examined the lives of five young Danish children, age one to five years, whose everyday lives situated in a particular society both differ from and are similar to elsewhere in the world. For instance, the discourses about child development and ideas on early childhood interventions share basic assumptions in the West, e.g. current discussions on child well-being in the UK are similar to those in Denmark (Burman, 2020). The concrete arrangements and composition of each child's everyday lives nonetheless vary.

The theoretical contribution concerning the social processes of young children's development of agency describes the concrete processes through which young children orientate in their daily lives not only as part of participating in the situations they are part of but also as part of contributing to developing and transforming these situations. The empirical analysis examines the extraordinary life conditions of five specific children, but its refinement of agency adds to the broader, more general discussions of the development of this group and includes a discussion of political, cultural and societal conditions for child development and the tasks involved in a shared care arrangement (Andenæs & Haavind, 2018). Consequently, although based on empirical sites in the Danish welfare state, the analysis has international relevance.

By analysing the agency of children through the lens of transitions in their everyday lives I have contributed to creating a more precise understanding of how young children act in their everyday life contexts and of their agency in how the abovementioned four aspects of social processes of embodied orientation unfold. In this way, I have contributed to the conceptualization of agency presented in the existing research literature by exploring agency as inherently embedded in social processes situated in historically developed social practices. This creates an alternative to the notion of agency as an individual process in which young children gradually become independent free agents. I have shown how agency comprises social processes situated in the conduct of everyday life and that the agency of young children is interrelated with the agency of caregivers. Moreover, I have illustrated how processes of embodied orientation in responsive ways act a stepping stone for children's possibilities for acting in more proactive and transformative ways. Hence, my research shows that being a historical responsive being is an important aspect of young children's development of agency.

In recent years, research and the professional practice of early childhood interventions have increasingly focused on the youngest children. The current political focus in Western societies on how to prevent risk in early childhood (Burman, 2020) manifests itself in preventive and compensatory intervention programmes based on research documenting the impact of risk factors (Love et al., 2002) and protective factors (Luthar et al., 2000; Rutter, 2000). This is why, particularly in the field of marginalization and inclusion, there is much to gain from employing theoretical frameworks and concepts capable of comprehending young children as intentional, agentic beings who already always contribute to influencing and co-producing their own and co-participants' life conditions.

Another contribution of general relevance is the broadening of diverse forms of communication in the exploration of young children's perspectives, which gives rise to new possibilities for including young children as active subjects in their own lives, in research and in professional practice aimed at enhancing children's possibilities in life, but also in early preventive interventions and in other everyday life contexts where children and professionals interact. Even though the concept of embodied orientation does not offer an unambiguous assessment of what situations mean to young children and why they act as they do, it does provide an incentive to further engage children, regardless of their age, in a shared exploration of their concrete possibilities in everyday life. Embodied orientation offers analytical possibilities for situating embodied ways of acting in the conduct of everyday life, contributing not only to theoretical development but to understanding how theorizing agency of young children is interrelated with epistemological, methodological and political consequences more broadly. The knowledge produced on young children's micromovements in daily living and the way they develop agency and not only contribute to creating and changing their own personal development but also contribute to transforming the social practices in which this development is situated contributes to the research fields of developmental psychology, childhood studies and parenting studies, as well as to the theoretical traditions of cultural-historical theory and psychology from the standpoint of the subject.

Notes

Chapter 1

1 https://www.ohchr.org/EN/HRBodies/CRC/Pages/CRCIndex.aspx (visited 16 September 2021).
2 This is a family hired by local authorities to regularly accommodate for a child in difficult life conditions in order to provide the child with a stable and appropriate developmental environment as well as to relieve the parents who often are in marginalized positions.

Chapter 4

1 https://www.dst.dk/en/Statistik/emner/borgere/husstande-familier-og-boern/boernepasning (visited 1 February 2022).

Chapter 6

1 https://www.retsinformation.dk/eli/lta/2019/798 (Danish Social Services Legislation, visited 1 November 2020).

Chapter 7

1 The No Child Left behind Act of 2001 in the United States is one example, https://www2.ed.gov/nclb/landing.jhtml (visited 11 October 2021).
2 The parents were from a low-income group and mainly comprised single mothers on welfare. This book only addresses poverty and inequality in terms of lack of network.

Chapter 8

1 https://www.unicef.org/sdgs (visited 11 July 2021).

References

Adair, J. K. (2014). Agency and expanding capabilities in early grade classrooms: What it could mean for young children. *Harvard Educational Review*, 84(2), 217–41. Doi: https://doi.org/10.17763/haer.84.2.y46vh546h41l2144

Ahnert, L., Gunner, M., Lamb, M. E., & Barthel, M. (2004). Transition to child care: Associations with infant-mother attachment, infant negative emotion, and cortisol elevations. *Child Development*, 75(3), 639–50.

Ahrenkiel, A., Holm, L., & Eilenberg, L. Ø. (2021). Children's language use in ECEC in a child perspective. *Ethnography and Education*, Latest articles. Doi: https://doi.org/10.1080/17457823.2021.1943699

Ahtola, A., Björn, P. M., Turunen, T., Poikonen, P. L., Kontoniemi, M., Lerkkanen, M. K., & Nurmi, J. E. (2016). The concordance between teachers' and parents' perceptions of school transition practices: A solid base for the future. *Scandinavian Journal of Educational Research*, 60(2), 168–81. Doi: 10.1080/00313831.2014.996598

Ainsworth, M. (1978). *Patterns of Attachment: A Psychological Study of the Strange Situation*. New Jersey: Lawrence Erlbaum.

Alderson, P., Hawthorne, J., & Killen, M. (2005). The participation rights of premature babies. *International Journal of Children's Rights*, 13, 31–50.

Andenæs, A., & Sundnes, A. (2019). Døgnet rundt: Utforskning av foreldres omsorg for barn. In A., Jansen & A. Andenæs (Eds.). *Hverdagsliv, barndom og oppvekst. Teoretiske posisjoner og metodiske grep*, pp. 226–50. Oslo: Universitetsforlaget.

Andenæs, A., & Haavind, H. (2018). Sharing early care: Learning from practitioners. In M. Fleer & B. van Oers (Eds.). *International Handbook of Early Childhood Education*, vol. 2, pp. 1483–502. Dordrecht: Springer.

Andenæs, A. (2011). Chains of care: Organizing the everyday life of young children attending day care. *Nordic Psychology*, 63(2), 49–67

Arnold, C., Bartlett, K., Giowani, S., & Merali, R. (2007). Is everybody ready? Readiness, transition and continuity: Reflections and moving forward. *Working Papers in Early Childhood Development*, No. 41, The Hague, The Netherlands: Bernard Van Leer Foundation.

Axel, E. (2011). Conflictual cooperation. *Nordic Psychology*, 63(4), 56–78.

Bach, D. (2017). The civilized family life: Childrearing in affluent families. In I. L. Gilliam & E. Gulløv (Eds.). *Children of the Welfare State: Civilising Practices in Schools, Childcare and Families*, pp. 194–235. London: Pluto Press. Anthropology, Culture and Society Anthropology, Culture and Society.

Beers, C. (2021). Case study of a preschool transition: An example of building resilience in times of uncertainty. *Early Years*, 41(2–3), 275–90. Doi: https://doi.org/10.1080/09575146.2018.1501554

Belsky, J. & Pluess, M. (2013). Genetic moderation of early child-care effects on social functioning across childhood: A developmental analysis. *Child Development*, 84(4), 1209–25. Doi: https://doi.org/10.1111/cdev.12058

Benard, B. (1999). The foundations of the resiliency paradigm. In N. Henderson, B. Benard & N. Sharp-Light (Eds.). *Resiliency in Action: Practical Ideas for Overcoming Risks and Building Strengths in Youth, Families, and Communities*. Gorham, ME: Resiliency in Action.

Bender, S. L., Pham, A. V., & Carlson, J. S. (2011). School readiness. In S. Goldstein & J. A. Naglieri (Eds.). *Encyclopedia of Child Behavior and Development*, pp. 1297–8. Boston, MA: Springer.

Bird, K. (2007). *The intergenerational transmission of poverty: An overview*. Overseas Development Institute, London SE7 1JD and Chronic Pewerty Re-search Center. ODI Working Paper 286, CPRC Working Paper 99.

Bjørnestad, E., & Os, E. (2018). Quality in Norwegian childcare for toddlers using ITERS-R. *European Early Childhood Education Research Journal*, 26(1), 111–27. Doi: https://doi.org/10.1080/1350293X.2018.1412051

Bjørnestad, E., & Samuelsson, I. P. (2012). *Hva betyr livet i barnehagen for barn under tre år? En forskningsoversikt. [What does the everyday life in child care mean to young children below age 3? A research review]*. https://www.regjeringen.no/globalassets/upload/kd/vedlegg/barnehager/rapporter20og20planer/forskningsoversikt_barn_under_tre_aar.pdf

Bleses, D., Jensen, P., Højen, A., & Dale, P. S. (2018). An educator-administered measure of language development in young children. *Infant Behavior and Development*, 52, 104–13.

Bourdieu, P. (2000). *Pascalian Meditations*. Stanford, CA: Stanford University Press.

Bowlby, J. (1998). *A Secure Base: Clinical Applications of Attachment Theory*. London: Routledge. 1. udgave: 1962.

Brooker, L. (2010). Constructing the triangle of care: Power and professionalism in practitioner/parent relationships. *British Journal of Educational Studies*, 58(2), 181–96. Doi: 10.1080/00071001003752203

Brooker, L. (2006). From home to the home corner: Observing children's identity maintenance in early childhood settings. *Children & Society*, 20(2), 116–27. Doi: 10.1111/j.1099-0860.2006.00019.x

Broström, S., & Hansen, O. H. (2010). Care and education in the Danish crèche. *International Journal of Early Childhood*, 42(2), 87–100. Doi: 10.1007/s13158-010-0010-x

Brownlie, J., & Leith, V. M. S. (2011). Social bundles: Thinking through the infant body. *Childhood*, 20(1), 196–210.

Burman, E. (2020). Decolonising childhood, reconceptualising distress: A critical psychological approach to (Deconstructing) child well-being. In M. Fleer, F. González Rey & P. Jones (Eds.). *Cultural-Historical and Critical Psychology. Perspectives in Cultural-Historical Research*, vol. 8. Singapore: Springer. Doi: https://doi.org/10.1007/978-981-15-2209-3_7

Burman, E. (2008). *Deconstructing Developmental Psychology* 2nd ed. New York: Routledge.

Burman, E. (1994). *Deconstructing Developmental Psychology*. New York: Routledge (Critical psychology).

Callaghan, J. E. M., Fellin, L. C., & Alexander, J. H. (2019). Promoting resilience and agency in children and young people who have experienced domestic violence and abuse: The 'MPOWER' intervention. *Journal of Family Violence*, 34, 521–37. Doi: https://doi.org/10.1007/s10896-018-0025-x

Chae, Y., Goodman, M., Goodman, G. S., Troxel, N., McWilliams, K., Thompson, R. A., Shaver, P. R., & Widaman, K. F. (2018). How children remember the strange situation: The role of attachment. *J Exp Child Psychol*, February, 166, 360–79. Doi: 10.1016/j.jecp.2017.09.001. Epub 2017 Oct 9. PMID: 29024847.

Chaiklin, S., Hedegaard, M., & Jensen, U. J. (Eds.) (1999). *Activity Theory and Social Practice: Cultural-Historical Approaches*. Aarhus: Aarhus University Press.

Charest, H. M., Bernier, A., Langevin, R., & Miljkovitch, R. (2019). Behavior problems in sexually abused preschoolers over a 1-year period: The mediating role of attachment representations. *Development and Psychopathology*, 31(2), 471–81. Doi: https://doi.org/10.1017/S0954579418000226

Chimirri, N. A., & Pedersen, S. (2019). Toward a transformative-activist co-exploration of the world? Emancipatory co-research in psychology from the standpoint of the subject. *Annual Review of Critical Psychology (Online)*, 16, 605–33. https://thediscourseunit.files.wordpress.com/2019/12/0605.pdf

Chimirri, N. A., Klitmøller, J., & Hviid, P. (2015). Studying the fabric of everyday life. *Outlines. Critical Practice Studies*, 16(2), 01–14. https://tidsskrift.dk/outlines/article/view/22992

Chimirri, N. A. (2013). Expanding the conduct of everyday life concept for psychological media research with children. In I. A. Marvakis, J. Motzkau, D. Painter, R. Ruto-Korir, G. Sullivan, S. Triliva, & M. Wieser (Eds.). *Doing Psychology under New Conditions,* pp. 355–64. Vaughan: Captus Press.

Christensen, P. H. (2004). Children's participation in ethnographic research: Issues of power and representation. *Children & Society*, 18, 165–76. Doi: 10.1002/CHI.823

Clark, A. (2003). Ways of seeing: Using the Mosaic approach to listen to young children's perspectives. In A. Clark, A. Kjørholt and P. Moss (Eds.). *Beyond Listening: Children's Perspectives on Early Childhood Services*, pp. 29–49. Bristol: Policy Press.

Clarke, A., & Moss, P. (2001). *Listening to Young Children: Using the Mosaic Approach*. London: National Children's Bureau.

Corsaro, W. A., & Molinari, L. (2005). *I Compagni. Understanding Children's Transition from Preschool to Elemntary School*. New York and London: Teachers College Press, Colombia University.

Corby, B., Millar, M., & Young, L. (1996). Parental participation in child protection work: Rethinking the rhetoric. *British Journal of Social Work*, 26(4), 475–790.

Csordas, T. J. (2008). Intersubjectivity and intercorporeality. *Subjectivity*, 22, 110–21.

Dannesboe, K. I., Westerling, A., & Juhl, P. (2021). Making space for 'learning': Appropriating new learning agendas in early childhood education and care. *Journal of Education Policy*, 1–19.

Dencik, L. (1999). Små børns familieliv: som de formes i samspillet med den udenomfamiliære børneomsorg. Et komparativt nordisk perspektiv. In L. Dencik, P. S Og Jørgensen (Eds.). *Børn og familie i det postmoderne samfund. [Children and Families in the Postmodern Society]*, pp. 242–72. Copenhagen: Hans Reitzels forlag.

Dreier, O. (2019). Generalizations in situated practices. In C. Højholt & E. Schraub (Eds.). *Subjectivity and Knowledge: Generalization in the Psychological Study of Everyday Life*, pp. 177–93. New York: Cham Springer. Theory and History in the Human and Social Sciences. Doi: https://doi.org/10.1007/978-3-030-29977-4

Dreier, O. (2011). Personality and the conduct of everyday life. *Nordic Psychology*, 63(2), 4–23.

Dreier, O. (2009). The development of a personal conduct of life in childhood. In T. Teo, P. Stenner & A. Rutherford (Eds.). *Varieties of Theoretical Psychology: International Philosophical and Practical Concerns*, pp. 175–83. Captus: Concord.

Dreier, O. (2008). *Psychotherapy in Everyday Life. Learning in Doing: Social, Cognitive and Computational Perspectives*. Cambridge: Cambridge University Press.

Dreier, O. (1997). *Subjectivity and Social Practice. Center for Health, Humanity and Culture*. Aarhus: Aarhus University Press.

Dumbrill, G. C. (2006). Parental experience of child protection intervention: A qualitative study. *Child Abuse & Neglect*, 30(1), 27–37. Doi: https://doi.org/10.1016/j.chiabu.2005.08.012

Edwards, A. (2020). Agency, common knowledge and motive orientation: Working with insights from Hedegaard in research on provision for vulnerable children and young people. *Learning, Culture and Social Interaction*, 26, 1–7. Doi: https://doi.org/10.1016/j.lcsi.2018.04.004

Edwards, A., Chan, J., & Tan, D. (2019). Motive orientation and the exercise of agency: Responding to recurrent demands in practice. In A. Edwards (Ed.). *Cultural-Historical Approaches to Studying Learning and Development*, 6. New York: Springer.

Egelund, N., & Mejding, J. (2004). *OECD PISA: Programme for International Student Assessment*. Copenhagen: Danish School of Education Press.

Elicker, J., Ruprecht, K. M., & Anderson, T. (2014). Observing infants' and toddlers' relationships and interactions in group care. In L. J. Harrison, & J. Sumsion

(Eds.). *Lived Spaces of Infant-Toddler Education and Care*, pp. 131–45. Dordrecht: Springer.

Elwick, S., Bradley, B., & Sumsion, J. (2014a). Infants as others: Uncertainties, difficulties and (im)possibilities in researching infants' lives. *International Journal of Qualitative Studies in Education*, 27(2), 196–213. Doi: https://doi.org/10.1080/09518398.2012.737043

Elwick, S., Bradley, B., & Sumsion, J. (2014b). Creating space for infants to influence ECEC practice: The encounter, écart, reversibility and ethical reflection. *Educational Philosophy and Theory*, 46(8), 873–85. Doi: https://doi.org/10.1080/00131857.2013.780231

Fabian, H., & Dunlop, A. W. (2007). *Outcomes of Good Practice in Transition Processes for Children Entering Primary School*. Working papers in Early Childhood Development, No. 42. The Hauge: Bernard Van Leer Foundation.

Fabian, H., & Dunlop, A. W. (Eds.) (2002). *Transitions in the Early Years. Debating Continuity and Progression for Children in Early Education*. London and New York: RoutledgeFalmer.

Faircloth, C. (2014). Intensive parenting and the expansion of parenting. In E. Lee, J. Bristow, C. Faircloth & J. Macvarish (Eds.). *Parenting Culture Studies*, pp. 25–50. New York: Palgrave Macmillan.

Fearon, R. P., Bakermans-Kranenburg, M. J., van Ijzendoorn, M. H., Lapsley, A. M., & Roisman, G. I. (2010). The significance of insecure attachment and disorganization in the development of children's externalizing behavior: A metaanalytic study. *Child Development*, 81(2), 435–56. Doi: https://doi.org/10.1111/j.1467-8624.2009.01405.x

Feng, X., Hooper, E. G., & Jia, R. (2017). From compliance to self-regulation: Development during early childhood. *Social Development*, 26(4), 981–95. Doi: https://doi.org/10.1111/sode.12245

Field, T. M., Vega-Lahr, N., & Jagadish, S. (1984). Separation stress of nursery school infants and toddlers graduating to new classes. *Infant Behavior & Development*, 7(3), 277–84. Doi: https://doi.org/10.1016/S0163-6383(84)80043-0

Fincham, E. N., & Fellner, A. R. (2016). Transitional practice: Teachers and children in-between classrooms in one early childhood centre. *Journal of Early Childhood Research*, 14(3), 310–23. Doi: 10.1177/1476718X14552874

Furedi, F. (2008). *Paranoid Parenting: Why Ignoring the Experts May Be Best for Your Child*, vol. 2. udgave, London: Continuum.

Gallagher, S. (2005). *How the Body Shapes the Mind*. Oxford: Clarendon Press.

Gartland, D., Riggs, E., Muyeen, S., Giallo, R., Afifi, T., MacMillan, H., Herrman, H., Bulford, E., & Brown, S. J. (2019). What factors are associated with resilient outcomes in children exposed to social adversity? A systematic review. *BMJ Open*, 9. Doi: 10.1136/bmjopen-2018-024870

Gladstone, G. L., Parker, G. B., & Malhi, G. S. (2006). Do bullied children become anxious and depressed adults?: A cross-sectional investigation of the correlates of bullying and anxious depression. *The Journal of Nervous and Mental Disease*, 194(3), 201–08. https://doi.org/10.1097/01.nmd.0000202491.99719.c3.

Gottlieb, A. (2000). Where have all the babies gone? Toward an anthropology of infants (and their caregivers). *Anthropological Quarterly*, 73(3), 121–32.

Graf, G. (2016). Conceptions of childhood, agency and the well-being of children. In G. Schweiger & G. Graf (Eds.). *The Well-Being of Children: Philosophical and Social Scientific Approaches*, pp. 20–33. Warsaw: De Gruyter Open.

Grienenberger, J., Denham, W., & Reynolds, D. (2015). Reflective and mindful parenting: A new relational model of assessment, prevention, and early intervention. In P. Luyten, L. C. Mayes, P. Fonagy, M. Target, & S. J. Blatt (Eds.). *Handbook of Psychodynamic Approaches to Psychopathology*, pp. 445–68. New York: The Guilford Press.

Groh, Roisman, G. I., van Ijzendoorn, M. H., Bakermans-Kranenburg, M. J., & Fearon, R. P. (2012). The significance of insecure and disorganized attachment for children's internalizing symptoms: A meta-analytic study. *Child Development*, 83(2), 591–610. Doi: https://doi.org/10.1111/j.1467-8624.2011.01711.x

Grummer-Strawn, L., Scanlon, M. S., & Kelley Fein, S. B. (2008). Infant feeding and feeding transitions during the first year of life. *Pediatrics* 122(5), S36–S42.

Guldbrandsen, L. M. (2012). Being a child, coming of age: Exploring processes of growing up. In M. Hedegaard, K. Aronsson, C. Højholt & O. S. Ulvik (Eds.). *Children, Childhood and Everyday Life. Children's Perspectives*, pp. 3–20. New York: Information Age Publishing Inc.

Haavind, H. (2019). Livsformsintervjuet: En veiviser til subjektive erfaringer [The life form interview: A guide to subjective experiences]. In A. Jansen & A. Andenæs (Eds.). *Hverdagsliv, barndom og oppvekst. Teoretiske posisjoner og metodiske grep [Everday Life, Childhood and Adolescence: Theoretical Positions and Methodological Measures]*, pp. 26–57. Oslo: Universitetsforlaget.

Haavind, H. (2011). Everyday life in psychology. *Nordic Psychology*, 63(2), 1–3. Doi: 10.1027/1901-2276/a000029

Haavind, H. (2006). Midt i tredje akt? Fedres deltakelse i det omsorgsfulle foreldreskap. *Tidsskrift for Norsk Psykologforening. [Norwegian Psychology Union Journal]*, 43(7), 683–93.

Haavind, H. (1987), *Liten og stor. Mødres omsorg og barns utviklingsmuligheter. [Small and Large. Mothers' s Care and Children's Development]*. Oslo: Universitetsforlaget.

Hackett, A., MacLure, M., & Sarah, M. (2020). Reconceptualising early language development: Matter, sensation and the more-than-human. *Discourse: Studies in the Cultural Politics of Education*, June, 1–17. Doi: 10.1080/01596306.2020.1767350

Heckmann, J. J., & Masterov, D. V. (2007). The productivity argument for investing in young children. *Review of Agricultural Economics*, 29(3), 446–93.

Heckman, J. J. (2006). Skill formation and the economics of investing in disadvantaged children. *Science*, 132, 1900–2.

Hedegaard, M. (2019). Children's perspectives and institutional practices as keys in a wholeness approach to children's social situations of development. In A. Edwards (Ed.). *Cultural-Historical Approaches to Studying Learning and Development*. Perspectives in Cultural-Historical Research, vol. 6, pp. 23–41. New York: Springer.

Hedegaard, M., & Fleer, M. (2019). Children's transitions in everyday life and institutions: new conceptions and understandings of transitions. In M. Hedegaard & M. Fleer (Eds.). *Children's Transitions in Everyday Life and Institutions (Transitions in Childhood and Youth)*, pp. 1–18. London: Bloomsbury Academic. http://dx.doi.org/10.5040/9781350021488.ch-001.

Hedegaard, M. (2014). The significance of demands and motives across practices in children's learning and development: An analysis of learning in home and school. *Learning, Culture, and Activity*, 3, 188–94.

Hedegaard, M. (2013). *Beskrivelse af småbørn [Descriptions of Young Children]*. Århus: Århus Universitetsforlag, 3. udgave.

Hedegaard, M. (2012a). The dynamic aspects in children's learning and development. In M. Hedegaard, A. Edwards & M. Fleer (Eds.). *Motives in Children's Development: Cultural-Historical Approaches*, pp. 9–27. New York: Cambridge University Press.

Hedegaard, M. (2012b). Children's creative modeling of conflict resolutions in everyday life as central in their learning and development in families. In M. Hedegaard, K. Aronsson, C. Højholt & O. S. Ulvik (Eds.). *Children, Childhood and Everyday Life. Children's Perspectives*, pp. 55–74. New York: Information Age Publishing Inc.

Hedegaard, M., Aronsson, K., Højholt, C., & Ulvik, O. S. (Eds.) (2012). *Children, Childhood and Everyday Life. Children's Perspectives*. New York: Information Age Publishing Inc.

Hedegaard, M. (2009). Children's development from a cultural-historical approach: Children's activity in everyday local settings as foundation for their development. *Mind, Culture, and Activity*, 16, 64–81.

Hedegaard, M., Fleer, M., Bang, J., & Hviid, P. (2008). *Studying Children – A Cultural Historical Approach*. Berkshire, UK: Open University Press.

Hedegaard, M. (2008a). A cultural–historical theory of children's development. In M. Hedegaard & M. Fleer (Eds.). *Studying Children: A Cultural-Historical Approach*, pp. 10–29. New York: McGraw-Hill Education.

Hedegaard, M. (2008b). Developing a dialectic approach to researching children's development. In M. Hedegaard & M. Fleer (Eds.). *Studying Children: A Cultural-Historical Approach*, pp. 30–45. New York: McGraw-Hill Education.

Hedegaard, M. (2002). *Learning and Child Development. A Cultural-Historical Study*. Aarhus: Aarhus University Press.

Heller, R., Chiero, L., Jesse, D., Puglisi, M. et al. (2019). Feeding infants and toddlers: A qualitative study to determine parental education needs. *Childhood Obesity*, 15(7), 443–50.

Hennum, N. (2014). Developing child-centered social policies: When professionalism takes over. *Social Sciences*, 3, 441–59.

Hogstad, I. & Jansen, A. (2020). Smart, vulnerable, playful or just disturbing? A discourse analysis of child involvement in palliative care. *Childhood*, 27(4), 468–82. Doi: 10.1177/0907568220918910

Holzkamp, K. (2013a). Basic concepts of critical psychology. In E. Schraube & U. Osterkamp (Eds.). *Psychology from the Standpoint of the Subject. Selected Writings of Klaus Holzkamp*, pp. 19–28. Basingstoke, England: Palgrave Macmillan.

Holzkamp, K. (2013b). Psychology: Social self-understanding on the reasons for action in the conduct of everyday Life. In E. Schraube & U. Osterkamp (Eds.). *Psychology from the Standpoint of the Subject: Selected Writings of Klaus Holzkamp*, pp. 233–341. Basingstoke, England: Palgrave Macmillan.

Holzkamp, K. (2013c). What could a psychology from the standpoint of the subject be? In E. Schraube & U. Osterkamp (Eds.). *Psychology from the Standpoint of the Subject: Selected Writings of Klaus Holzkamp*, pp. 46–59. Basingstoke: Palgrave Macmillan.

Hopwood, N., Elliot, C., & Pointon, K. (2021). Changing the world for children with complex feeding difficulties: Cultural-historical analyses of transformative agency. *Cultural-Historical Psychology*, 17(2), 155–66. Doi: https://doi.org/10.17759/chp.2021170215

Hopwood, N., & Mäkitalo, Å. (2019). Learning and expertise in support for parents of children at risk: A cultural-historical analysis of partnership practices. *Oxford Review of Education*, 45(5), 587–604. Doi: https://doi.org/10.1080/03054985.2018.1553776

Howes, C. (2011). Children's social development within the socialization context of child care and early childhood education. In P. K. Smith & C. H. Hart (Eds.). *The Wiley-Blackwell Handbook of Childhood Social Development*, 2nd ed, pp. 246–62. Hoboken, NJ: Blackwell Publishing Ltd.

Hugo, K., McNamara, K., Sheldon, K., Moult, F., Lawrence, K., Forbes, C., Martin, N., & Miller, M. G. (2018). Developing a blueprint for action on the transition to school: Implementation of an action research project within a preschool community. *International Journal of Early Childhood*, 50(2), 241–57. Doi: 10.1007/s13158-018-0220-1

Hultgen, F., & Johansson, B. (2013). Making sense of participation in cultural activities for children. *Information Research*, 18(3).

Hviid, P. (2008). 'Next year we are small, right?' Different times in children's development. *EuAnnan Journal of Psychology of Education*, 23(2), 183–98.

Højholt, C., & Røn Larsen, M. (2021). Conflicts, situated inequality and politics of everyday life. *Culture & Psychology*, 27(4), 591–611. Doi: https://doi.org/10.1177/1354067X21989950

Højholt, C., & Kousholt, D. (2020). Contradictions and conflicts: Researching school as conflictual social practice. *Theory & Psychology*, 30(1), 36–55. Doi: https://doi.org/10.1177/0959354319884129

Højholt, C. (2018). Children's perspectives and learning communites. In I. M. Hedegaard, K. Aronsson, C. Højholt & O. Skær Ulvik (Eds.). *Children, Childhood, and Everyday Life: Children's Perspectives,* 2 udg., s., pp. 93–111. Charlotte, NC: Information Age Publishing.

Højholt, C., & Kousholt, D. (2018). Children participating and developing agency in and across various social practices. In I. M. Fleer, & B. van Oers (Eds.). *International Handbook of Early Childhood Education,* Bind 2, s. pp. 1581–98. Springer. Springer International Handbooks of Education Series. Doi: https://doi.org/10.1007/978-94-024-0927-7_82

Højholt, C., Juhl, P., & Kousholt, D. (2017). The collectivity of family conduct of life and parental self-understanding. In I. S. Garvis, & E. E. Ødegaard (Eds.). *Nordic Dialogues on Children and Families.* Routledge. Evolving Families. Doi: https://doi.org/10.4324/9781315561981

Højholt, C. (2012). Communities of children and learning in school: Children's perspectives. In M. Hedegaard, K. Aronsson, C. Højholt, & U. S. Ulvik (Eds.). *Children, Childhood, and Everyday Life. Children's Perspectives,* pp. 199–215. Charlotte, NC: Information Age Publishing Inc.

James, S., Jenks, C., & Prout, A. (1998). *Theorizing Childhood.* Cambridge & Oxford: Polity Press.

Jennings, P. A., DeMauro, A. A., & Mischenko, P. P. (2019). *The Mindful School: Transforming School Culture through Mindfulness and Compassion.* New York: The Guilford Press.

Jensen, B. (2009). A Nordic approach to Early Childhood Education (ECE) and socially endangered children. *European Early Childhood Education Research Journal,* 17(1), 7–21.

Johansson, B., & Hultgren, F. (2015). *Rum för de yngsta: barns och föräldrars delaktighet i kulturverksamheter [Spaces for the Youngest Children. Parents' and Childrens' Participation in Cultural Activities].* Borås: Högskolan i Borås.

Johansson, E. (2011). Introduction: Giving words to children's voices in research. In E. Johansson & E. J. White (Eds.). *Educational Research with Our Youngest: Voices of Infants and Toddlers.* Dordrecht: Springer.

Johansson, E., & Emilson, A. (2010). Toddlers' life in Swedish preschool. *IJEC,* 42, 165–79.

Johansson, I. (2007). Horizontal transitions: What can it mean for children in the early years? In A. W. Dunlop & H. Fabian (Eds.). *Informing Transition in the Early Years. Research, Policy and Practice,* pp. 151–68. Maidenhead: The Open University Press.

Juhl, P., & Westerling, A. (Eds.) (forthcoming). *(Re)configuration of Parenthood. Political Agendas Entangling Everyday Family Life.* Singapore: Routledge.

Juhl, P. (2019). Preverbal children as co-researchers: Exploring subjectivity in everyday living. *Theory & Psychology,* 29(1), 46–65

Juhl, P. (2018). Early childhood education in Denmark: Contested issues. In S. Garvis, S. Phillipson & H. Harju-Luukkainen (Eds.). *International Perspectives on Early Childhood Education: Early Childhood Education in the 21st Century,* vol. 1, pp. 42–53. Abingdon: Routledge.

Juhl, P. (2016). Parenting on the edge: Ideals and practices of parental involvement. In A. Sparrman, A. Westerling, J. Lind & K. I. Dannesboe (Eds.). *Doing Good Parenthood: Ideals and Practices of Parental Involvement,* pp. 41–52.

New York: Palgrave Macmillan. Studies in Family and Intimate Life. Doi: 10.1007/978-3-319-46774-022

Juhl, P. (2015). Toddlers collaboratively explore possibilities for actions across contexts: Developing the concept conduct of everyday life in relation to young children. In G. B. Sullivan, J. Cresswell, A. Larrain, A. Haye & M. Morgan (Eds.). *Dialogue and Debate in the Making of Theoretical Psychology*, pp. 202–10. Vaughan: Captus Press Inc.

Juhl, P. (2014). *På sporet af det gode børneliv: Voksnes bekymring og børns perspektiver på problemer i hverdagslivet. [On the trail of the good childhood]*. PhD thesis, Roskilde University.

Kagan, S. L., & Neuman, M. J. (1998). Lessons from three decades of transition research. *The Elementary School Journal*, 98(4), 365–79.

Kelly, Y., Sacker, A., Del Bono, E., Fransesconi, M., & Marmot, M. (2011). What role for the home learning environment and parenting in reducing the socioeconomic gradient in child development? Findings from the Millennium Cohort Study. *Arch Dis Child*, 96, 832–7. Doi: 10.1136/adc.2010.195917

Kervin, L., Turbill, J., & Harden-Thew, K. (2017). Invisible to visible: Mapping the continuum of literacy learning experiences in an early years setting. *Journal of Early Childhood Literacy*, 17(4), 465–84. Doi: 10.1177/1468798416638139

Kienig, A. (2002). The importance of social adjustment for future success. In H. Fabian & A. Dunlop (Eds.). *Transitions in the Early Years: Debating Continuity and Progression for Young Children in Early Education*, pp. 23–37. New York, NY: RoutledgeFalmer.

Kilgo, J., Richard, N., & Noonan, M. J. (1989). Teaming for the future: Integrating transition planning with early intervention services for young children with special needs and their families. *Infants and Young Children*, 2(2), 37–48. Doi: https://doi.org/10.1097/00001163-198910000-00006

Klein, S. P., Kraft, R. R., & Shohet, C. (2010). Behaviour patterns in daily mother–child separations: Possible opportunities for stress reduction. *Early Child Development and Care*, 180(3), 387–96. Doi: 10.1080/03004430801943290

Klette, T., & Killen, K. (2019). Painful transitions: A study of 1-year-old toddlers' reactions to separation and reunion with their mothers after 1 month in childcare. *Early Child Development and Care*, 189(12), 1970–7.

Koch, A. B. (2012). Idealet om det glade og afstemte barn. Pædagogers blik for trivsel i børnehaven. *Nordisk Barnehageforskning. [Nordic Day Care Research]*, 5, nr. 2 (1), 1–26.

Kousholt, D. (2019). Children's everyday transitions: Children's engagements across life contexts. In M. Hedegaard & M. Fleer (Eds.). *Children's Transitions in Everyday Life and Institutions*, pp. 145–65. London: Bloomsbury Academic (Transitions in childhood and youth).

Kousholt, D. (2018). Family problems: Exploring dilemmas and complexities of organizing everyday family life. In K. Aronsson, M. Hedegaard, C. Højholt & O. S. Ulvik (Eds.). *Children, Childhood and Everyday Life. Children's Perspectives*, pp. 113–28. New York: Information Age Publishing Inc.

Kousholt, D. (2016). Collaborative research with children: Exploring contradictory conditions of conduct of everyday life. In E. Schraube & C. Højholt (Eds.). *Psychology and the Conduct of Everyday Life*, pp. 241–58. Singapore: Routledge.

Kousholt, D. (2012). Family problems: Exploring dilemmas and complexities of organising everyday family life. In H. Mariane, K. Aronsson, C. Højholt & O. S. Ulvik (Eds.). *Children, Childhood, and Everyday Life: Children's Perspectives*, pp. 125–39. Charlotte, NC: Information Age Publishing.

Kousholt, D. (2011). Researching family through the everyday lives of children across home and day care in Denmark. *Ethos*, 39(1), 98–114. Doi: 10.1111/j.1548-1352.2010.01173

Kousholt, K., & Thomsen, R. (2013). Dialectical approaches in recent Danish critical psychology. *Annual Review of Critical Psychology*, 10(1), 359–90.

Kvale, S., & Brinkmann, S. (2015). Interview: *Det kvalitative forskningsinterview som håndværk. [Interview. Qualitative Research Interview as Craft]*. Copenhagen: Hans Reitzels Forlag.

Køster, A., & Winther-Lindqvist, D. A. (2018). Personal history and historical selfhood: The embodied and pre-reflective dimension. In A. Rosa & J. Valsiner (Eds.). *The Cambridge Handbook of Sociocultural Psychology*, pp. 538–55. England: Cambridge.

La Paro, K. M., & Pianta, R. C. (2000). Predicting children's competence in the early school years: A meta-analytic review. *Review of Educational Research*, 70(4), 443–84. Doi: https://doi.org/10.3102/00346543070004443

Lam, M. S., & Pollard, A. (2006). A conceptual framework for understanding children as agents in the transition from home to day care centre. *Early Years*, 26(2), 123–41. Doi: 10.1080/09575140600759906

Lansdown, G. (2005). The evolving capacities of the child. *Innocenti Insights*, 11, UNICEF.

Laughlin, L. (2010). *Who's minding the kids? Child care arrangements: Spring 2005/summer 2006*. Current Population Reports, pp. 70–121. In US Census Bureau. US Census Bureau. https://files.eric.ed.gov/fulltext/ED585393.pdf

Lee, E. (2014). Experts and parenting culture. In E. Lee, J. Bristow, C. Faircloth & J. Macvarish (Eds.). *Parenting Culture Studies*, pp. 1–24. New York: Palgrave Macmillan.

Lee, N. (2001). The extensions of childhood: Technologies, children and independence. In I. Hutchby & J. Moran-Ellis (Eds.). *Children, Technology, and Culture: The Impacts of Technologies in Children's Everyday Lives*, pp. 153–69. Routledge (Future of childhood series).

Lee, N. (1998). Towards an immature sociology. *The Sociological Review*, 46(3), 458–81.

Legerstee, M. (1992). A review of the animate-inanimate distinction in infancy: Implications for models of social and cognitive knowing. *Early Development and Learning*, 1(2), 59–67.

Leggett, N., & Ford, M. (2016). Group time experiences: Belonging, being and becoming through active participation within early childhood communities. *Early Childhood Education Journal*, 44(3), 191–200. Doi: 10.1007/s10643-015-0702-9

Lind, J., Westerling, A., Sparrman, A., & Dannesboe, K. I. (2016). Introduction: Doing good parenthood. In A. Sparrman, A. Westerling, J. Lind & K. I. Dannesboe (Eds.). *Doing Good Parenthood, Ideals and Practices of Parental Involvement*, pp. 1–15. New York: Palgrave Macmillan.

Love, J. M., et al. (2002). *Making a Difference in the Lives of Infants and Toddlers and Their Families: The Impacts of Early Head Start*. Washington: Department of Health and Human Services.

Lugo-Gill, J., & Tamis-lemonda, C. (2008). Family resources and parenting quality: Links to children's cognitive development across the first 3 years. *Child Development*, 79, 1065–85.

Luthar, S. S., Cicchetti, D., & Becker, B. (2000). The construct of resilience: A critical evaluation and guidelines for future work. *Child Development*, 71(3), 543–62.

Luyten, P. et al. (2017). *Handbook of Psychodynamic Approaches to Psychopathology*. New York: The Guilford Press.

Løkken, G. (2008). *Toddlarkultur : om ett- och tvååringars sociala umgänge i förskolan*. 1. uppl. Studentlitteratur.

Løkken, G. (2004). Greetings and welcomes among toddler peers in a Norwegian barnehage. *IJEC*, 36, 43–58.

Løkken, G. (2000). Tracing the social style of toddler peers. *Scandinavian Journal of Educational Research*, 44(2), 163–76.

Macvarish, J. (2014). The politics of parenting. In E. Lee, J. Bristow, C. Faircloth & J. Macvarish (Eds.). *Parenting Culture Studies*, pp. 76–101. New York: Palgrave Macmillan.

Marschall, A. (2013). Who cares for whom? Revisiting the concept of care in everyday life of post-divorce families. *Childhood*, 21(4), 517–31. Doi: https://doi.org/10.1177/0907568213496656

Martiny, K. M. (2017). Varela's Radical Proposal: How to embody and open up cognitive science. *Constructivist Foundations*, 13(1), 59–67. http://constructivist.info/13/1/059

Mashford-Scott, A., Church, A., & Tayler, C. (2012). Seeking children's perspectives on their well-being in early childhood settings. *International Journal of Early Childhood*, 44(3), 231–47. Doi: 10.1007/s13158-012-0069-7

Masten, A. S., & Barnes, A. J. (2018). Resilience in children: Developmental perspectives. *Children*, 5(7), 98. Doi: https://doi.org/10.3390/children5070098

McDevitt, S. E., & Recchia, S. L. (2020). How toddlers new to child care become members of a classroom community. *Early Child Development and Care*, 192(3), 481–98.

McNamee, S., & Seymore, J. (2012). Towards a sociology of 10–12 year olds? Emerging methodological issues in the 'new' social studies of childhood. *Childhood*, 20(2), 156–68.

Melhuish, E. C., Sylva, K., Sammons, P., Siraj-Blatchford, I., Taggart, B., & Phan, M. (2008). Effects of the home learning environment and preschool center experience upon literacy and numeracy development in early primary school. *Journal of Social Issues*, 64, 157–88.

Melhuish, E. C., Sylva, K., Sammons, P., Siraj-Blatchford, I., & Taggart, B. (2001). *The effective provision of pre-school education project, Technical paper 7: Social/behavioural and cognitive development at 3–4 years in relation to family background.* London: Institute of Education/DfES.

Mercer, N., & Littleton, K. (2007). *Dialogue and the Development of Children's Thinking.* London: Routledge.

Mercieca, D., & Mercieca, D. P. (2013). 'How early is early?' Or 'How late is late?': Thinking through some issues in early intervention. *Educational Philosophy and Theory*, 46(8), 845–59. Doi: 10.1080/00131857.2013.787587

Merleau-Ponty, M. (1964). *The Primacy of Perception: And Other Essays on Phenomenological Psychology.* Chicago: Northwestern University Press.

Mierendorff, J. & Grunau, T. (2021). COVID-19 and 'The Making Of' Family in (Post-) Welfare State Contexts. Conference paper, presented at the conference 'Doing and making of family in, through, and with education & social work', Trier, Germany, 22 September 2021.

Ministry for Children, Education and Gender Equality. (2016). *Master for en styrket pædagogisk læreplan. [Strenghtening the curriculum].* Denmark, Copenhagen.

Morgan, D. H. G. (2011). *Rethinking Family Practices.* London: Palgrave Macmillan UK.

Mumford, K. H., & Kita, S. (2016). At 10–12 months, pointing gesture handedness predicts the size of receptive vocabularies. *Infancy*, 21(6), 751–65. Doi: 10.1111/infa.12138

Munck, C. (2018). *How children act through materiality across age thresholds in ECEC.* Conference paper. Childhood and Materiality, 7–9 May 2018, Jyväskylä, Finland.

Murray, L., & Cortés-Morales, S. (2019). *Children's Mobilities: Interdependent, Imagined, Relational.* London: Palgrave MacMillan.

Mørck, L. L., & Hunniche, L. (2006). Critical psychology in a Danish context. special issue: critical psychologies. *Annual Review of Critical Psychology (Online)*, 5. www.discourseunit.com/arcp/5

Norman, K., & LeVine, R. A. (2008). Attachment in anthropological perspective. In R. A. LeVine, R. S. New & M. A. Malden (Eds.). *Anthropology and Child Development: A Cross-Cultural Reader*, pp. 127–42. Oxford: Blackwell.

Nygren, P. (1999). *Professionel omsorg for børn og familier. [Professional Care for Children and Families].* København: Dansk Psykologisk Forlag.

Oberhuemer, P., & Schreyer, I. (2018). *Early Childhood Workforce Profiles in 30 Countries with Key Contextual Data.* Germany, München: Staatsinstitut für Frühpädagogik. www.seepro.eu

O'Hagan, C. (2010). *Inequalities and privileges: Middle-class mothers and employment.* Doctoral Thesis, University of Limerick, September 2010. https://ulir.ul.ie/bitstream/handle/10344/1649/2010_O%27Hagan%2c%20Clare.pdf?sequence=5

Orrmalm, A. (2020a). Culture by babies: Imagining everyday material culture through babies' engagements with socks. *Childhood*, 27(1), 93–105. Doi: 10.1177/0907568219881676

Orrmalm, A. (2020b). Doing ethnographic method with babies – Participation and perspective approached from the floor. *Children & Society*, 34(6), 461–74. Doi: https://doi.org/10.1111/chso.12380

Osterkamp-Holzkamp, U. (1991). Emotion, cognition, and action potence. In C. W. Tolman & W. Maiers (Eds.). *Critical Psychology. Contributions to an Historical Science of the Subject*, pp. 102–33. Cambridge: Cambridge University Press.

Osterkamp-Holzkamp, U. (1979). Erkendelse, emotionalitet, handleevne [Recognition, emotions and action potens]. In O. Dreier (Ed.). *Den kritiske psykologi [Critical Psychology]*, 237–348. København: Rhodos.

Parsons, J. & Bales, R. F. (1956). *Family: Socialization and Interaction Process*. UK: Oxfordshire.

Pellegrini, A. (2009). *The Role of Play in Human Development*. New York: Oxford University Press.

Peterson, S. M., & Yates, T. M. (2013). Early childhood relationships and the roots of resilience. *Encyclopedia on Early Childhood Development*, Montreal, Quebec: Centre of Excellence for Early Childhood Development and Strategic Knowledge. Cluster on Early Child Development; 2013: 1–6. http://www.childencyclopedia.com/documents/Yates-PetersonANGxp1.pdf.

Phoenix, A. (2017). Unsettling intersectional identities: Historicizing embodied boundaries and border crossings. *Ethnic and Racial Studies*, 40(8), 1312–19. Doi: 10.1080/01419870.2017.1303171

Piaget, J. (1989). *The Child's Conception of the World*. Totowa: Rowman & Littlefield.

Pontecorvo, C., Fasulo, A., & Sterponi, L. (2001). Mutual apprentices: The making of parenthood and childhood in family dinner conversations. *Human Development*, 44(6), 340–61. Doi: https://doi.org/10.1159/000046155

Pratt, S., & George, R. (2005). Transferring friendships: Girls' and boys' friendships in the transition from primary to secondary school. *Children & Society*, 19, 16–26.

Ramey, C. T., & Ramey, S. L. (2004). Early learning and school readiness: Can early intervention make a difference? *Merrill-Palmer Quarterly*, 50(4), 471–91.

Recchia, S. L. (2012). Caregiver-child relationships as a context for continuity in child care. *Early Years: An International Research Journal*, 32(2), 143–57.

Recchia, S. L., & Dvorakova, K. (2012). How three young toddlers transition from an infant to a toddler child care classroom: Exploring the influence of peer relationships, teacher expectations, and changing social contexts. *Early Education & Development*, 23(2), 181–201. Doi: 10.1080/10409289.2012.630824

Reddy, V., & Trevarthen, C. (2004). What we learn about babies from engaging with their emotions. *Zero to Three*, 24(3), 9–15.

Rimm-Kaufman, S. E., & Pianta, R. C. (2000). An ecological perspective on the transition to day care centre: A theoretical framework to guide empirical research. *Journal of Applied Developmental Psychology*, 21(5), 491–511.

Robinson, M., & Dunsmuir, S. (2010). Multi-professional assessment and intervention of children with special educational needs in their early years: The contribution of educational psychology. *Educational and Child Psychology*, 27(4), 10–21.

Rogoff, B. (2003). *The Cultural Nature of Human Development*. New York: Oxford University Press.

Rogoff, B. (1996). Developmental transitions in children's participation in sociocultural activities. In A. J. Sameroff & M. M. Haith (Eds.). *The Five to Seven Year Shift: The Age of Reason and Responsibility*, pp. 273–94. Chicago, IL: University of Chicago Press.

Romagnoli, A., & Wall, G. (2012). 'I know I'm a good mom': Young, low-income mothers' experiences with risk perception, intensive parenting ideology and parenting education programmes. *Health, Risk & Society*, 14(3), 273–89.

Rutter, M. (2000). Resilience reconsidered: Conceptual considerations, empirical findings, and policy implications. In J. P. Shonkoff & S. J. Meisels (Eds.). *Handbook of Early Childhood Intervention*, 2nd ed, pp. 651–82. Cambridge: Cambridge University Press.

Røn Larsen, M., & Stanek, A. (2015). Young children and their conduct of everyday life. *Nordic Psychology* 67(3), 195–209. Doi: https://doi.org/10.1080/19012276.2015.1062256

Sandseter, E. B. H., & Kennair, L. E. O. (2011). Children's risky play from an evolutionary perspective: The anti-phobic effects of thrilling experiences. *Evolutionary Psychology*, 9(2), 257–84.

Sannino, A. (2022). Transformative agency as warping: How collectives accomplish change amidst uncertainty. *Pedagogy, Culture & Society*, 30(1), 9–33. Doi: 10.1080/14681366.2020.1805493

Schatzki, T. (1996). *Social Practices: A Wittgensteinian Approach to Human Activity and the Social*. Cambridge: Cambridge University Press.

Schmidt, L. S. K. (2017). *Pædagogers samfundsmæssige roller i forældresamarbejde [The Societal Role of Educators in Parental Collaboration]*. Roskilde: Absalon University College, Center for Social Education.

Schraube, E. (2013). First-person perspective and sociomaterial decentering: Studying technology from the standpoint of the subject. *Subjectivity*, 6(1), 12–32. Doi: 10.1057/sub.2012.28

Scraube, E., & Osterkamp, U. (2013). *Psychology from the Standpoint of the Subject: Selected Writings of Klaus Holzkamp*. New York: Palgrave Macmillian.

Schwartz, I. (2014). *Hverdagsliv og livsforløb: Tværprofessionelt samarbejde om støtte til børn og unges livsførelse. [Everyday Life and Life Courses: Interdisciplinary Collaboration about Supporting Children and Youth in Conducting an Everyday Life]*. Denmark, Aarhus: Klim.

Scott-Little, C., Kagan, S., & Frelow, V. (2006). Conceptualizations of readiness and the content of early learning standards: The intersection of policy and research? *Early Childhood Research Quarterly*, 21(2), 153–73.

Seland, M., Sandseter, E. B. H., & Bratterud, A. (2015). One-to-three-year-old children's experience of subjective well-being in day care. *Contemporary Issues in Early Childhood*, 16(1), 70–83.

Selby, J. M., & Bradley, B. S. (2003). Infants in groups: A paradigm for the study of early social experience. *Human Development*, 46, 197–221. Doi: 10.1159/000070370

Shotter, J. (2011). Embodiment, abduction, and expressive movement: A new realm of inquiry? *Theory & Psychology*, 21(4), 439–56. Doi: 10.1177/0959354310372992

Sieben, A., & Yıldırır, A. (2020). Cultural spaces of popularized psychological knowledge: Attachment parenting in Turkey. *Culture & Psychology*, 26(3), 335–57. Doi: 10.1177/1354067X19861055

Singer, Elly. (1993). Shared care for children. *Theory & Psychology*, 3(4), 429–49. Doi: https://doi.org/10.1177/0959354393034003

Sirois, S., & Mareschal, D. (2002). Models of habituation in infancy. *Trends in Cognitive Science*, 6(7), 293–8. Doi: 10.1016/S1364-6613(02)01926-5

Slade, A., Grienenberger, J., Bernbach, E., Levy, D., & Locker, A. (2005). Maternal reflective functioning, attachment, and the transmission gap: A preliminary study. *Attachment & Human Development*, 7(3), 283–98. Doi: https://doi.org/10.1080/14616730500245880

Sommer, Pramling Samuelsson I., & Hundeide, K. (2010). *Child Perspectives and Children's Perspectives in Theory and Practice*. Netherlands: Springer. Doi: https://doi.org/10.1007/978-90-481-3316-1

Sonne, T., Kingo, O. S., & Krøjgaard, P. (2016). Empty looks or paying attention? Exploring infant's visual behavior during encoding of an elicited imitation task. *Infancy*, 21(6), 728–50. Doi: 10.1111/infa.12141

Spradley, J. (1980). *Participant Observation*. New York: Holt, Rinehart and Winston.

Stanek, A. H. (2019). Children's proximal societal conditions: Analysed through a case of an exclusion process in elementary school. In I. A. Marvakis, S. Batur, S. Kessi, D. Painter, E. Schraube, E. S. Bowler & S. Triliva (Eds.). *Annual Review of Critical Psychology: Special Issue: Kritische Psychologie*, 16, pp. 849–72. https://discourseunit.com/annual-review/arcp-16-kritische-psychologie-2019/

Staton, S., Rankin, P. S., Harding, M., Schmith, S. S., Westwood, E., LeBourgeois, K. M, & Thorpea, J. (2020). Many naps, one nap, none: A systematic review and meta-analysis of napping patterns in children 0–12 years. *Sleep Medicine Review*, 50(2020), 101247. Doi: https://doi.org/10.1016/j.smrv.2019.101247

Steckermeier, L. C. (2019). Better Safe than Sorry. Does agency moderate the relevance of safety perceptions for the subjective well-being of young children? *Child Indicators Research*, 12(1), 29–48.

Steele, M., & Steele, H. (2017). Attachment disorders. In Patrcik Luyten et al. (Eds.). *Handbook of Psychodynamic Approaches to Psychopathology*, pp. 426–44. New York: The Guilford Press.

Stern, D. (2000). *The Interpersonal World of the Infant: A View from Psychoanalysis and Development Psychology*. New York: Basic Books.

Stern, W. (1914). *Psychologie der frühen Kindheit bis zum sechsten Lebensjahre. Mit Benutzung ungedruckter Tagebücher von Clara Stern*. Leipzig: Quelle & Meyer.

Stetsenko. (2020). Critical challenges in cultural-historical activity theory: The urgency of agency. *Kul'turno-Istoricheskaia Psikhologiia*, 16(2), 5–18. Doi: https://doi.org/10.17759/chp.2020160202

Stetsenko, A. (2019). Cultural-historical activity theory meets developmental systems perspective: Transformative activist stance and natureculture. In A. Edwards (Eds.). *Cultural-Historical Approaches to Studying Learning and Development*. Perspectives in Cultural-Historical Research, vol. 6, pp. 249–62. New York: Springer.

Stetsenko, A. (2017). *The Transformative Mind: Expanding Vygotsky's Approach to Development and Education*. New York: Cambridge University Press.

Stetsenko, A. (2008). From relational ontology to transformative activist stance on development and learning: Expanding Vygotsky's (CHAT) project. *Cultural Studies of Science Education*, 3, 471–91.

Sumsion, J., Harrison, L. J., & Stapleton, M. (2018). Spatial perspectives on babies' ways of belonging in infant early childhood education and care. *Journal of Pedagogy*, 9(1), 109–31. Doi: 10.2478/jped-2018-0006

Sumsion, J., Stratigos, T., & Bradley, B. (2014). Babies in space. In L. J. Harrison & J. Sumsion (Eds.). *Lived Spaces of Infant-Toddler Education and Care: Exploring Diverse Perspectives on Theory, Research and Practice*, pp. 1–16. Dordrecht: Springer (International Perspectives on Early Childhood Education and Development).

Sumsion, J., & Goodfellow, J. (2012). 'Looking and listening-in': A methodological approach to generating insights into infants' experiences of early childhood education and care settings. *EuAnnan Early Childhood Education Research Journal*, 20(3), 313–27.

Tebet, G., & Abramowicz, A. (2019). Finding a place for babies and their spatialities. In T. Skeleton & S. C. Aitken (Eds.). *Establishing Geographies of Children and Young People*, p. 1. Singapore: Springer (Geographies of Children and Young People).

Teo, T. (2016). Embodying the conduct of everyday life: From subjective reasons to privilege. In E. Schraube & C. Højholt (Eds.). *Psychology and the Conduct of Everyday Life,* pp. 111–23. NY: Routledge.

Thorne, B. (2008). Editorial. What's an age name? *Childhood*, 15(4), 435–9.

Thorne, B. (2001). Pick-up time at Oakdale Elementary school: Work and family from the vantage point of children. In R. Hertz & N. Marshall (Eds.). *Working Families: The Transformation of the American Home*, pp. 354–76. Berkeley and Los Angeles, CA: University of California Press.

Tolman, C. W. (2009). Holzkamp's critical psychology as a science from the standpoint of the human subject. *Theory & Pscyhology*, 19(2), 149–60. Doi: 10.1177/0959354309103535

Traum, L. C., & Moran, M. J. (2016). Parents' and teachers' reflections on the process of daily transitions in an infant and toddler laboratory school. *Journal of Early Childhood Teacher Education*, 37(4), 331–50. Doi: 10.1080/10901027.2016.1241967

Ulvik, O. S., & Gulbrandsen, L. M. (2015). Exploring children's everyday life: An examination of professional practices. *Nordic Psychology*, 67.

Ulvik, O. S. (2007). *Seinmoderne fosterfamilier: En kulturpsykologisk studie av barn og voksnes fortellinger [Postmodern Foster Families. A Cultural Psychological Study Children's and Adults' Perspectives]*. Oslo: Unipub forlag.

Valsiner, J. (1997). *Culture and the Development of Children's Actions*. New York: John Wiley & Sons, Inc.

Vandenbroeck, M., & De Bie, M. (2006). Children's agency and educational norms: A tensed negotiation. *Childhood – A Global Journal of Child Research*, 13(1), 127–43. Doi: https://doi.org/10.1177/0907568206059977

Visak, T. (2016). Does welfare trump freedom? A normative evaluation of contextualism about how to promote welfare. In G. Schweiger & G. Graf (Eds.). *The Well-Being of Children: Philosophical and Social Scientific Approaches*, pp. 34–48. Warsaw: De Gruyter Open.

Vogler, P., Crivello, G., & Woodhead, M. (2008). *Early Childhood Transitions Research: A Review of Concepts, Theory, and Practice. Working paper No 48*. The Hague: Bernard van Leer Foundation.

Vygotsky, L. S. (1998). The collected works of L. S. Vygotsky. In T. M. J. Hall & R. W. Rieber (Eds.). *Child Psychology*, vol. 5. New York: Kluwer Academic and Plenum Publishers.

Vygotsky, L. S. (1988). *Child Psychology. The Collected Works of L. S. Vygotsky*, vol. 5, trans. M. J. Hall & R. W. Rieber (Ed. English translation). New York: Kluwer Academic and Plenum Publishers.

Væver, M. S., Krogh, M. T., Smith-Nielsen, J., Christensen, T. T., & Tharner, A. (2015). Infants of depressed mothers show reduced gaze activity during mother-infant interaction at 4 months. *Infancy*, 20(4), 445–54. Doi: 10.1111/infa.12082

Waldenfels, B. (2008). The role of the lived-body in feeling. *Continental Philosophy Review*, 41(2), 127–42. CrossRef. Google Scholar.

Waller & Bitou. (2011). Research with children: Three challenges for participatory research in early childhood. *EuAnnan Early Childhood Education Research Journal*, 19(1), 5–20.

Westerling, A., & Juhl, P. (2021). Collaborative instrumentalization of family life – How new learning agendas disrupt care chains in the Danish welfare state. *Nordic Psychology (Online)*, 73(2), 136–52. Doi: https://doi.org/10.1080/19012276.2020.1817768

Wilson, S. L. (2001). Attachment disorders: Review and current status. *The Journal of Psychology*, 135(1), 37–51. Doi: 10.1080/00223980109603678

Winter, S. M., & Kelley, M. F. (2008). Forty years of school readiness research: What have we learned? *Childhood Education*, 84, 260–6.

Winther-Lindqvist, D. A. (2021). Caring well for children in ECEC from a wholeness approach – The role of moral imagination. *Learning, Culture and Social Interaction*, 30(Part B), 100452. Doi: https://doi.org/10.1016/j.lcsi.2020.100452

Winther-Lindqvist, D. (2019). Becoming a school child: A positive developmental crisis. In M. Hedegaard & M. Fleer (Eds.). *Children's Transitions in Everyday Life and Institutions*, pp. 47–70. London: Bloomsbury Academic. (Transitions in childhood and youth).

Winther-Lindquist, D. (2017). The role of play in Danish child care. In C. Ringsmose & G. Kragh-Müller (Eds.). *Nordic Social Pedagogical Approach to Early Years: International Perspectives on Early Childhood Education and Development*. pp. 95–114. Switzerland: Springer International Publishing. Doi: 10.1007/978-3-319-42557-3_6

Woods, P. (1990). *The Happiest Days? How Pupils Cope with Schools*. London: Routledge.

Woodhead, M. (2005). Early childhood development: A question of rights? *International Journal of Early Childhood*, 37, 79–98.

Woodhead, M. (1999). Reconstructing developmental psychology – Some first steps. *Children & Society*, 13, 3–19.

Xu, Y. (2006). Toddlers' emotional reactions to separation from their primary caregivers: Successful home–school transition. *Early Child Development and Care*, 176(6), 661–74. Doi: 10.1080/03004430500147581

Yeboah, D. A. (2002). Enhancing transition from early childhood phase to primary education: Evidence from the research literature. *Early Years*, 22(1), 51–68.

Index

action possibilities 152–5
agency 39–41
    competences and risk factors 20–1
    embodied orientation 189–90
    interrelatedness 195–7
    orientating and transformative actions 36–9
    resilience 21–2
    responsiveness and transformative actions 191–2
    situated and social process 25–9
    supporting 200–2
agentic contributions 73–6, 100–1, 191
attachment theory 15–20, 128, 145, 203

babyhood 4, 15, 26, 30
Befindlichkeit 35, 42–4

children
    and adults 106–8
    community 76–8, 96–8
    nursery for 68–71
    parental expectations 112–13
    parental task 163–5
    perspectives 12–13, 26, 29, 34, 44, 53–6, 59, 187, 189, 198
collectividual 33
condition discourse 42
conduct of everyday life 6, 13, 34, 41, 44–8, 50, 55, 58–60, 65, 93, 103–8, 111–12, 117, 123–4, 130, 141, 143, 147, 162, 189–90, 199–200, 205
conflict escalation 150–2
contributions to change 9–11

Danish Daycare Act 66
Day Care Act 164
day care centre 66–7, 71, 84, 87, 89–92, 95–6, 98–9, 113–15, 117, 131, 152–6, 169–70

early childhood education and care (ECEC) 5, 11, 20, 41, 65–7
    everyday life in 67–8
    family and 163–5, 202–3
    professionals 95, 170–3, 180
    and support 80–1
ecological validity 19
embodied orientation 3–4, 13, 22, 34–5, 40–5, 57–61, 70–1, 86, 102, 104, 130, 132, 135, 137, 147, 149, 151, 159, 188–94, 196, 199, 204–5
epistemic asymmetry 56
externalized aspects of reasons 43

family life 12–13, 48, 52, 121–3, 126–7
    daily routines 143–5
    dynamics 143–4
    early childhood interventions 124–6
    and ECEC 163–5, 202–3
    prioritization 136–8
    protection and variations 140–3
    relationship 144–5
    shared care practice 123–4
    space and possibilities 138–40
family nursery 69, 72–4, 76–80, 84, 104, 109–11, 117, 126, 128–31, 134, 137–40, 144, 147–8, 151–2, 193, 195
friendships 25, 92–4, 169

geneticism 52
grandparents day 174

home learning environment 164
horizontal transitions 24–5
human existence 47–8

inequality 23, 67, 163–4, 172, 184, 203
infant psychology 16–17
infant research 15–17
intentional orientation 36–7

internal transitions 25
interrelatedness 36, 41, 43, 48, 108, 195–7
intersubjective understanding 56–8, 189, 194, 199

language problem 57–8

meaning-making process 81, 162
microgenetic process 7, 10, 12, 22, 24, 51–3, 88, 101
microgenetic transitions 24, 101
micro-movements 5, 10, 12, 24–5, 27–8, 36, 38, 65, 101, 132, 191, 205
mothers' group 177–81
mutual interest 69, 71–2, 76, 97

nursery group 81–4

ontological symmetry in human relations 56
orientation process 3, 8, 23, 37, 45, 65, 69, 76, 84–7, 99, 103, 129, 131–2, 176, 184, 193

parents/parental/parenthood/parenting 122–3, 125–6, 137, 158, 163, 168, 171–3, 182–3, 201, 206
   determinism 201–2
   ECEC professionals and 198
   expectations 112–13
   family and ECEC 202–3
   and respite parents 176
   in Scandinavia 157, 163
   self-understanding 163, 167–8, 176, 181–2
   task 163–5
play activities 67, 94–6
professional practice 122, 188, 196–8, 200–3, 205
professional work 199–200

Programme for International Student Assessment (PISA) 66
psychological process 189
public family nursery 68–71

reason discourse 42
reflective and mindful parenting 168
research 29–30
resilience 6, 15–16, 21–2, 30
responsiveness 39, 191–2
risk factors 7–8, 19–21, 30, 60, 151, 197, 199, 205
risk-resilience discourse 128, 202–3

social practice 6–7, 37, 40–1, 44–6, 49–52, 54–6, 59, 65–6, 68, 76, 79, 83, 86–8, 100–1, 107–8, 121, 125, 151, 166, 176, 182, 188–9, 191, 199, 202, 204–6
   family nursery as 72–3
Sustainable Develop Goals 198

third-person perspective 51
toddlers 15, 17, 25, 27–8, 55, 70–1, 81, 104, 177
traditional variable psychology 42, 51
transformative actions 36–9, 147, 189–92
transitions
   conditions 109–11, 155–6
   conduct of everyday life 103–6
   conflict of interest 106–8
   day care centre and home 114–15
   defined 23
   demands 155–6
   in everyday living 53–5, 87–90
   horizontal 24–5
   internal 25
   planned activities 96–8
   vertical 23–4

vertical transitions 23–4

www.ingramcontent.com/pod-product-compliance
Lightning Source LLC
Chambersburg PA
CBHW062217300426
44115CB00012BA/2098